The Promise of the Suburbs

The Promise of the Suburbs

A VICTORIAN HISTORY IN LITERATURE AND CULTURE

Sarah Bilston

Yale UNIVERSITY PRESS

New Haven & London

Yale University Press books may be purchased in quantity for educational, business, or promotional use. For information, please e-mail sales.press@yale.edu (U.S. office) or sales@yaleup.co.uk (U.K. office).

Set in Adobe Garamond type by IDS Infotech, Ltd.
Printed in the United States of America.

Library of Congress Control Number: 2018945019
ISBN 978-0-300-17933-0 (hardcover : alk. paper)

A catalogue record for this book is available from the British Library.

This paper meets the requirements of ANSI/NISO Z39.48–1992 (Permanence of Paper).

10 9 8 7 6 5 4 3 2 1

Contents

Acknowledgments

First, many thanks to the Trinity College students who have taken my courses on Victorian London over the years, generously sharing my obsession with the city and the suburbs. Especial thanks to Cristina Conti for a summer of research assistance. Thanks to Trinity's librarians for helping me locate sources and navigate databases, above all Jeff Liszka and Erin Valentino. Thanks too to the librarians at the British Library, Yale University Library, the WiKo (Berlin), Girton College, Cambridge, and the Alexander Turnbull Library (New Zealand).

Thanks to my wonderful colleagues in Trinity's English department for twelve years of friendship, advice, and constructive criticism. This is a book about, in part, finding new communities, new support networks; the English department has offered me this in the United States, and I'm more grateful to the occupants of 115 Vernon than I can say. Trinity College generously funded my research assistant and provided a completion grant in the fall of 2017. I am forever grateful to Allan K. Smith.

Thanks to Kate Flint, Stefanie Markovits, David Rosen, and Talia Schaffer for their immensely helpful comments on the manuscript. Thanks to the anonymous reviewers at *Victorian Literature and Culture* and *Victorian Review* for remarks on earlier versions of my work, and to Yale University Press's reviewers for suggesting new directions, new lines of inquiry. Janine Barchas, Kate Bergren, Patrick Brantlinger, Guido Calabresi, Stephanie Kuduk Weiner,

Linda Peterson, Ben Polak, and Chloe Wheatley offered helpful suggestions and asked pointed questions along the way. Mark Bills was a fascinating resource on William Powell Frith, and I thank him for a memorable tea at Gainsborough's House in Sudbury, Suffolk. Thanks to Sarah Miller and Ash Lago at Yale University Press for wonderful editorial support, to Kathleen Anderson for pitching the book, and to Alison MacKeen for encouraging me to turn my scattershot ideas into a book on the Victorian suburbs in the first place.

An elderly friend named Margaret Tyrrell died in 2011 and left me a remarkable library of books on Victorian London. Twenty-six boxes arrived by boat one steamy August afternoon. Every month I find new treasures on my shelves; I gratefully acknowledge her kindness and lifelong commitment to the city she loved.

Barbara Bilston was the first to take me to London. She has cheered this book, and me, on for decades; a million thanks to her for inspiring my love of the past. Lastly, thanks to Daniel Markovits, my husband, who was always willing to read one more draft. My deepest love and thanks to him, and our children Maisie, Rosa, and Karl, for listening to me speak of suburbia. This book is for them.

The Promise of the Suburbs

Introduction
THE "HORROR" OF SUBURBIA

She learnt to speak with horror of Suburbia.

—E. M. Forster, *A Room with a View* (1908)

Lucy Honeychurch knows that suburbia is a dreadful place. Raised in genteel, semirural society, Lucy thinks the dull, vulgar suburbs threaten the circles "of rich, pleasant people" among whom she moves as fog threatens the pinewoods encircling London. Lucy's ideas about suburbia were far from unusual in 1908—indeed, it was a virtual axiom at the turn of the twentieth century that suburbia was an architectural blight, a cultural wasteland, a national embarrassment. Three years before Forster published *A Room with a View,* T. W. H. Crosland sneered in *The Suburbans:* "In the whole arid area of Suburbia you shall not find a building that meets the eye graciously, or that does not bespeak a vile taste and a stingy purse"; "economy . . . coupled with flaring vulgarity is the keynote of the region." H. G. Wells loathed what he called "the catastrophic multitudinousness of suburban development" so much he sent his Martians to annihilate the Thames commuter belt first in *The War of the Worlds* (1897).[1]

In an episode from season 5 of *Mad Men* (2012), Don Draper remarks that Saturday night in the suburbs is when "you really want to blow your brains out." Such cracks about suburban life sound modern, but they are as old as the suburbs themselves. Lucy Honeychurch repeats a near-century-old commonplace in *A Room with a View,* for representations of suburban areas as crushingly dull and tasteless may be found as early as the 1820s, the earliest decades of suburban growth. By the 1850s, the association of suburbia with

1. Grantham Road, c. 1911; a sweeping terrace in Stockwell.
This image was reproduced by kind permission of Lambeth Archives department.

dullness and vulgarity had already passed into stereotype—Emily Eden's 1859 novel, *The Semi-Detached House,* takes great comic pleasure in puncturing its heroine's ready-formed ideas about her new home in "Dulham." One might be tempted to argue, of course, that the long-standing association of suburb and dullness reflects reality; that the suburbs really were that dreadful. But the very longevity, the tenacity of the associative connection between suburbs and tedium, suburbs and tastelessness, invites suspicion—an emerging 1820s suburb was a very different place from a 1920s suburb connected to the center by trains, and North London's thousand-year settlement of Tottenham was very different from the new suburb of Pentonville, or for that matter Bristol's Clifton, Birmingham's Edgbaston, or Manchester's Chorlton-cum-Hardy. Camille Pissarro's luminous 1871 painting of Sydenham—a rapidly expanding suburb from the 1850s onward, following the reconstruction of Crystal Palace in the area and the opening of the Sydenham railway—reminds us that suburbs did not immediately become rows of identikit terraces.

Moreover, if suburbia was really so bad, why would so many people move there over the course of the century, changing the face of the nation in the process? The story of "urbanization" is in many ways one of *sub*urbanization, as villages and towns morphed in the course of mere decades into areas

2. Camille Pissarro (1830–1903). *The Avenue, Sydenham 1871.* Oil on canvas, 48 × 73 cm. Bought 1984 (NG6493). © National Gallery, London/Art Resource, NY.

connected to the center by transportation networks, while open land in between and around built-up areas was sold and built into terraces, quadrupling the population of the metropolis in a century. So why did suburbia gain its enduring reputation as a place of dullness and sterility, vulgarity and horror? *The Promise of the Suburbs* seeks to answer this question, locating as it does so a counter discourse, a different set of ideas about the suburbs as places that facilitated creative self-expression and enabled new communities formed around shared interests rather than birth networks.

VICTORIAN MODERNITY AND SUBURBAN GROWTH

Britain became an urban nation in the nineteenth century, meaning that more people lived in cities than in the countryside by 1851, the year of the Great Exhibition. By 1901, at Queen Victoria's death, three-quarters of the population was registered by the census as urban dwelling; the population of London alone swelled from under one million in 1800 to four and a half million in 1900, with one-fifth of the entire population of England and Wales living inside Greater London.[2] In the face of dizzying change, the concepts of city and of country came to hold especially "great force," Raymond Williams has argued, becoming laden with ideas about society's values, its hopes and dreams—as well as its deepest anxieties, doubts, and fears. Life in the country and life in the city were invariably described as different: the country was associated with peace, with sanctuary, tradition, and childhood, the city with "progress, modernisation, development."[3] Many writers mourned the loss of the rural past, seeing Britain's transition to an urban present as the national equivalent of a painful, tortured, but ultimately inescapable growth into adulthood.

The opposition of country and city was not dreamed up in the nineteenth century, needless to say; the two have been contrasted since classical times. Indeed, in a memorable journey on what he calls an "escalator," Williams shows us that repining over the loss of a rural idyll has been a literary pastime for centuries, if not millennia—since the Garden of Eden, perhaps.[4] Shakespeare's *As You Like It* takes its characters into the restorative Forest of Arden for refreshment and therapy, before returning them to the more straining, if sophisticated, life of the court. Williams explores the reasons for the accretion of meanings in the ideas of country and city over centuries—the ways in which cultures draw on beliefs about their difference to help get a grip on a changing world, finding stability by reinforcing rhetorical continuity.

Williams also points out that even as certain ideas cling through time—the country as peaceful or bucolic idyll, the city or town as place of energy, sophistication, change—such seemingly stable ideas persist precisely because they are open to subtle modification by different periods, cultures, moments; they would not last, in other words, if they were not so very malleable. The idea of a rural village in the sixteenth century is very different from the idea of a rural village in the twenty-first, even if similar words are used, even when both are associated with peace and tranquility. When Romantic and Victorian writers contrasted country and city they surely knew they were drawing on centuries-old traditions. The forests, towns, villages, and cities they saw were not the kinds of settlements their ancestors knew, and the encircling realities of industrial modernity—the evolving transportation and information networks, the brick-built homes, the factories, the smokestacks whose pollution smeared the landscape—produced a rural existence very far from Virgilian Arcadia or Shakespearean Arden. Unpicking the threads of Victorian writing about the country and the city requires attention both to tradition, then, and to difference; to the specificity of the sub/urbanizing Victorian world.

To the Victorians, the change that was happening so dramatically outside (and in many ways, inside) their doors was not merely the expansion of what could be called the town, the city, or the country but something else as well—the development of a new space, or more properly a space that expressly called into question the binary of country and city that had structured life and ways of thinking about the human experience of modernity for centuries. On the margins between country and city, changing the experience of both, was the suburb, a word whose classical Latin origins—*suburbium*—appeared in Anglo-Norman as *suburb, subarbe,* and *subburbe,* according to the *Oxford English Dictionary;* the idea of the suburbs as a place on the edge of town and city was certainly not new by the time Victoria came to the throne in 1837. Chaucer's Canon's Yeoman admits to living "in the suburbes of a toun . . . / Lurkynge in hernes and in lanes blynde, / Whereas thise robbours and thise theves by kynde / Holden hir pryvee fereful residence" at the end of the fourteenth century.[5] Byron's 1817 *Beppo* terms a lady "vulgar, dowdyish, and suburban"—and, as John Clubbe acidly observes, "the last adjective he intends to be no more a compliment than the two that precede it."[6] *Suburban* is used adjectivally in an 1819 article in the *Times* about the profligate behavior caused by, and surrounding, suburban fairs; the first *Times* advertisement I've found for the soon-to-be-much-mocked "desirable suburban residences" dates to 1826.[7] Implications of criminality that dated at least as far back as Chaucer lingered throughout the century, but an association with middle-class aspiration was to become increasingly dominant.

The term "suburban" had long been in use, but the Victorians treated "their" suburbs as emphatically a phenomenon of modernity—as a built environment distinctive of the age, of now, of the "new." To choose a suburban home was to move *toward* opportunity: the first generations of suburbanites left, not the city, as in our own time, but the countryside. As H. J. Dyos and D. A. Reeder put it, "London grew by sucking in provincial migrants because jobs were either better paid there or thought to be so. . . . [London offered] a more persuasive legend of opportunity than could be found anywhere in the country."[8] The suburbs took on important new cultural meanings and were associated with new problems—squawking green parrots, children dragging sticks along the railings, too-loud pianos, straggly venetian blinds, gravel, scarlet geraniums, yelling potboys—as they occupied hitherto unimaginable amounts of geographical space.[9] Population growth began early, the total population of England and Wales swelling from about nine million in 1801 to nearly eighteen million in 1851, which may partly explain the rapid expansion of the suburbs from 1790 onward; other precipitating factors include "plentiful supplies of cheap finance for builders" (which may, F. M. L. Thompson theorizes, be responsible for "an initial impulse to suburban building in the 1820s"), and the development of omnibus routes, soon followed by tram and rail.[10] While transportation links undoubtedly fueled growth, routes only opened up once a need was clearly established; it was extremely difficult to start up a rail line in London because the metropolis was already so heavily built. Buying the necessary land or forcing a compulsory purchase, through an Act of Parliament, was expensive and difficult.[11] In the case of Camberwell, for instance, Dyos observes that because of the difficulty early rail companies experienced in generating good returns, "the locomotive was in truth practically middle-aged before it appeared."[12] Still, rail lines undoubtedly helped the suburbs grow, and at a speed contemporaries found shocking.

A final important factor in the expansion of the suburbs was the emerging demand—which become particularly powerful from the 1820s and '30s onward—for areas that offered legible and consistent class markers. Ideology and economics subsequently came to reinforce one another, as a growing cultural preference for houses whose architectural properties could be quickly decoded was helped along by the fact that groups of uniform homes were quicker and cheaper to construct than detached houses of varied architectural style.[13] The more demand increased for suburban housing, in other words, the more reason developers had to produce standardized, architecturally uniform terraces with duplicated layouts.[14]

This is not to say that all Victorian suburban homes looked precisely the same—far from it, though there were marked commonalities across suburban areas aimed at each class (the expected class of occupants was typically deduced from a range of factors, including geography, existing housing stock, proximity to amenities, and nuisances). Early suburban homes were typically expansive single-family dwellings aimed at the upper-middle class: these "villas" (as they were termed) had every "mod con." An elaborate "Design for an Italian Villa," published in *The Builder's Practical Director*, for instance, included not only a drawing room, dining room, breakfast parlor (or library), hall, inner hall, lobby, terrace, cellars, kitchen, scullery, bedrooms, boudoirs, and dressing rooms but also a tower with a curved roof whose lantern would "serve the purpose of ventilating the smoking-room." A slightly more modest "Design for a Suburban Villa" comprised three bedrooms, a dining room, drawing room, porch, hall, kitchen, and scullery, plus space for a china closet (though, the editor notes sagely, "the lower part of the China closet will probably be appropriated for wine"). This property "may be erected of stock bricks and cement for the sum of £1500"; the cost of erecting the larger property was estimated at £3,000.[15]

Smaller semidetached homes, with gardens front and back, became increasingly popular after the middle of the century in rapidly growing middle-class areas like Maida Vale, Blackheath, Greenwich, and Camberwell. These homes, many of which line the streets of London to this day, often claimed the name "villa," drawing newspaper derision, as we shall see presently. Lower-middle and respectable working-class homes were typically two-story, with little decoration, and a scullery and washhouse to the rear. Ruskinian Gothic shaped suburban styling of all classes through much of the period, though later Victorian suburban homes were often influenced by the Queen Anne Revival style deployed in Bedford Park, the first speculatively built garden suburb (see fig. 18). Trees and plantings were an integral part of such turn-of-the-century suburbs that aimed to speak back, through design, to the redbrick homes of the eighteenth century, with ironwork detailing and picturesque groupings in place of regular rows.

THE SUBURBS AS "DULHAM"

When suburban homes appear in well-known Victorian novels, they tend to be either dull, ridiculous, monstrous, or all three—think of Wemmick's Walworth miniature castle with a drawbridge (and cannon) in *Great Expectations,* Charles Pooter's six-roomed "Home Sweet Home" by the Holloway railway, "The Laurels," in *Diary of a Nobody.* The tedious Victorian suburb, wearying in its architectural sameness, seems embodied in the image circa 1911 of Grantham Road, Stockwell, near the start of this chapter, where each house appears as a gabled copy of its peers. Dickens called such architecture, as early as 1841, in *Barnaby Rudge,* "bold-faced, with great staring windows . . . planned with a dull and wearisome regard for regularity."[16] Lucy Honeychurch would surely have agreed.

Roland Barthes has argued that we must press on textual images, treating them as "polysemous; they imply, underlying their signifiers, a 'floating chain' of signifieds, the reader able to choose some and ignore others. Polysemy poses a question of meaning and this question always comes through as a dysfunction. . . . Hence in every society various techniques are developed intended to fix the floating chain of signifieds in such a way as to counter the terror of uncertain signs; the linguistic message is one of those techniques."[17] The meanings immanent in the Victorian usages of the term "suburban"—of the suburbs first as a semicriminal borderland, then as a place that appealed to, and capitalized upon, middle-class aspiration—intend to fix the meaning of what was, in truth, dizzyingly various, growing rapidly, changing by the year, impossible to define. Some suburbs were, at heart, older, well-established villages—Richmond was evoked by Mary Elizabeth Braddon as a sort of affluent paradise at the turn of the twentieth century, for instance, though she described Camberwell as more urban, lower-middle class, and plagued by pollution. (Camberwell she termed Edenic at mid-century.) Other suburbs were Victorian creations, growing rapidly to accommodate office workers, and many were ethnically various—bustling Bayswater was known by its contemporaries as "Asia Minor" because of its large numbers of "rich and cultured Orientals": the *Bayswater Chronicle* remarked that to shop in a Bayswater bazaar was to mingle with "every class, every age . . . almost every nationality."[18] Vastly different streets existed in close proximity: in Edith Nesbit's *Story of the Treasure Seekers* (1899), a family's upward social trajectory is expressed by leaving a declining semi (or, as the young hero Oswald grandly terms it, an "ancestral home on the Lewisham Road") for a redbrick villa a mile or so away in Blackheath. Rich Shortlands in Bromley was a very different place from urban Battersea, on the south banks of the Thames, battling the olfactory challenges of Price's Candle Factory, yet both could be described as "suburban." This does not mean that life in the two places was alike, though both were designated *suburban* in contemporary guidebooks. Indeed, the differences between areas, and within areas, not to mention over time, were so significant it may seem surprising the term "suburban" acquired such a fixed and flattened meaning in the first place.

In truth, Victorians were intensely conscious of the gap between what the new suburbs were designed to offer—consistency, legibility—and what they *were.* Consider, for instance, Grantham Road, Stockwell. This "typical" late Victorian street may look like unending Dulham in one black-and-white photograph, a scene of homogeneity and sameness, but a close-up of number 37 offers a tantalizing glimpse of the individual lives unfolding behind its façades. A brief dip into the census returns for 1911 reinforces the point, for residents reveal a remarkable range of nationalities, backgrounds, employments, and means. Florence Brannan, a thirty-eight-year-old woman from Lincolnshire, resided at number 37, possibly alone (on census night her husband of sixteen years and child were not with her); Brannan's neighbors included a "fine etcher," a sculptor, an oilman, at least three self-supporting female typists, male and female clerks from many different businesses, domestic servants, a pastry cook, a tax assessor, a book binder, a gelatin capsule maker, a caterer at an art school, and numerous widows "of private means," including one from

3. Grantham Road, c. 1911; close-up of number 37.
This image was reproduced by kind permission
of Lambeth Archives department.

Kingston, Jamaica. Other residents hailed from New Zealand, Germany, France, Switzerland, Ireland, Aberdeenshire, Glamorganshire, Yorkshire, Lancashire, Durham, Cornwall, Dorset, Devonshire, Guernsey, Surrey, Essex, Suffolk, Norfolk, Leicestershire, Gloucestershire, Somerset, Berkshire, Kent, and all over London. Visitors were recorded that night from South Africa, France, and Spain. The architect James Lloyd Worrsell boarded at number 8.

And Grantham Road was far from unusual. The suburbs were remarkably diverse: Thompson has observed that, whatever the dream of suburbia, "the nineteenth-century suburban reality was a social patchwork."[19] Or, as Erika Diane Rappaport expresses it, in more positive terms, "suburban districts were often as internally heterogeneous as any large urban area. Islington, Hackney, Clapham, and Brixton were quite unlike the western suburbs of Bayswater and Kensington, and even these areas, although sharing certain characteristics, were not identical."[20] Hampstead was known for its artistic community, and Maida Vale and Bayswater welcomed large Jewish populations, for instance, so that, in the suburbs, people from very different communities found themselves living in proximity. Architectural sameness certainly did not reflect, or produce, sameness of human beings. Indeed, the longing for clear class markers in suburban homes surely bespeaks an effort to make what was palpably new and in process appear fixed and stable. The effort to fit in at all costs constitutes an urge to connect by those who feel dislocated. Arthur Morrison's short story "Behind the Shade" (1894), a tale of two women who die of starvation sooner than sell the vase of plastic fruit that anchors their last claim to respectability, makes this point to tragic effect. Writing about the suburbs in the nineteenth century often drives to expose the "keeping up appearances" character of suburban life—or, to put it another way, to explore the slippage between the supposedly secure class identity of a locale and its residents' mixed and various lives.

If a photograph tells only a partial story of the Victorian suburb, so does the familiar textual image of Dulham, repeated so often, from early in the period, with so much disdain. A Victorian writer's association of the suburbs with the dull, identikit, and tasteless tells us little about the people who actually lived in the suburbs or the brick-and-mortar reality of the suburbs themselves. But it has a great deal to tell us about the speaker's attitudes to rapid social change, especially the decline of the older elites and the ascendance of a new, mobile middle class, with still-emerging tastes, preferences, and practices. The short answer to the question I posed a few pages ago, in other words, is that the image of the dull, silly, tasteless suburb reflects and embodies anxiety about the middle class and its efforts to establish and understand itself in the nineteenth and early twentieth centuries. It is a rhetorical position, not an actual fact.

THE SUBURBS AND THE MIDDLE CLASS

Aristocratic dismay at suburbia as a physical manifestation of growing middle-class economic and cultural power is not, perhaps, terribly surprising. But the decline of the aristocracy over the course of the nineteenth century has been well documented, most famously by David Cannadine, and still dislike of suburbia blazed fiercely at the turn of the twentieth century. Moreover, middle-class writers and suburban-dwelling authors themselves actively participated in shaping and burnishing the image of the dull and vacuous suburb. While birth certainly still mattered, aristocrats were no longer driving the cultural narrative. So how are we to account for the intense disdain for suburbia expressed so regularly by members of the intelligentsia and the suburbanite middle class?

John Carey's *Intellectuals and the Masses* (1992) offers signposts toward a possible explanation. Carey contends that Victorian intellectuals, anxious that meritocratic advance should track worth and virtue, in place of birth and breeding, came to set a high value on signals of worthiness and achievement they felt they possessed. General literacy levels rose, particularly in the wake of the 1870 Education Act (the difference, Carey observes, between the "mob" and the "masses" is literacy). Now that a large population could read, intellectuals increasingly defined themselves as those who did *more* than read—as men (sometimes women) whose reading practices and tastes were distinctive. The education levels of the majority were for the most part basic: a new "alternative culture was created for them," Carey remarks, pointing out that Lord Northcliffe "aimed the *Daily Mail* specifically at clerks."[21]

As the "masses" read stories of adventure and news oriented around "human interest" (family and domestic life), intellectuals placed a higher value on news about politics and business, on literature that was allusive and complex, on texts that required a tertiary education to appreciate. The masses were unthinking consumers of low culture, and they firmly associated mass tastes with the body, not the mind; animated by unfettered emotions, the masses were fascinated by violence and sex and buying things—out-of-place, useless things, like cacti, green parrots, and monkeys. Intellectuals defined themselves, by contrast, as altruistic, self-disciplined, other regarding, cerebral, civilized—and as residents, not of a "suburb," but of a locale with a rich historical past that was currently experiencing growth. Leigh Hunt repackaged Kensington as "the old court suburb" in 1855, during a period of rapid suburban expansion, stressing its difference from the new suburbs, the places that were building villas with curved roofs and smoking rooms; the gesture is typical. "Suburbia" was—and probably remains—where other people live. We shall see throughout this book that writers introduce the suburban areas they like and live in by name, articulating the generalized "suburbs" and "suburbia" as alternative vulgar dystopias inhabited by aliens.

What Carey calls "the imaginative project of rewriting the masses" by writers and intellectuals involved connecting the majority with newly built homes: the suburbs were a visible manifestation of massed human beings, after all, and clerks (who were rarely educated at the great public schools) were especially likely to live in the more recently built areas. Matthew Arnold's account of the cultured, and of the differences between the Barbarians, the Philistines, and the Populace, surfaces regularly in texts that speak of suburbia, as Lara Baker Whelan has argued, apparently seeming to express what the newly literate masses embodied. Culture, Arnold famously remarked, is "the best which has been thought and said in the world"; its opposite is "our stock notions and habits, which we now follow staunchly but mechanically, vainly imagining that there is a virtue in following them staunchly which makes up for the mischief of following them mechanically."[22] To many critics, the bowler-hatted clerks crowding the sidewalks into London, the women and servants disappearing into duplicated terraced houses, seemed powerful signs of a mechanical population following practices mechanically. To such critics, the suburb's rapid expansion appeared a terrifying, concrete manifestation of the takeover of the Philistines, or uncultured middle classes, each new row of terracing an assault on the tastes of the cultured. The "spoliation" of key writers' own suburban areas lent grist to the mill, as Carey notes: "The ruined childhood paradise becomes a familiar refrain in writer's biographies and autobiographies."[23] Speaking of suburbia with disdain, as a place of consumerism, tastelessness, and dullness, by first aristocratic, then intellectual elites, was part of a broader effort to draw a boundary line between the Philistines and the cultured, the unworthy and the worthy, the many and the favored few.

Forster, though no lover of the suburbs, seems to have seen that disdain for the suburbs involved enacting the position of "cultured": Lucy, after all, *learnt* to speak with horror of suburbia. Her hatred is imbibed from and reinforced by the circle in which she moves. She deploys the fruits of her lessons as a means of securing a foothold in a society that is, in truth, a little above her—after all, the narrator tells us, her father was a solicitor. Expressing distaste for suburbanites and their tastes means, or appears to mean, that you are separated from the masses, even when you are not: "Windy Corner" teeters on the very edge of suburbia, as Cecil Vyse all too uncomfortably recognizes. Speaking with disdain about the suburbs is a rhetorical and political gesture, then, an effort to position oneself within the hushed, magical circle of the elite, that "small group of people with exquisite sensibility," even if you live in Peckham yourself.[24] The Victorian yoking of the suburb with the dull and vulgar clerk or the foolish consumerist woman were not so much reflections of a lived reality as associative connections every bit as freighted as that of the Arcadian shepherd with the countryside or the liar with classical Rome.[25]

THE SUBURBS IN VICTORIAN FICTION

Fredric Jameson has argued that modernist aesthetics were a way of rendering acceptable to a population the otherwise "distressingly alien reality" of the modern world; modernism, he suggested, was "a final and extremely specialized phase of that immense process of superstructural transformation whereby the inhabitants of older social formations [were] culturally and psychologically retrained for life in the market system." Nicholas Daly's work has developed the insight, showing how late-century novels assisted readers to "acclimatize to certain historical shifts in social organization, imperial power, and commodity culture."[26] Suburban popular fiction—a genre developing from the 1820s onward, yet one that has received little critical attention to date—worked, analogously, to help readers explore how the suburbs were represented, to recognize the politics in play in their representation, and to manage their own residence in a place so tightly bound up with unworthiness. Plots set in the suburbs invariably turn on understanding the "truth" behind the stereotypes, on testing experience against cultural messages, on distinguishing the worthy from the not so worthy using a range of metrics open only, interestingly, to suburbanites. A typical plot involves the arrival of an alien, his or her assessment by a landlady, and the subsequent, awkward coming together of different worlds. In one strand, a particular suburb is a dangerous landscape the visitor must escape, a place of labyrinths, a terrifying, threatening terrain. This strand of suburban popular fiction grows in importance over the course of the century, when it is picked up and deployed to powerful effect by writers like George Gissing.

But there is a second strand of suburban popular fiction, one far less well known; one that will require a turn to nonfiction, as we shall see, to fully unpick its threads. Women authors in particular were especially likely to present a sympathetic reading of suburbia, returning to suburban homes as scenes of possibility, community, agency, and choice; deploying, challenging, and even countering the stereotype of suburbia as vulgar, tasteless, self-regarding, and dull. These more positive representations of suburban life are often depicted as unfolding, not in a place designated by the narrative "the suburbs," but in areas that were, in fact, suburbanized: Bayswater, Camberwell, Richmond, and so on. Indeed, while use of the term "suburb" (or suburban, suburbanism, suburbia) in a literary passage typically opens into a set of concerns about the changing economic and social order and the politics of representation, use of a named suburban area allows a writer to map out a new territory where a new middle-class resident makes new life choices. My book aims to complicate our understanding of suburban stereotypes and to restore a different articulation of suburban life to the conversation. If Victorian writing about the suburbs helped contemporaries acclimate to a new social and architectural landscape, it also helped some imagine what new lives could be pursued in a still-unfolding, still-unmapped space.

I've chosen to concentrate on the capital's suburbs for this book because the writers whose suburban lives and stories first interested me (Braddon, Jane Loudon, Jane Ellen Panton) lived in London's suburbs and wrote at length about these areas. Future research could well turn on how the residents of Birmingham's Edgbaston or Bristol's Clifton, or any of the other rapidly growing suburbs around the nation's cities, wrote about their landscape. The vibrancy of Victorian suburban living is a truth hiding in plain sight, though more positive images of the suburb may take some work to find in other city's suburbs, just as in London: Victorians lived in the suburbs but found representing it fraught. Periodicals aimed at late-century middle-class amateur photographers, for instance, are replete with references to suburbs all over the nation, revealing the depth of suburban engagement in a new, up-to-date art form: apparatus is wanted in Broughton (Salford), new photography groups are advertised in Moseley (Birmingham), competition winners are praised in Rottingdean (Brighton), amateur exhibitions are promised in Clifton (Bristol). Yet there are few images of suburban streets or interiors in the magazines' pages; editors recommend rural lanes, seascapes, historic buildings, foreign climes, slum misery, posed family groupings, and pets as subject matter (a dog in evening dress met with especially high regard). As the editor of the *Amateur Photographer* put it, " 'Every old cottage is to a certain extent a work of art, every new one an abomination.' "[27] It can seem hard to find Victorians who made England's suburbs the focus of their art, but they certainly exist. This book is an effort to return some of the nation's many voices to the conversation.[28]

THE SUBURBS IN HISTORICAL AND LITERARY CRITICISM

A hearty loathing of suburbia surfaces in analyses and studies of the architectural and social phenomenon penned long years after Victoria's death. F. M. L. Thompson's pioneering 1982 historical study, *The Rise of Suburbia,* memorably portrays suburbia as a beast—"mindless, creeping . . . with [an] apparently insatiable capacity for devouring land, destroying the countryside, and obliterating scenery. . . . The ceaseless activity of the builders, the alarming rapidity with which they turned pleasant fields into muddy, rutted building sites, the confusion of hundreds of building operations going on simultaneously without any discernible design . . . were in themselves frightening portents of disorder and chaos as if a machine had escaped from its makers and was careering wildly out of control." Shifting from an image of chomping monster to mindless machine, Thompson braids Victorian and modernist anxieties together: "The suburbs appeared monotonous, featureless, without character, indistinguishable from one another, infinitely boring to behold, wastelands of housing as settings for dreary, petty, lives without social, cultural, or intellectual interests, settings which fostered a pretentious preoccupation with outward appearances, a fussy attention to the trifling details of genteel living, and absurd attempts to conjure rusticity out of minute garden plots."[29] Thompson affects to describe reality, but he channels nineteenth-century and Edwardian discourse, ending with the "fussy" wife or maiden aunt from a Gissing or Forster novel, "absurdly" interested in the "trifling" details of her domestic existence. Each of the images Thompson deploys—suburbia as monster, suburbia as machine, suburbia as fussy domestic absurdity—would be familiar to a reader a full century earlier. Thompson has taken nineteenth- and twentieth-century criticisms and sucked them up into his own prose; inevitably, they freight his conclusions about the ultimately deplorable consequences of suburban growth.

Most literary critics have seen, for the most part, only a startling absence of literary engagement with the Victorian suburbs before the end of the nineteenth century.[30] Gail Cunningham argues, "Although the term 'suburb' was used from Shakespeare and Milton onwards . . . it was not until the final decades of the nineteenth century that writers turned to suburban life as a subject of imaginative investigation."[31] Lynne Hapgood's *Margins of Desire* (2005) begins from a similar premise: "The unfolding of this strange phenomenon [suburbanization] was first recognised in the mid-nineteenth century, although it was not until the 1880s and 1890s that it became a positive social fact: an entirely new kind of society was evolving on the very doorstep of Britain's capital city."[32] Cunningham's work on suburban narrative positions authors of the late nineteenth century as architects of "the new imaginative category suburban," one that was substantially shaped by the experience of observing and living among "newly massed middle classes."[33] Cunningham usefully engages a range of fin de siècle texts, from music hall song to H. G. Wells's fiction, but her emphasis on the newness of both the category and the lived experience underestimates the impact of suburbanization on the totality of the period. Suburbanization was a phenomenon that Victorian society had been experiencing, and responding to, for at least eight decades by the time of Victoria's death. Literary narratives engaging suburbia from these eight decades in fact exist: they have received scant critical attention, yet they constitute a crucial tradition without which the more famous late nineteenth-century texts of suburbia—by Forster, Gissing, Wells, Doyle, Grossmith—cannot be adequately understood.

Partly because the suburban works we know are all by men, literary critical work on suburbia has also tended to insist that suburbia's development was something with which men, male values, and male writers alone were concerned. Todd Kuchta argues in *Semi-Detached Empire* (2010) that the story of literary suburbia is a story of masculine experience. Admitting that his own "study takes up a distinctly masculine problematic," he argues: "Catherine Jurca's claims that U.S. suburban fiction is 'a male-authored and frequently male-focused body of literature' is no less true of the British context, whether in the traditional fiction of suburbia or in the more obliquely suburban narratives I examine."[34] Kuchta's text is useful for the way in which it illuminates the close relationship between suburban and imperial anxieties, but the claim that suburban fiction focuses on exclusively masculine problematics misses a rich literary vein. If we read what Kuchta calls "the traditional fiction of suburbia" by Gissing and Grossmith we should expect to find masculine anxieties laid bare. The iconic suburban man was, Kuchta suggests, the hapless clerk personified in George and Weedon Grossmith's *Diary of a Nobody* (1892); Whelan makes a similar point when she observes that "the picture of the suburbs that emerges from 1880 through the First World War is the image with which modern readers are . . . familiar—the suburb as trivial, dull, bourgeois, pretentious, an object of mockery."[35] But it depends, as always, who "paints the lion." To locate narratives that engage "feminine problematics"—to read how women responded to industrial modernity and the changing landscape around them, to the new homes they inhabited and the new roles they took up inside those homes—we need to search among the many thousands of popular novels, advice texts, home manuals, and periodical articles published by women. For women writers explored very different figures—the suburban ingénue, for instance, thrilled by urban adventures, or the suburban wife, making friends and finding connections among a socially and culturally heterogeneous group. Women writers also paint a very different picture of the suburb as not so much dull and vulgar as socially complex, emotionally challenging, aesthetically stimulating. Suburban life provides fertile territory for self-making—for meeting new people, for finding communities based on shared interests, and for learning new skills, that even open into, by the end of the century, professional work. *The Promise of the Suburbs* brings women's voices, women's words, back into the conversation, reading fiction and nonfiction together in order to understand how new genres of writing articulated a range of London-based experiences that, taken together, contest the heretofore seemingly unitary narrative of suburban dreadfulness.

Broadly speaking, the book proceeds chronologically. Chapter 1 examines the rise and fall of John Claudius Loudon's suburban optimism in the 1830s and '40s. Chapter 2 explores the setting of the stereotype of suburban dullness in the printing presses of the late 1820s and the exploration of that stereotype in early (and even pre-) Victorian fiction. Chapter 3 explores the evolution of suburban plots in fiction around the middle of the century, turning on the lives and practices of landladies and boarders, the coexistence of strangers, the business of moving house, and the challenges of interpreting local practices and suburban decorative codes. Even as the suburbs' reputation as a place of dullness and oppressive sameness was hardening, the suburbs were giving rise in literature to plots of unexpected meetings and interclass, intercultural communities.

Chapter 4 explores women's advice literature on suburban home decoration as a powerful—and personally empowering—counter to the forces of industrialization and capitalism; at the same time, commercial engagement is presented as a means for women to become part of modern communities and experience the city. Chapter 5 focuses on women's writing about the suburban garden as a space of aesthetic experimentation, active labor, and personal freedom, gardening as an activity that brings women out of their houses and, through shopping at nurseries, onto the streets. Chapter 6 turns to the writing of a single author, Mary Elizabeth Braddon, who wrote for suburban readers, lived most of her long life in suburbia, and negotiated for decades between stereotypes of suburbs and what different suburban areas offered contemporary women. Braddon's work exemplifies two strains of discourse, one centered around the suburbs as tasteless and threatening, the other around the suburbs as generative and networked, a conduit (for women especially) from birth networks into personal and professional communities. The very existence of suburban problems gives women a vocation, in Braddon's work as in suburban design literature, with professional work offered tentatively as the answer, the solution, the future.

My final chapter, concentrating on the last decades of the nineteenth century, tipping into the first decades of the twentieth, centers around the writing of Jane Ellen Panton and Julia Frankau. Now hardly known, these once-famous women made their names writing (and fighting) about the suburbs: both had difficult personal histories, and both found in the new suburbs literary inspiration and practical aid. Panton especially discovered, in the suburb of Shortlands in the borough of Bromley, a community that allowed her to detach from her famous artist father and evolve a new professional writing identity. Panton and Frankau exemplify, to my mind, the two fronts of the semidetached house: similar at first sight, they were profoundly different in their life experiences and the challenges they surmounted. Still, for both of them, as for many writers considered in this book, the suburbs were artistically generative and practically useful, not a place of shut doors and silent streets but a networked world where new stories could be written, new lives lived, new professional identities established.

To be sure, some writers and residents no doubt disliked their suburban lives. Many reformers and writers critiqued haphazard building practices, rapacious speculators, and duplicitous auctioneers, not to mention the startling incursion of the railways: Dickens, in *Dombey and Son* (1848), offered a memorable and strongly negative account of the arrival of the train in Camden Town, terming it a "great earthquake" that "rent the whole neighborhood to its centre."[36] The separation of the worlds of work and home, and the practice of commuting, must have produced marital and family problems; Talia Schaffer has argued, in "Sensational Story," that Ellen Wood's *East Lynne* (1861) is a working out of exactly this issue in Victorian marriages. But from as early as the 1820s, even as some presented the suburbs as dull and vulgar, and/or a monstrous incarnation of greed, a horrifying disruption with the past, others associated the suburbs with economic and creative opportunity, celebrating the access suburbs gave residents to the tools and industrial and commercial scenes of modern life. Fictions and nonfictions explore the experiences of living in, not dully identikit, but socially and culturally heterogeneous communities, where people connect with and learn from other classes, countries, and faiths.

The very homogeneity of much suburban architecture, meanwhile, the duplicated floor plans, serves a startling narrative purpose, for it allows characters to see how much they have in common. Suburban plots turn on the ways in which the suburban landscape forces meetings between strangers that yield unexpected results. In nonfiction advice texts on suburban home decoration and gardening, the duplicated landscape again yields rewards, for here the suburban home is presented as a veritable apprenticeship space, where housewives learn the skills and develop the practices that can facilitate the leap into professional work in areas connected with the home, such as landscape gardening and interior design. Duplicated floor plans actively facilitate the kinds of standardized skill gaining that lay at the heart of the newly conceptualized professions; the woman who learned to decorate a home in Camberwell could apply her skills to Lewisham or Bayswater. It is not accidental that the first ever exhibition in England of women's professional achievements, held in Bristol, in 1885, chose a suburban home for its backdrop.

There were many different ways of speaking of suburbia, only some of which we have heard. But insofar as the suburb was, John Carey argues, for later poets a locale for writers who wish to "[avoid] and [undercut] the kind of dignity that males have appropriated," it is to the suburbs we must go if we want to hear new voices telling new stories about the landscapes and possibilities of modern life.[37]

CHAPTER I

John Claudius Loudon and the New Suburban Landscape

> It happens, in the progress of civilisation, and the changes that society is continually undergoing, that, at a certain stage, mankind arrive at a similar point to that from which they set out, only in a more improved and refined form; and as, in a rude state, they congregated together in encampments or in villages, for mutual protection and security, so, in a refined state, they congregate together in towns and suburbs, for business and refined enjoyment.[1]

At the end of the nineteenth century, the suburbs were routinely represented as an architectural manifestation of the stuffiest of all middle-class Victorian values, as places where oppressive domesticity prevailed, where the joys of intellectual companionship and creative innovation were stifled. At first blush, the reasons for this seem obvious: many suburban areas were, after all, designed to separate homes from places of commerce and industry. Judith Flanders notes that in the early Birmingham suburb of Edgbaston "the leases . . . were clear: no retail premises were permitted, nor was professional work to be undertaken in these houses."[2] The familiar image of the suburban street is of a row of houses unbroken by social gathering places; over time, Lynne Hapgood argues, the physical separation of home and work seemed to reinforce the emerging ideology of the sanctified home, so that, by the end of the period, "suburban streets laid out in rows of domestic housing, whether small working class developments or more spacious villas with gardens," appeared to be "manifestations of the traditional middle-class belief in home and family."[3] Certainly, as we shall see later in the book, many later Victorian writers, particularly men, evoked fin de siècle suburbia as a place to escape.

Yet whatever the theory or the dream of suburbia, individual suburbs varied widely, as did blocks and streets, over the course of the century. Some, like

4. Shoolbred's department store on Tottenham Court Road. Mary Evans Picture Library.

rapidly urbanizing Bayswater, were to become bustling hubs, with department stores, tailors, milliners, and boutiques, and were home to a range of classes and ethnicities. Others, like Bromley, in Kent, attempted to preserve an affluent character by preventing the development of a working man's train service. In all areas, residents managed daily interactions with servants, delivery boys, shopkeepers, and door-to-door salesmen, commercial interactions that called the supposed separation of public and private into question. That separation was blurred further by rapidly expanding transportation networks that moved suburbanites into and all over the city: as Erika Rappaport points out, the shopping crowds of the West End were substantially formed of suburban women, while later Victorian men commuted to work. Suburban journeyings began early: omnibuses began to transport people from Paddington to the City four times a day from 1829, and "by the late 1830s, over fifty vehicles traveled between Bayswater and the City"; "by 1851 one could also ride directly to Tottenham Court Road," and so shop in new large department stores like Shoolbred's.[4]

John Claudius Loudon was a Bayswater resident. He was also one of the century's most important garden writers, author of the successful *Suburban Gardener* (1838), itself one of the first texts to address the landscape and interests of a new suburban readership. Loudon, a promoter of a suburban way of life, tends to be regarded as yet another advocate for reserved domesticity and the sanctified home, a writer obsessed with maintaining both class and gender hierarchies through the material boundaries of walls and hedges.[5] And yet, as the epigraph to this chapter reveals, Loudon's 1838 book suggests that modern housing no longer needs to keep things out: whereas once people "congregated together in encampments or in villages, for mutual protection and security," Loudon protests that the defensive circle of the English village is no longer necessary. Protection and security can take a back seat to the middle-class pursuits of business and pleasure.[6] Indeed, the suburban landscape allows residents to connect with one another: Loudon celebrates the possibilities for forming friendships with neighbors and the vistas of an industrial landscape just beyond the suburban periphery. Consequently, the straight rows of suburbia are, for Loudon, a vibrant manifestation of England's move into an exciting present: artificial boundary lines are valuable because they make the space more manageable for the evening gardener returned home from work. With walls in place, a brand-new spade, and Loudon's book in hand, a suburban gardener, male or female, may enjoy the delights of self-directed enterprise as a complement to professional life and as a contrast to an older agrarian existence, where land cultivation was about food production as opposed to aesthetics. The modern gardener performs, through flower cultivation and bulb forcing, that he or she is a man or woman of the present, not the past.

Loudon's admiration for industry and advance seems all the more striking when the 1838 edition of the text is laid beside *The Villa Gardener* (1850), the posthumously released version of *The Suburban Gardener.* As we shall see presently, this later work, edited by Loudon's wife, Jane, an important garden writer in her own right, erases expressions of admiration for the industrial landscape and celebrations of suburban community. Paying attention to this deleted material indicates how suburbia's promise began to be revised in the light of shifting cultural attitudes to the home, the family, and the middle class around the middle of the century.

THE RISE OF SUBURBIA AND THE DECLINE OF THE RURAL

Loudon's responses to the country and the cities in the 1830s are best understood in the light of broad demographic trends. Studies of Victorian suburbia's extraordinarily rapid growth tend to read the phenomenon in the light of hand-wringing about the public sphere generally and urbanization specifically. Flanders identifies the "rejection of city life" as a crucial "impetus for the growth of suburbia"; Whelan argues that "the ideal suburb was supposed to be, above all things, a haven from urban chaos."[7] And indeed, urban flight lies at the heart of what suburban development claimed to offer, for if the towns and newly industrialized cities were busy, noisy, and crime-ridden, suburbia's appeal lay in the ways it preserved residents from urban problems while allowing access to industrial and commercial jobs and facilities.

Yet demographic and population studies of the period show that the rapid growth of the suburbs was not simply produced by flight from city life; flight from the countryside was a substantial piece of the puzzle. As Jeffrey G. Williamson's detailed *Coping with City Growth* shows, migration from country to city underpinned urbanization across all classes.[8] David Feldman concurs: "At least 40 per cent of the demographic growth of urban Britain in the nineteenth century can be attributed to movement away from rural areas . . . indeed, from the 1840s net out-migration from agricultural areas was so great that between 1851 and 1911 they suffered an absolute decline in population."[9] Meanwhile, natural increase fueled the cities' growth; R. I. Woods points out that "this was itself a reflection of biases in the age- and sex-selective nature of rural-urban migration, which tended to pick out the young and active and to leave behind the elderly or less ambitious."[10]

What Jack Simmons has termed the "huge migration away from the centre of London" characterized the *last* quarter of the century, and helps explain the growth of the suburbs farthest from the city center.[11] But as H. J. Dyos has shown in his influential study of the expansion of Camberwell, the suburbs closer to the city were the destination of many arriving from the countryside in the early decades of industrial growth: "The growth of the suburb since the beginning of the century" was chiefly produced by a "stream of migrants," of whom about 28 percent came "from the neighbouring south-eastern counties of Sussex, Hampshire, Berkshire, Essex, Suffolk, and Norfolk"; 40 percent from "adjacent areas of metropolitan Middlesex and extra-metropolitan Surrey and Kent"; and most of the rest from farther north. Dyos concludes that "the cumulative effect of these prodigious transfers of population was to create urban communities in which not more than half their members had been born within South London at all."[12] It was only at the end of the century, when Camberwell had become seriously congested, that migrants began to move out.[13]

The pattern of early movement into the suburbs from surrounding rural areas was common: according to F. M. L. Thompson, "the mid-nineteenth-century pattern of internal migration . . . shows that at least two-thirds of the residents of south London and Liverpool suburbs, and presumably other suburbs likewise, had moved to the suburbs from neighboring and largely rural areas and had not moved out from the central zone."[14] Historical and demographic analyses reveal, in other words, that in spite of critics' undoubted anxiety about the cities and the suburbs and the ongoing idealization of the rural in Victorian poetry, novels, and periodicals, Britain's population was voting with its feet and moving into the suburbs as fast as it could.[15]

Early Victorian literature about the new suburban areas frequently expresses ambivalence not just about the city, then, but also about the countryside. The rural is often represented as out of touch with the modern world: the suburbs are hymned by Loudon, for instance, precisely for the distinctively new, nonrural opportunities they present. The suburbs facilitate consumerism, he suggests, not to mention new forms of community and the chance to foster new skills through new technologies. The suburban experience he presents is shaped around participation in the opportunities of the city, rather than proximity to the countryside, and his suburbanites assert through the very food they eat and the way they prune their plants they are *not* rural dwellers. Loudon's suburbia is a space in which residents are able to signal, by the streets they walk along, the tools they pick up, and the activities in which they participate, that they are the products of an advanced nation and a modern world.

CULTIVATING MODERNITY IN THE SUBURBAN GARDEN

The Suburban Gardener is an extraordinarily detailed articulation of the pleasures and possibilities of suburban living in the early years of Victoria's reign. Notably, Loudon's title page describes the book as a work "for the instruction of those who know little of gardening and rural affairs"; as early as 1838, Loudon projects a reader who was detached not just from horticulture but also from rural tradition.[16] Yet, while this might imply an *already* suburbanized readership, the text presumes a landscape in flux; Loudon's work describes how to build and shape the new houses. Suburban home development is conceived repeatedly in the text as both producing and consolidating distance from the rural, and to this end Loudon insists on the difference between the act of villa gardening and "mere" rural toil. Indeed, distancing the two—and celebrating the modernity of the former—is central to the book's project. Suburban gardening is evoked as a quintessentially new skill, a scientific, aesthetic, intellectual, and above all text-oriented act.

Loudon, a farmer's son, had come a long way by 1838; a glance at his biography is a helpful reminder that many different, individual stories lie behind the large-scale narrative of suburban expansion. Enduring and overcoming multiple financial disasters, the amputation of an arm, severe rheumatism, and laudanum addiction, this Bayswater resident became a successful landscape gardener, author of numerous well-received texts, and editor of (at one time) five separate monthly publications. (It is said that this indefatigable Victorian, still striving to right the wrecked boat of his finances in 1843, died literally standing on his feet.)[17] He built his house, 3–5 Porchester Terrace, in 1825, and the home is often credited as the building that popularized the "semi" in Victorian London. The Porchester Terrace house is two homes designed to look like a single, larger building (Loudon called it a "double detached"): he explains in his manual that "the entrances to the two houses are on opposite sides . . . the porches not being so conspicuous, and it being utterly impossible to see any considerable part of both at the same moment, from any point of view, the illusion is more complete."[18]

In his earlier publications, Loudon gave high value to the rural above the man-made: in his 1806 *Treatise on Forming, Improving, and Managing Country Residences,* he remarked on the charm of "glittering dew on the gossamer of grass or shrubs"; "a thousand other beauties belong to the country, which happily art can neither create, deform, nor annihilate." At this stage in his writing career, he lauded the rural availability of natural beauty to men and women of all classes: the charms of an early morning "may be enjoyed by the peasant on his native mountains, as completely as by the wealthy and noble in all the splendour of artificial magnificence."[19]

By 1838, Loudon was renegotiating his conception of the outdoors. In *The Suburban Gardener,* the countryside is no longer the preeminent space for contemplation of higher aesthetic pleasures—the suburban garden is. As he elevates the garden, he separates it from work associated with the countryside. Suburban gardening is not about digging, tilling, and food production, Loudon contends; it is about aesthetics, self-cultivation, and gentle exercise. He does discuss "simple or rude" work in the garden but dismisses such manual labor as unworthy of attention. "To dig, to hoe, and to rake, are not operations requiring much skill; and the amateur gardener will, perhaps, chiefly value them for their use in preparing for crops, or in encouraging the growth of crops already coming forward," he observes, before moving into more interesting suburban skills such as pruning and taking cuttings.[20]

The shift is not accidental; Loudon consistently values the production of aesthetically pleasing trees, flowers, and shrubs above food.[21] His analysis of fruit rearing is not about maximizing yields but about how to stage and contain the fruits so that they do not take up much room.[22] The decision for a freshly retired businessman to cultivate fruits or "culinary vegetables" is, Loudon suggests, simply "to afford exercise," a "beau ideal" for one who is "fond of plants."[23] The suburban resident buys food in the markets (Loudon is quite explicit about this) and cultivates figs and other ornamental fruits or vegetables in his or her garden for charm and challenge. Food production is thus set at a distance in the countryside; the suburban resident is evoked as consumer, not producer.

Yet Loudon does not take the challenges of gardening lightly: gardening is hard, good gardening is very hard, and he looks to modern discoveries to help resolve problems. In the areas of fruit production, cuttings, bulb forcing, and so forth, "scientific and practical knowledge" will, he insists, help gardeners see tangible and positive results ensue from their endeavours.[24] And in the case of cuttings, "a very little scientific light thrown on the subject leads to rules for operating, which will turn chance into certainty in almost every case that can occur to ordinary practitioners, and, consequently, will greatly enhance the pleasure of performing the operation, from the consciousness that the labour bestowed will not be thrown away."[25] Stressing the benefit of "a very little scientific light," as Loudon does repeatedly, intervenes into the way the act of gardening is learned; by disseminating the supposedly required science in an appropriately apportioned form, his book accords itself a critical role in the learning of horticulture.[26] Working with the land is not passed on through experience and family, like farming, but becomes instead a skill learned from Loudon's own book. The idea that the reader begins from a position of ignorance, knowing "little of gardening and rural affairs," is therefore less an authentic point of origin than a means of rendering vivid the reader's ability to be changed; turned, through reading, into a gardener. The gardener thereby constructed is a leisured amateur, one who dabbles for pleasure and aesthetics, not for profit or yield.

Happiness is, Loudon assures his reader, the prize for engaging the intellectual faculties in the garden, because the gardener's labors almost certainly will yield desired results; difficulties will be encountered but overcome. This type of happiness grows best in the suburbs, Loudon contends, because of the very confinement of the suburban plot: "The master of a suburban villa . . . finds enjoyment, not only in his family, friends, and books, but in his garden, and in the other rural objects which he can call his own, and which he can alter at pleasure, at a trifling expense, and often with his own hands. It is this which gives the charm of creation, and makes a thing essentially one's own."[27] The walled garden asserts by its construction that it encloses nature and renders it contained, cultured, civilized—precisely what the suburbs themselves demonstrated as they extended their reach into the countryside. In the suburban villa, "rural objects" could be owned and controlled; the smallness of the garden meant that the gardener became more effectively its "master." Technology facilitates this process for Loudon; he regularly recommends the new mowing machines to keep lawns trim and strongly advocates the purchase of a particular tool because, he suggests, it makes transplanting so entertaining that gardeners cannot stop themselves from doing it for fun.[28]

Wealthy landowners with expansive parklands are, he argues, *less* likely to be happy than suburbanites: they are more likely to use gardeners, and thus they do not enjoy the pleasures of invoking science in solving problems and are more likely to take on food production.[29] He seems to take a particular delight in the idea that landowners end up with worse food than suburban residents, because while the latter choose from a wide range of foods produced by many different growers in the markets, landowners are limited to what they can produce: "It may reasonably be calculated on, that every year, from unforeseen casualties, some crop will be found to fail, and others to be of inferior quality."[30] The rural peasant he valorized in *A Treatise* is replaced by the suburban dweller who, like his precursor, derives far greater pleasure from his surroundings than his more affluent contemporaries: "The master of a suburban residence, however small may be his demesne, may . . . procure health and enjoyment at the same time, with more certainty than the possessor of a larger property; because his grounds lie more in his hands, and he can superintend every change himself."[31] The ability to "master" the plot is a pleasure especially available, in Loudon's opinion, in the suburbs.

Early suburbanites typically came, as we have seen, from the country, not the city. Similarly, the *ideal* of the suburbs grew out of its departure from a rural, rather than an urban, experience. The charm of the suburban plot in *The Suburban Gardener* is precisely that it embodies a move away from the rural past, an opportunity to participate in and benefit from modernity; brick walls, creating a confined plot of land, are both practically useful and a means of marking out newness, difference. Yet Loudon's celebration of brick walls and hedges has long been interpreted as an effort to preserve the family from "prying eyes." Leonore Davidoff and Catherine Hall, for instance, contend that "in concrete terms of walls and hedges he promoted the privacy so important to suburban life; prying eyes and too much interest in other people's business took away from the charms of domesticity. Communal living with its echoes of the easy and promiscuous sociability of the poor was alien."[32] Marjorie Garson (who terms the Victorian home "an escape from the capitalist marketplace and the payoff for one's alienated labour in it") agrees that the interest Loudon shows in peripheries, walls, hedges, and boundaries becomes "a subliminal trope that dominates his thinking," a way of inscribing the lines of class that must be kept out, bounded, limited.[33] Garson, Hall, and Davidoff all agree that familial privacy is an important way for families to show off their leisured status in Loudon's work, and that the seclusion of the woman is valorized as a preeminent signal of mobility. The virtuous woman must be "like the plant in the pot," Davidoff and Hall observe, "limited and domesticated, sexually controlled, not spilling out into spheres in which she did not belong nor being overpowered by 'weeds' of social disorder."[34]

These critics and historians have tended to walk in the footsteps of the great urban historian Donald Olsen, who argued in the late 1970s that maintaining privacy was a near-universal Victorian preoccupation and a major defining factor in the shape and narrative of the suburbs. In the service of this idea, Olsen quotes a contributor to the *Building News* (1858) who remarked: "After travelling five miles from the Bank, we begin to grow impatient of gardens desecrated to semi-public use, and to demand a plot, however small, for the special delectation of our own family. . . . The ground wasted for supposed general use would in most cases be enough, if allotted in separate portions, to render each house semi-detached at least."[35] Notably, the language of "desecration" and "wasting" is missing from Loudon's text; Loudon positively favors public spaces given over to "general use." For example, he is impatient with the new phenomenon of locked squares "only accessible to the occupiers of the surrounding houses; whereas on the Continent they are open to all persons whatever," and argues that one of suburbia's chief pleasures is easy access to communal recreation spaces, such as a botanical garden, commercial nursery, or public orchard.[36] And the pleasure of these spaces is, interestingly enough, not an uplifting encounter with flowers but rather the opportunity to develop "cheerfulness . . . from the labours continually going forward there." Loudon argues that a "cultivated botanic garden" is preferable to a public square full of "fine plants, trees, fountains, statues, and other objects" because the square lacks "the peculiar animation" of a space full of workers.[37]

Loudon's delight in enjoyment offered by public outdoor spaces may lead us, in fact, to ponder the writer's motivations in the *Building News:* given the nature of the publication, perhaps the speculative gentleman saw in land given over to "semi-public use" opportunities for commercial development, or the potential for squeezing out a few "semi-detached houses" for rent. Loudon, with different motives in play, finds delight in the coexistence of nature and bustling activity in a public orchard. This makes his reading of the suburban garden—as an opportunity to combine the outdoors with industrial advance—less surprising. The charm of both spaces lies in their blending of private and public, the harmonious juxtaposition of plants with brick.

For Loudon, suburbia is fundamentally a space of connectedness both with the industrial moment and with other people. In the suburbs, factories may be glimpsed, which Loudon terms—in marked contrast to his contemporary, Charles Dickens—"magnificent masses": living near a factory should not be ruled out, Loudon contends, and may even be deliberately chosen, if the building is well designed.[38] In *The Old Curiosity Shop* (1841) factory chimneys are described as an "endless repetition of the same dull, ugly, form," their smoke "the horror of oppressive dreams," while the miserable suburban developments nearby are blackened with coal dust, their gardens sinking "under the hot breath of kiln and furnace."[39] Nell and her grandfather, longing for the countryside, find only a terrible absence of rural peace on their journey through the heartland of the nation. But Loudon's vision couldn't be more different.

The suburbs are places not of death and dying but of living in Loudon's *Suburban Gardener.* The suburban landscape is fundamentally conducive to growth—of plants, new interests, new insights, new friendships. In the chaotic cities residents do not always know their neighbors, Loudon contends, but in the suburbs they do, and cosy neighborliness is also central to his vision of what suburbia offers.[40] He opines that "not only is social intercourse essential to the happiness of grown-up persons; but, as children must mix with the world sooner or later, it is better that they should do this with their neighbours, and under the eye of their parents, than that it should be deferred till they leave the parental roof."[41] If city dwellers find themselves lost in the teeming millions of the city, their children assaulted by risks, rural residents too may find themselves lost—albeit for quite different reasons. Loudon lauds the suburban life over the life of comparable income in the countryside because of the greater opportunities to connect with friends and experience crowds:

> One immense advantage of a suburban residence over one isolated in the country consists in its proximity to neighbours, and the facilities it affords of participating in those sources of instruction and enjoyment which can only be obtained in towns: for example, public libraries and museums, theatrical representations, musical concerts, public and private assemblies, exhibitions of works of art, &c. The suburban resident, by his locality, has an opportunity of witnessing these spectacles with as much ease as the distant wealthy proprietor has, by means of his establishment of horses and carriages. The small proprietor and the farmer in the interior of the country, on the other hand, are comparatively shut out from participating in the enjoyments which constant intercourse with society procures; as well as from receiving that refinement of mien and of manners which it produces.[42]

Far from advocating retired domesticity and decrying "promiscuous sociability," Loudon's vision of the new suburbs turns on the opportunities for socializing through the use of the roads and railways, which Loudon memorably calls "one of the finest artificial features of the moving kind."[43] Given their curious beauty, who *wouldn't* want to live near railways? Dickens evoked the new trains in *Dombey and Son* as virtual monsters, approaching with "two red eyes, and a fierce fire, dropping glowing coals; an irresistible bearing on of a great roaring and dilating mass." Loudon, rather more prosaically, remarks: "We have been much struck with the effect of the carriages passing along the line of the Manchester railway, as seen from the beautiful villas, particularly one erected from a design by Mr. Barry, situated on the high bank which overlooks the valley through which that railway is conducted."[44] Here, as so often occurs in *The Suburban Gardener,* Loudon raises his voice to hymn the aesthetics of modernity visible from the suburban peripheries.

Forging an ideal of middle-class identity in the form of the suburban gardener, Loudon presents the suburbanite as a master of the universe.[45] The suburban garden is a space in which to prove middle-class affiliation and to forge middle-class traits of patience, diligence, and consumerism. As happiness replaces production as the end goal of gardening, so an entire class may experience the "refined enjoyment" that Loudon sees defining a new, advanced age. His discourse of modernity allows him to transform manual labor and food production into skills for the middle classes. Technology and science allow dabbling in areas traditionally associated with the lower classes both because dirt may be minimized and because the skill is learned from a purchased text, not from family. Far from wistfully recalling the rural or enforcing family seclusion, Loudon celebrates the suburban outdoors as a space in which all meanings of "recreation" are in play, as a place of pleasurable pastime and a place for remaking oneself and the land. Given that modernity became later associated with alienation and isolation, with fundamental schisms (between, as Nicholas Daly summarizes, "people and things"), it is remarkable that Loudon celebrates the modernity of suburbia as an opportunity to connect with people, with the land, and with the commercial and technological possibilities of a new age.[46]

WOMEN'S ROLE IN LOUDON'S SUBURBAN GARDEN

After directing his book to the edification of those who "know little of gardening and rural affairs," Loudon adds that the book is "more particularly for the use of ladies."[47] He presumes a female readership from the beginning; indeed, he appears to expect that women will seek information on the choice of a house, or "the Situation on which to form one . . . the Laying out, Planting, and general Management of the Garden and Grounds; the whole adapted for Grounds from One Perch to Fifty Acres and upwards in Extent."[48] The book as a whole is long, dense, and complex: the introduction alone consists of eight pages of closely typeset explanations. From the outset, Loudon frames gardening as an intellectually as well as physically challenging activity in which women can fully participate.

Modern critics—Marjorie Garson especially—have assumed that Loudon cannot possibly mean that women should involve themselves in the more physical aspects of gardening, and that his address to women at the text's opening is therefore a feint.[49] In fact, gardening texts aimed directly at women commonly covered detailed discussions of physical tasks. Jane Loudon's own gardening books (as we shall see in more detail presently) give advice on some of the more potentially insalubrious aspects of gardening, including "manuring the hot-beds" and spadework; J. B. Whiting observes in *The Manual of Flower Gardening for Ladies* (1849) that even if women are not doing all the work themselves, they need to know about every aspect of creating and structuring it.[50] Whiting contends that "the labours which the landscape gardener has to superintend are trenching, ploughing, or digging; planting; road and walk making; cutting and relaying turf; laying down land into permanent grass; forming ponds or reforming the course of brooks or rivers; removing earth; draining; well-digging; together with every branch of hydraulics which may be useful for the convenience or embellishment of a country residence."[51] The language of feminine delicacy that Loudon adopts in the text must be set, then, beside what seems to have been a widespread expectation that women needed rigorous training in all aspects of gardening. The address to women in the subtitle of his book is not merely a polite bow but a recognition of women's gardening practices.

Loudon claims that the position of the middle-class suburban woman is, like that of a man, especially conducive to happiness. For an upper-class lady, entertainment must be sought in "airings in her carriage" and "recreation in her pleasure-ground"; shepherded from place to place, her activities are circumscribed by the importance of maintaining the class hierarchy through limited interactions with others.[52] The suburban housewife, on the other hand, enjoys the satisfaction of achieving small successes with her own hands, opportunities for neighborly friendships, and "the personal management of her household affairs."[53] To Loudon, suburbia appeals to women because it offers opportunities for self-determining action, not because it preserves them from urban problems or prying eyes. Indeed, he argues at the start of his book that the suburban housewife's "enjoyments are the same as those of her husband": while he certainly takes at face value the idea that the husband will go into work each day and the wife will stay at home, the suburban garden is one where both spouses meet to pursue personal fulfillment in substantially similar activities.[54]

Women gardeners are in fact Loudon's beau ideal of the female suburbanite—these hard-working individuals will help Loudon beautify the nation, possibly even the world: "If we can succeed in rendering every lady her own landscape-gardener, which we are confident we can do, we shall have great hopes of effecting a general reform in the gardening taste, not only of this country, but of every other for which this work is calculated: and we intend it for circulation in the temperate climates of both hemispheres."[55] In pursuit of this goal, he presents trained professional women as, intriguingly, especially likely to succeed, because, in them, "natural" feminine good taste meets systematic aesthetic training: "We venture to assert that there is not a mantuamaker or milliner, who understands her business, that might not, in a few hours, be taught to design flower-gardens with as much skill and taste as a professional landscape-gardener; and so as to produce incomparably better results than are now generally to be seen in the flower-gardens of the great majority of British country residences."[56] Some upper-class ladies may be led astray by their taste for sumptuous finery, he observes, which will lead them to put too many rich-looking objects in the same room (or garden). Professional women trained in aesthetics—those, crucially, able to navigate economic constraints—are less likely to fall into this trap. Furnishing a home involves a trained awareness of "what to aim at, . . . what is practicable, and what is impracticable, within the limits to which we are circumscribed by locality, income, or other circumstances."[57] The mantuamaker and the milliner, experienced navigators of both requirements, are well positioned to become the best landscape gardeners and leaders of Loudon's suburban charge. Professional women and suburban gardens will together, Loudon suggests, ensure the health of the nation.

Certainly Loudon combines pronouncements on the value of professional training and self-determining action for suburban women with references to women's physical delicacy. Often when he invokes the term "lady" he clusters around it associations of frailty that jar with the text's avowed intention to turn women into educated, active landscape gardeners: "Tying up and trimming flowers are operations generally undertaken by the ladies of the family," he observes, "but the pruning of shrubs and trees, and tying up to stakes such as require it, invite the hand of the master."[58] "Master" here takes on its familiar meaning of the masculine hand's superior control; the "modernity" of this moment lies precisely in the separation of women's and men's responses to the organic. The middle-class wife asserts through mere "tying and trimming" that she is leisured and no "gatherer," that her family has socially advanced. In passages like these, Loudon endorses a gendered hierarchy of activity.

Yet these moments are comparatively few and far between: on the whole, Loudon makes little reference to the differences between what men and women should or can do, so that his occasional bows to women's frailty seem largely rhetorical. At most, they guarantee the text's social respectability: he renders gardening consistent with emerging ideals of the delicate leisured woman, thereby attempting to ensure that the suburbanite woman gardener is able to continue her work with impunity. Loudon's female suburbanite gets on with the designing and the planting, then comes indoors periodically to ask her husband for help in chopping back shrubs—just as the master sometimes asks "the man" for help with the heaviest digging. Both sexes, in other words, are asked to navigate a boundary line of class and physical activity. In a world in which physical activity is becoming heavily freighted with class meaning, Loudon works to suggest that the suburban garden is one place where the pleasures of free movement for both sexes may become possible.

REVISING THE SHAPE OF MIDDLE-CLASS LIFE: THE VILLA GARDENER

In 1850, *The Suburban Gardener* was posthumously released in revised form as *The Villa Gardener,* edited by Loudon's wife, Jane. What John himself planned for the text must remain unknown; in her preface, Jane observed that he intended "to alter the work considerably, by omitting a portion of the Suburban Gardens, and inserting more descriptions of Villas," though we cannot know precisely which sections he planned to leave out.[59] Certainly, the new work is (mercifully) shorter. But the abbreviations come at a cost, for while *The Suburban Gardener* embraces a broad range of suburban experiences—Loudon incorporated extraordinary detail on the needs and characteristics of "first-rate" to "fourth-rate" homes, on double-detached and single-detached homes, on homes of different acreage—the updated *Villa Gardener* is far more focused on the life of a more narrowly defined middle-class occupant. Loudon does still recognize that suburban residents have different means and needs. But the shift in title is not accidental. Offering opportunities to beautify the "villa," the text is more fundamentally aspirational. And the vision of suburban living is substantially changed.[60]

A comparison between the old and newer editions serves to point out what makes the earlier, 1838 *Suburban Gardener* so remarkable, most particularly its energetic defense of the modern. The earlier text's lively embrace of railways and manufacturing spaces is gone by mid-century, as are the celebrations of commercial nurseries, botanical gardens, and other public spaces. *The Villa Gardener*'s conception of suburban space is more oriented around privacy and far less interested in the ways in which suburbia allows proximity to other people: while passages on the value of gates to keep out prying eyes are not new, they acquire a new prominence in a text that no longer celebrates suburban friendships. The earlier text navigated between the pleasures of community and the value of privacy, but the later manual says virtually nothing on community at all. *The Villa Gardener* looks to public spaces only for architectural and landscape inspiration, and it uses discussion of the public to foreground the ways in which the private must look different.

The references to the mantuamaker and milliner have also disappeared. The professional woman worker Loudon celebrated in 1838 has been replaced with a far more leisured figure: "There is not *any lady* who can design a pattern, and embroider a gown, that might not, in a few hours, be taught to design flower-gardens with as much skill as a professional landscape-gardener," he observes.[61] *The Villa Gardener* continues to address itself "more particularly to ladies" in the subtitle, but the passage about a woman's particular delight in managing her own household affairs is erased; Loudon's 1850 text outlines only the pleasures of suburbia for men. The references to ladies that do linger in the text of *The Villa Gardener* posit women's interaction with the garden as either faintly fraught (as when voluminous dresses catch on nails) or paint women moving through the gardens and greenhouses in search of shady places to sit.[62] This is not to say that the 1850 text does not anticipate a woman's activity in the garden at all; aside from the continued prominence of the subtitle (indeed, the words are actually rendered in enlarged type on the title page), Jane Loudon's own *Ladies' Companion to the Flower Garden* is (perhaps unsurprisingly) quoted repeatedly. But nonetheless there is a significant change in emphasis in the representation of women's roles, a shift away from discussions of women's pleasure and need for self-fulfillment. There is no mention of professional women's especially useful skills.

This change, combined with the erasure of celebrations of bustling community, significantly reframes what the text has to offer. *The Suburban Gardener* presented the 1838 reader with a vision of suburbia in which the shape of the streets and the choice of a home enabled self-determining action and a productive blending of public and private, nature with brick, where women and men came together to experience what modernity had to offer. Loudon's posthumously published voice submerges the joyous experience of the public in a more reserved, private space. *The Villa Gardener* is a much warier text. Women all but disappear into the new, quieter home; only a flourish of skirts remains. In the title, the "suburban" is reduced to the "villa," and with it goes the earlier emphasis on architectural range; the reframed text speaks to a shift away from the suburban as a space of choice.

Loudon's 1850 suburb is positioned in counterpoint to the city, rather than the country. While the 1838 suburb was a space of bustling modernity, oriented around public streets and parks, the 1850 suburb is, rather, a "self-contained [world]," as Hapgood puts it, made "safe from London's dangers, where the sanctity of family life and the pre-eminence of love flourish in *rus in urbe* surroundings."[63] Tellingly, Loudon's entire discussion on how suburban rows constitute a move away from the defensive past has also been removed. Loudon's final text is shaped by a form of cultural defensiveness that finds expression not in the comforting huddle of a village circle but in the confines of a single private house.

What changed? Loudon's later vision of the suburb is certainly more consistent with a growing cultural ideal of the home as a place of refuge from the threats of the modern world (threats explored, for instance, in Condition of England novels by Dickens, Gaskell, and others through the 1840s). We can't know if Loudon's perspective changed for biographical reasons, if an editor stepped in, if the dying Loudon found the rapidly changing character of Bayswater disturbing, or what part Jane played in the rewriting and cutting of the text.[64] All we can know for certain is that John Claudius Loudon ranged along an interpretive spectrum, reading the suburb first as a site of opportunity and modernity, later as a place of sanctity and retreat. At all times, this indefatigable Bayswater resident presented the suburbs growing around him as an important phenomenon to explore and a proving ground for middle-class identity: his treatment of modernity may shift, but he continued to present the ideal suburb as a place of middle-class thriving. Not everyone agreed, as we shall see in the next chapter. The notion of the suburbs as the preserve of the dull, tasteless, and small-minded was already a cultural commonplace.

CHAPTER 2

Setting Suburban Stereotypes
1820s–1850s

Turn-of-the-century texts like George Gissing's *In the Year of Jubilee* (1896) and *The Whirlpool* (1897), T. W. H. Crosland's *The Suburbans* (1905), and H. G. Wells's *Ann Veronica* (1909) evoke the suburban landscape as an anonymous dystopia. Here the values of mass culture and fussy women predominate: professional men lack community and are forced into the uncongenial practice of commuting through an atomized space whose landscape signifies wider social disintegration. This unease, read without reference to earlier literature on suburbanization, is regularly characterized as the product of a fundamentally proto-modernist—or at least anti-Victorian—sensibility. When writers like Gissing and Wells evoke the suburban landscape as stultifying and boring, critics tend to view such characterizations as grounded in a "critique of modern urban society and [a] rejection of Victorian values at the end of the nineteenth century," as A. James Hammerton has put it.[1] Critical interpretations of such texts thereby situate dissatisfactions with the shape and characteristics of the landscape within a crucially fin de siècle battle, stressing that the "long, unlovely rows of semi-detached villas" became a crucial image for emerging modernists of the worst the previous era's industrializing, democratizing zeal had to offer.[2]

Yet ninety years before Leonard Bast dragged out his miserable existence in *Howard's End,* the idea of suburbia as deadening, culturally sterile, petit bourgeois Dulham was a literary commonplace.[3] Dating as far back as the late 1820s, in the work of Edward Bulwer-Lytton, suburbia is evoked by some as a cultural wasteland dominated by the values of women and the bourgeois. By the 1840s and 1850s, notions of suburbia as boring, aesthetically sterile, populated by the masses, and hence dull were so familiar as to be a stereotype—a word whose contemporary usage was emerging at just the same time. Indeed, the relationship between the meaning of the word "suburb" and the newly metaphorical use of the term "stereotyping" was an intimate one, for it was precisely through a new awareness of the processes of commercialism and mass production that the modern meaning of stereotyping gained currency. Victorian writers, disturbed at the promises of suburbia stamped out tirelessly in the print press and in auctioneer's pamphlets, used the language of a mechanized process to describe what they saw, calling the age-old puffery surrounding commodification "stereotyping." At the same time, writers sought to rebut the commercially produced stereotypes of utopian suburbia with stereotypes of deadening suburbia in a process of replacement that intriguingly replicated the two-step mechanics of stereotype production itself. To talk about "the suburb" in the first half of the century was to talk about a word whose meaning an aristocratic elite was struggling to wrest back from the forces of commercialization by engaging the language and the tools of industrial modernity. Decrying suburbia at the fin de siècle placed a speaker in a long literary and cultural tradition, then; Gissing, Wells, Crosland, and Forster inherited images and terms of culturally and aesthetically arid, bourgeois suburbia that had been in circulation for decades. Rather than emerging as a proto-modernist reaction against Victorian middle-class ideals of domesticity, or even as a response to the rapid development of lower-middle-class suburban housing from the 1870s onward, the language of suburban aridity was produced in the first place to overset and repudiate the auctioneer's stereotype.[4] Indeed, it is quite literally in the mechanized presses of the 1820s that the narrative of suburbia begins.

THE CONSTRUCTION OF THE SUBURBS AND THE SUBURBAN STEREOTYPE

As F. M. L. Thompson argued in "The Rise of Suburbia," the "great suburban sea-change" began in the middle of the eighteenth century, but it was only in "the years after Waterloo" that "modern suburban development got properly under way on a significant scale."[5] The mass construction of homes was, of course, only one of many forms of mass production emerging in the

1820s and '30s. Printing was another, and discussions of both new print practices and suburban building coincide along the axis of industrial unease. Standardization, the loss of old skills, whether in typesetting or construction, and the tastes and demands of the masses emerge as common concerns. Moreover, mass-produced printing was felt dangerously to enable the business of speedy suburban construction: critics of suburban development repeatedly decried the standardized texts stamped out by land developers, speculators, and auctioneers for aiding in the commodification—and hence debasement—of the home. Indeed, intriguingly, discussions of suburbia were one place where the word "stereotype" made the jump from its literal to its metaphorical meaning, as authors searched for a term to describe the proliferation of idealized descriptions of middle-class homes produced for commercial gain.[6] In an article on the characteristics of modern advertising in the *Dublin Review* (1849), for instance, the author skates the edges of the two meanings of "stereotype" (as an industrial-era printing phenomenon and an excessively repeated phrase or idea) to describe the frequent appearance of the supposedly ideal middle-class home in contemporary newspaper advertisements: a "man who advertises a house to let, does not even tell us that it had 'a dining-room and drawing-room, and four best bed-rooms, besides servants' ditto, and excellent offices,' all which we suppose the 'Times' keeps stereotyped, for its advertisements of semi-detached villas, at Clapham or Croydon."[7] The *OED* dates the first appearance of the metaphorical meaning of "stereotyping" to the 1840s; I have not found it in common use in this manner before the early 1850s.[8] The *Dublin Review* article from the late 1840s captures the word in transition. Thus while suburbia was obviously not the only industrial artifact to produce a shift in the meaning of "stereotype," it was in the room at the birth. The *Dublin Review* article suggests that the home advertisement—particularly the *Times*'s soon-to-be-infamous "houses to let" section—was one place where readers saw on a daily basis the commercial enterprise of selling and renting homes rendered in print form, and where the unvarying nature of the advertisements' prose seemingly duplicated the unvarying nature of the suburban homes themselves. Describing the first as "stereotyped" eased the passage into describing the second as stereotyped also, not least because the worries surrounding the two industries corresponded closely. "Stereotyping" was not just an industrially produced word, then; it was one whose shifting meaning spoke to its ability to capture discomfort with the fundamental shape and directions of industrial modernity.

"RUS IN URBE"

The stereotypes of inimical, dull, deadening suburbia that were to become pervasive moreover possess the striking feature that, from the earliest years, the form of their construction mimicked the mechanical process of print stereotyping. Stereotypes of enervating suburbia were almost always framed by an expression of concern about the commercialized image of *delightful* suburbia found in the auctioneer's pamphlet or the newspaper advertisement. Rather as the print stereotyping process was a two-step process, in which a metal cast was created from a papier-mâché mold, so the literary stereotyping of deadening suburbia itself engaged two steps, with a final shape created as the inverse of a preexisting form. This is not to say that writers always or necessarily termed their own portraits of suburbia "stereotypes." But from the first, the images of suburbia that were to become commonplace in literary texts—of suburbia as dreary, dull, poorly built, packed with crooks and sharks—were presented as alternatives to the stamped-out images of ideal gentlemen's residences propagated by speculators, developers, and auctioneers.

The anger Bulwer-Lytton expressed at the pettiness and materialism of the aristocracy, his conviction that class warfare was not only inevitable but also sanctionable between the haves and have-nots (terms he famously coined in *Lucretia*), did not result in sympathetic representations of what one might call the democratizing impulse of suburbia.[9] Instead his fictions treat the suburbs as a deeply unpleasant product of what he termed "our sickly civilization" in *Night and Morning* (1841), a place where exploitation of and crime against the virtuous was rampant.[10] His fictions regularly ridicule and reject the near-utopian claims made for middle-class suburbia, especially in advertisements—its putative opportunities for peace and quiet, retired living, and limited encounters with others of a similar class and sensibility. Indeed, characters who speak of these idyllic qualities are virtually always criminal. Bulwer-Lytton was one of the very first writers to note and seek to combat idealized images of suburbia propagated to sell houses en masse, and his distaste for the increasing cultural force of the tastes and aesthetics of the "new" middle classes in the 1820s, '30s, and '40s anticipates by decades plots and preoccupations of the fin de siècle. In particular, his evocation of the spider-like woman lurking within the suburban villa, waiting to lure in the passing unwary young man, was to become a literary commonplace. In this, its earliest form, however, the woman's villainy lies less in her sexual predations than in her distasteful willingness to commodify her home.

In *The Disowned* (1829), the young hero (who, in his disowned state, goes by the name Clarence Linden) is repeatedly tricked on his arrival in London by a dubious character named Morris Brown, who attempts to sell any number of useless goods—mustard, a green parrot—in order to part Linden from his money. After failing to stick Linden with a hefty bill for unnecessary perishable items, the entrepreneurial Mr. Brown next lures him with promises of a suburban lodging—"a charming little abode, sir, situated in the suburbs of London, quite *rus in urbe,* as the scholars say; you can have a delightful little back parlor, looking out upon the garden, and all to yourself, I daresay." The suburban home is thus one more useless commodity that Brown tries to foist on Linden—and at last his point finds its mark. The friendless Linden, looking to find his way to climb "a high step in the world's ladder," imagines that the modern suburbs offer the best possible residence for one lacking patronage, one who must therefore turn to "regular methods of adventure and enterprise" to establish himself.[11]

The joke underlying Brown's claim of "rus in urbe" is of course that the Latin phrase is far from confined to scholars—that it is, in fact, the cornerstone of the commercialized appeal of the suburbs (Thomas Gray used the phrase wryly in a letter to describe the area of Hampstead and Highgate, as early as 1759, as "rus-in-urbe-ish").[12] The suburban lodging to which Linden is introduced immediately gives the lie to Brown's inflated claims and, by expansion, those made for suburbia itself: "At the suburbs towards Paddington, Mr. Brown stopped at a very small house; it stood rather retired from its surrounding neighbours, which were of a loftier and more pretending aspect than itself, and, in its awkward shape and pitiful bashfulness, looked exceedingly like a schoolboy . . . shrinking with all possible expedition into the obscurest corner he can discover. Passing through a sort of garden, in which a spot of grass lay in the embraces of a stripe of gravel, Mr. Brown knocked upon a very bright knocker at a very new door."[13]

The dream of rus in urbe is shown here in debased form, as "a sort of garden" with "a spot of grass," the hope for respite from pollution reduced to nothing more than a selling point. The very grass seems to suffer the "embraces" of the faddish gravel; Bulwer-Lytton's description of the home and its miserable environs conveys a sense of deep unease at exposure to the modern world. The "shrinking" schoolboy Bulwer-Lytton conjures suffers "pitiful bashfulness" and even struggles to hide himself in an obscure corner, all terms that evoke intense social awkwardness in a situation full of threat. The home seems to loathe what it has become, the space it is forced to inhabit, the neighboring buildings to which it is exposed. In characterizing the house in this way, Bulwer-Lytton implicitly sketches the situation of *all* males in the suburban landscape—as not only awkward but diminished. For here, as in many late Victorian texts, suburbia is evoked as a world where men are, as Hammerton argues, "emasculated and ridiculous."[14] (Apart from Forster's tragic Leonard Bast, one thinks of Mr. Morgan in Gissing's *In the Year of Jubilee,* Mr. Jordan in "The Prize Lodger," Ella D'Arcy's hectored and dying Catterson in "A Marriage," or, in a text I discuss in chapter 3, the prodigiously deceived hero of Wilkie Collins's *Basil* [1852]). Linden should learn from the home's own emotions of pathetic self-loathing, the narrative implies, and get out of suburbia as quickly as possible, or he will become not only unhappy but unmanned.

The hero's moment of standing by the door, followed by "symbolic threshold-crossing" into a sinister space dominated by a bourgeois woman's values and aesthetics, is one that was often repeated at the fin de siècle. "As men pass from the free, masculine space of town and street, through the transitional front garden and into the domestic interior they enter a world alien to their nature," Gail Cunningham observes; the moment of passing through the front door is a moment of entering into a world where women's concerns—which seem fundamentally the overthrow of men's traditional privileges—predominate.[15] For suburban spider-women here, as in late Victorian texts, invariably have both secret plans and bad taste, which somehow become so fused that possession of one seems virtually to guarantee the existence of the other. The act of passing inside the door necessarily entails exposure to a strangely decorated space: threat is typically "signaled through images of darkness and gloomy interiors revealing small but potentially malignant female figures," Cunningham continues.[16] This is exactly what happens to Bulwer-Lytton's 1829 hero: "Up a singularly narrow staircase, into a singularly diminutive drawing-room, Clarence and his guide [Mr. Brown] were ushered. There, seated on a little chair by a little work-table, with one foot on a little stool and one hand on a little book, was a little, very little lady."[17] This extraordinary little creature, Mrs. Copperas, is every bit as spider-like as Ella D'Arcy's odd, colorless Nettie Hooper in "A Marriage," and just as set on luring in her prey. But there is a crucial difference: Bulwer-Lytton's villainess sets her lures with offers of gentility and not, like Nettie—or Collins's Margaret Sherwin—with sexual promise.

Living in a suburban home in the nineteenth century was, Kate Flint has argued, theoretically a sign of "one's ability to purchase leisure," and thus potentially a way to buy "at least in the imagination, into the tradition and culture of the aristocracy."[18] Bulwer-Lytton makes clear the commercial underpinnings of Mrs. Copperas's aspirations by endowing her descriptions of her house from the first with advertiser jargon. Thus, for instance, she displays a land developer or real estate agent's generous notions of geography: "We possess accommodations of a most elegant description: accustomed to the genteelest circles, enjoying the pure breezes of the Highgate hills . . . you will find our retreat no less eligible than unique," she informs Linden, who is then introduced to two rooms, each the size of a box.[19] Needless to say, the Paddington home has little in common with the more elegant hills of north London. And, as the text progresses, every interaction between Linden and his host is a further opportunity for the narrator to reveal similar "truths." The tea is heavily watered down; the Butler "de Warens" is really a footboy; the "company" Mrs. Copperas flaunts is "chiefly in commercial life"; Mr. Copperas himself is, for all Mrs. Copperas's cooings, a vulgar "stock-jobber"; and Mrs. Copperas is constantly betraying herself (by publically admonishing her son, for instance) in ways that reveal she is no "lady."[20]

Indeed, while Mrs. Copperas does not have a sexual interest in Linden, for Bulwer-Lytton her willingness to open up her home, and commercialize it, is functionally akin to a debased sexual exchange. "You are desirous, sir, of entering into the bosom of my family," the lady declares effusively on first meeting Linden: the language of intimacy and sentiment fits uncomfortably with the fact that Mrs. Copperas is simultaneously observing the new lodger to determine how much he can afford to pay (in the end she is, the narrator observes coolly, "not above three times as extortionate as she ought to have been").[21] In this novel, as in other Bulwer-Lytton texts, the sense of threat introduced by such corrupted suburban fraudsters is further heightened by images of sexual danger in the suburban landscape, which is closely associated with the alien feminine. Thus in *Night and Morning,* for example, published in the early 1840s, a suburban lodging room is rendered all the more disturbing through an image of sexual control: "There was an air of heated discomfort in the thick, solid moreen curtains; in the gaudy paper, in the bright-staring carpet, in the very looking-glass over the chimney piece, where a strip of mirror lay imprisoned in an embrace of frame covered with yellow muslin."[22] Rather like the gravel outside Mrs. Copperas's house, here the "embrace" of the mirror's frame confines. It is surely not accidental that the embracing frame is attired in flaunting, brightly colored muslin ("a bit of muslin" being a common synonym for prostitute), and the passage begins with an image of a fly paper hanging from the ceiling "swarmed with flies," to further hint at the dangers of temptation. The language of disgust and repulsion that Bulwer-Lytton's narrator employs is not only disgust at middle-class tastes, then (at the "bright-staring carpet" and "gaudy paper" that have not had time to fade, at the lack of a long-established garden to offer shade and sanctuary). The values of the middle classes are also aligned in this novel, as in *The Disowned,* with the very worst commercial exchanges, so that renting out a house becomes perilously close to renting out the body, with the prostituting woman possessing near-lethal power.

Bulwer-Lytton's gentlemen inevitably respond to suburbia with disgust (Paul Clifford, who becomes a highwayman, is the exception that proves the rule). In *Night and Morning,* which begins with the widowhood of a lady unable to prove the lawful nature of her marriage, the narrative concentrates on the hardship experienced by the lady's proud sixteen-year-old son, Philip, in loathsome suburbia. The boy escapes the suburban house as much as he possibly can, wandering the streets listlessly (but admirably) in search of opportunities for restoring the family fortunes. Linden, however, is conveniently relieved from further suburban horrors by an encounter with a wealthy gentleman: having saved the gentleman's life from dangerous burglars, he is led into a more "honest" life of affluence and aristocratic patronage, where claims of elegance are backed up by fact and where commercial inducements hold less sway. Uncovering the "truth" of bourgeois suburbia—as tasteless, vulgar, and commercialized—is a process that ultimately resituates it as reliably, reassuringly beneath the aristocratic in the social and cultural hierarchy; the hero's own sterling qualities make the restoration of him and his values a foregone conclusion. Linden is so deeply conscious of good taste that he never seems seriously at risk of becoming the pitiful schoolboy: he sees easily through the Copperases' stratagems from the first. He is also immediately recognized by *real* gentlemen for the man of taste he is and, through a combination of good luck and bravery, achieves his rewards. The lot of the bourgeois men in the novel is rather different: they are either fraudsters or dupes or both, either in cahoots with or manipulated by women, so that their very weakness becomes a further mechanism through which the values and tastes of the aristocratic male are restored.

Yet the experience of threat to those values and tastes is an originary point to which the novels repeatedly return. *The Disowned* begins with a fierce and impassioned diatribe on the need to escape the encroaching ravages of the suburban landscape, imagining the parceling up of land into plots as a sort of invasion, a direct assault. The tale is set in the later years of the eighteenth century, and it asks the reader to hearken back to the days when areas now developed were peaceful fields: standing in a patch of countryside on the very edge of the city, Clarence Linden inveighs against what will happen next. He blames all those he believes are involved in chopping up England's ground—and "feelings"—into a world of terraces: "Is it the puny and spiritless artisan, or the debased and crippled slave of the counter and the till, or the sallow speculator on morals, who would mete us out our liberty, our happiness, our very feelings, by the yard and inch and fraction? No, no; let *them* follow what the books and precepts of their own wisdom teach them; let them cultivate more highly the lands they have already parcelled out by dikes and fences, and leave, though at scanty intervals, some green patches of unpolluted land for the poor man's beast and the free man's foot."[23] This passage reveals that Linden is no friend to "the debased and crippled slave of the counter and the till . . . the sallow speculator on morals," or to any other entity engaged in the process of suburbanizing the nation. But he also explicitly connects commercial and entrepreneurial activities with a loss to *him* of the rights of the "free man's foot": "our liberty, our happiness, our very feelings" are attacked, he believes, by the processes of land subdivision and suburbanization. Notably, Linden and the novel highly value the city, which is described as a world of zesty, interesting civilization, of culture and society, of "all genial companionship"; the text is no enemy to the urban itself, perceiving the city as a space of exciting freedom (for men).[24] The countryside meanwhile occupies an equivocal position both here and in other Bulwer-Lytton novels for, while explicitly hymned, rural pastimes are evoked as painfully—indeed, in *Night and Morning,* even fatally—boring.[25] The defense of the freedom to ramble in *The Disowned* is less about sniffing country air than it is about a world whose spatial order is changing in ways that point to deeper, more structural shifts.

For at this point, around the years of Victoria's accession, the assaults Bulwer-Lytton identifies do not stem from reasons common in later texts—the uncongenial practice of commuting, for example. His image of disgusting suburbia is nested instead in a rejection of its emerging presentation as a modern-day ideal, which is to say a rejection of commerce and capitalism and above all the great, slow fading of the aristocracy. Linden's concern with the invading suburban is underwritten by a libertarianism that really aims to maintain "freedoms" only an upper-class male can fully enjoy. Linden's nebulous association of the suburban with the alien or prostituting woman is ultimately a way of first characterizing and then unmanning the encroaching middle classes, in an effort to reinforce their subservient position in the deferential order.

LETTING AND LEAVING THE SUBURBAN HOME

How did the middle classes react to the assault on their new homes? John Claudius Loudon, as we have seen, cautiously pulled back from his defense of suburban living as a place of joyous modern opportunity, though he remained the suburbs' advocate; others joined in the growing chorus of criticism. In 1859, George Augustus Sala published a satirical nonfiction take on London's development entitled *Gaslight and Daylight: With Some London Scenes They Shine Upon* (1859). Sala's examination of the "Houses to Let" pages in the *Times* is, on the face of it, an immensely critical response to the commodification of suburbia: the parceling up of land into plots, the parceling up of homes into goods, and the absolute necessity of becoming an informed consumer in a modern world. Like Bulwer-Lytton, Sala frames his stereotypes of deadening suburbia with reference to texts that advertise its supposedly utopian promise. But Sala is no aristocrat, and here and in other middle-class texts of the period a male speaker stages his own bewilderment in the face of sharp practices, characterizing himself repeatedly as victim, not perpetuator, of suburban growth.

In general, Victorians did not own their houses but took short leases and moved as their own financial circumstances—and the class affiliation of their street—changed.[26] This practice of constant moving, and all that moving involves—advertising, dealing with agents, hiring movers, selling and buying new furnishings—fit oddly with the emerging ideology of the home as an almost church-like space, removed from the world of commerce, dedicated to preserving the sanctity of the family.[27] John Tosh has argued in his study of middle-class masculinity that the practice of constant moving may in fact have reinforced men's "nostalgia for the home of their dreams" and "sentimental attraction to childhood, when home was imagined to have been as a 'real' home should be."[28] Sala makes the strangely commercial realities of home life in the modern era very clear by comparing houses to other consumable goods in a passage of intense Victorian self-mockery: "We change our dresses, our servants, our friends and foes—how can our houses expect to be exempt from the mutabilities of life? We tire of the old friend, and incline to the new; the old baby is deposed in favour of the new baby; the fat turnip silver watch our father gave us, gives place to a gold Geneva—we change, and swop, and barter, and give up, and take back, and long for, and get tired of, all and everything in life—why not of houses too? So the Supplement of the 'Times' can always offer Houses to Let; and we are continually running mad to let or hire them, as vice versa six months hence, perhaps we shall be as maniacally eager to hire or to let."[29] Sala never uses the term "stereotype," but here, as in the *Dublin Review* article of a decade earlier, we see contemplation of newspaper advertisements prompting observations on the practices and the character of industrial modernity, particularly the use of repetition and puffery in advertisements. "A spade isn't a spade in 1859, but something else," asserts Sala, "and with our house agents, a house is not only a house but a great many things besides": "A House to Let may be a mansion, a noble mansion, a family mansion, a residence, a desirable residence, a genteel residence, a family residence, a bachelor's residence, a distinguished residence, an elegant house, a substantial house, a detached house, a desirable villa, a semi-detached house, a villa standing in its own grounds, an Italian villa, a villa-residence, a small villa, a compact detached cottage, a cottage ornée, and so on, almost *ad infinitum.*"[30]

Criticism of advertisers' duplicitous use of language precedes discussion of suburbia's supposed "reality"—which, as in Bulwer-Lytton's novels, is forged in the terms of yet more stereotypes. The characters Sala creates—bored bachelors sucking on meerschaums, maiden ladies twittering in crumbling homes, criminally inclined fraudsters like "the Earl of Elbowsout"—are designed to point to the distance between elevated language and a debased reality.[31]

Sala's images of fake suburban mansions chime with those of other literary contemporaries, of course—Wemmick's castle in *Great Expectations,* for instance, or the "assemblages of palaces" and "flaunting" stucco homes Dickens detours to critique, in a passage on Clerkenwell, in *Barnaby Rudge.* But they also hearken back to texts of a full three decades earlier: "First, of the Mansion. What manner of house would you imagine that to be? I take it to be situate at Kew, possibly at Chiswick, peradventure at Putney. Red brick, stone window casings, a great many chimney-pots, a steep flight of steps before the door. Perhaps the advertisements says that it is 'approached by a carriage drive.' I can see that carriage drive, the mangy gravel, weeds and grass springing up between; the brown ragged lawn in the middle; the choked-up flowerbeds, with pieces of broke bottles and fractured tobacco-pipes."[32] As in earlier texts, Sala stresses the socially distant environs of the suburban home, then turns our attention to the poor exterior (the "mangy gravel," the sad-looking lawn), before moving inside the front door to discuss characters who are blood relations of Mr. and Mrs. Copperas. In a long line of scoundrel tenants, he imagines "Captain Vere de Vere Delamere, and his family, who paid nobody," and "the celebrated Mr. Nix, who said he belonged to the Stock Exchange, and removed in the midst of winter, and at the dead of night, taking with him, over and above his own furniture, a few marble mantel-pieces, register stoves, and other trifles in the way of fixtures." Stockbrokers are particularly likely to live in suburbia, he observes, because of their constitutional desire to impress and their deep-dyed vulgarity: "The 'villa standing in its own ground' is generally suggestive of stock-brokers. Great people are these stock-brokers for villas; for driving mail-phaetons, or wide-awake looking dog carts."[33] Sala's study concentrates in the first place on "uncovering" the underpinnings of the home advertisement—the ways in which both the original developer and the advertiser or auctioneer conspire to produce false images of the homes, then the proliferation of these textual images on page after page, edition after edition of the newspaper—before turning to the complicity of the fraudsters who live in the homes. (Many novels of the period stage similar scenes, where supposedly desirable homes are shown to be built on fraudulence. In Charlotte Eliza Riddell's 1861 *City and Suburb,* for instance, we are introduced to the Upases, a house that, when last let, was "described . . . as a desirable residence of genteel elevation (perhaps the reader knows what [the house-agent] meant)."[34] Riddell explains that excessive gravel was applied beneath the house in an attempt to offset the problems of the clay bed in North London. The "palaces" Dickens mentions, meanwhile, in *Barnaby Rudge,* are built on swamps.) Sala's method of combating the oft-repeated image of a "desirable residence" is to stamp out familiar replacement images of suburban aesthetic aridity, cultural debasement, and white-collar criminality, centering the critique of suburbia on the fact that it is both inhabited and commercialized by the tasteless and aspirational.

But notably, while Bulwer-Lytton's well-born heroes move through suburbia with distaste, yet comparative ease, Sala returns repeatedly to stories of his own hapless failures in the face of the suburbs' fraudulent practices. "Start not, reader, while I whisper in your ear," he murmurs at one point: "The Italian villa is a shabby little domicile, only Italian in so much *as it possesses Venetian blinds.* I know it for I, who speak, have been egregiously sold, lamentably taken in, by this mendacious villa."[35] If suburbia is a criminal enterprise, he implies, he has fallen a victim to it himself: in a tacit reply to observers of Bulwer-Lytton's ilk, Sala firmly situates responsibility for all such crimes *elsewhere.* Admitting his own social aspirations (he was, after all, tempted by the Italian villa), he stresses that he is guilty neither of the physical development of suburbia nor, for that matter, of the crime of bad taste (he does not admire venetian blinds): others, of a criminal—mostly lower-middle or working—class are guilty of both. Resisting Bulwer-Lytton's broad characterization of the suburban middle-class as either duplicitous or failed, then, he gives voice to a positive middle-class male identity grounded in experience. Exposed regularly to the realities—the depredations—of a commercial age, he suggests that such exposure ultimately produces an informed, world-weary participant. His use of suburban stereotypes stages both his familiarity with the commercial practices of the age *and* the fact that, through experience, he has learned to interpret them appropriately himself. Aligning himself with aristocratic stereotypes is a way of signaling his connectedness to traditional elite values while also demonstrating his ability to function in the modern world, because he has participated in it and learned its ways.

Other middle-class writers at mid-century employed similar strategies, characterizing the middle-class man as one who makes mistakes—who falls for suburban ruses—then learns from his errors. Charles Whitehead's "Suburban Retreat" (1847), a short story from *Bentley's Miscellany,* is a case in point, a cautionary tale about a middle-class academic husband who allows himself to be enticed from his city lodging into the suburbs by a foolish—and ultimately chastened—wife. Mrs. Rushworth is convinced by all the specious arguments in favor of suburban residence: the suburbs, unlike the city, are healthy, she declares. When Mr. Rushworth points out they haven't caught typhus (or been stifled, or poisoned) in twenty years of city living, his wife insists he's looking dreadfully—perhaps even fatally—ill. Then an interfering friend dwells on the extra space and domestic facilities they will enjoy in suburbia: "Six rooms, *such* rooms, and a lean-to kitchen. A copper in it? Bless you, yes. All the washing can be done at home. I should call it a long garden." Ease of public transportation and accessibility to London are also touted: there are "omnibuses passing every minute at less than a stone's throw," explains Mrs. Rushworth's friend.[36] Rushworth's wife adds some more loud whispers about the unhealthy looks of the forty-seven-year-old narrator, and the fish swallows the bait.

But as night follows day, the suburban retreat is anything but; Mrs. Rushworth's friend's use of advertising jargon necessarily precedes disillusionment. As soon as Mrs. Rushworth gets better acquainted with her new house, her language begins to change, and the smallness of the accommodation is an immediate sign of the joke that must inevitably unfold: "She reported that the rooms were certainly not large, but they were so snug; that the kitchen was a perfect culinary love, and that the house was so openly situated, back and front, that if we didn't get air enough there, we should be suffocated in a windmill."[37] The comedy here depends on the reader's understanding that "snug" is a developer's synonym for "tiny," that "a culinary love" means miniature, and that the whole place is most appallingly drafty. To make the point even clearer, Rushworth piteously makes us feel what he is losing: "Never shall I forget the feeling that came upon me when everything was cleared out, and I paced alone over the ribbed dust on the floor of my empty sitting-room. . . . Why not have rested contented here! It was an ample, cheerful, bustling street, full of life and gaity from seven in the evening til midnight. Neither was the bedroom so close as my wife had pronounced it, and as I, like a fool, had been persuaded to believe it. There was a good, honest, brick-and-mortar look-out from the window."[38] Rushworth here reframes the image of the city for the reader as "good, honest": the urban street is not a place where Bill Sikes or Fagin prey but rather "ample, cheerful, bustling," "full of life and gaity." Washing the city free from its familiar associations with the criminal, reconnecting with Bulwer-Lytton's love of the urban streets, Rushworth relocates crime and dishonesty firmly inside the suburbs.[39]

The rooms turn out to be so small that Rushworth is constantly banging himself on the furniture: the home is overrun with pests and poorly built, so that there is "a great stain of damp, like a map of Lincolnshire," on the wall of their bedroom.[40] Within hours of his arrival Rushworth finds himself harangued by itinerant salesmen and dunned for the previous inhabitant's taxes, and soon his only entertainment is trying to put off the dubious characters who daily assault his home. These assaults are, he assures his reader, infinitely more alarming than those in the city, and so much more disturbing: "What a wretched mistake, or a base calumny it is to call London a noisy place, if by that be meant anything in its disparagement. There is a vast quantity of sound going forward, I admit; but it is a fine blended harmonious clamour and chatter, if I may so express myself; a sort of homogenous hubbub which offers an admirable substitute for silence. But your vile suburbs can offer nothing but the deadness of the grave, or the rude raw bellowings of a cattle-market, or a raree-show, except at nine o'clock at night . . . no utterance in nature is so terrible as the cry of the suburban pot-boy."[41] Both husband and wife become faintly unhinged in the face of all this—as does Sarah, their domestic, who can't stop counting cats. The serious decline of Mrs. Rushworth is signaled by her willingness to talk over the wall to the large family next door and her sage contemplation of a mangle purchase. Rushworth's life finally takes a turn for the better when he and his wife return, intensely relieved, to their former urban dwelling: significantly, it is only on his resumption of life in his old lodgings that the narrator is able to complete his great book, a history of the pyramids of Egypt. (If only Mr. Casaubon's problems were so easily resolved.)

"The early years of Victoria's reign were widely thought at the time to be bringing about the triumph of the middle classes," observed Martin J. Wiener in his foundational work *English Culture and the Decline of the Industrial Spirit:* "Marx and Engels went so far as to assert in 1850 that 'the only remaining aristocracy is the bourgeoisie.'" Yet as Wiener notes, while in broad terms this shift was clearly well under way, it happened "not before the aristocracy had succeeded in both prolonging its reign and educating its successors in its world view."[42] Texts like Whitehead's and Sala's draw on and reproduce not only Bulwer-Lytton's stereotypes of tedious or criminal suburbia but also the shape of their construction—that is to say, like Bulwer-Lytton's, these mid-century stories of suburbia, written by members of the new elite—intellectuals—trace an arc of hope to disillusionment, where hope is exploited and manipulated by advertisers and developers, where a "true" stereotype (of suburban criminality and dullness) emerges latterly to dispel a "false" one (of suburban promise). The discovery that homes are fundamentally commodities in the modern world becomes a fact the stories strain to uncover, a passage through which order, peace, and productivity are finally restored. Rejecting suburbia entirely, or living within it as a sadder and wiser man, seem the only available options. To be a middle-class man of "taste" in the early Victorian years was to adopt the worldview of the aristocrat about this astonishingly fast-paced modern phenomenon.

Stereotyping is an effort to neutralize and control, to restore legibility. At a historical moment in which individuals were increasingly resisting the totemic denominations of self conferred by the class system (Charles Taylor, in *Sources of the Self,* identifies "recognized particularity" as one of three key facets of modern individualism), stereotyping, with its apparent claim to reduce personality back to groups and types, seems to restore social legibility.[43] The stereotyping of suburbia in the early to mid-Victorian years was one way of attempting to limit the increasing cultural force of the middle classes: the stultifying suburb was a stereotype employed in the service of an aristocratic ideology that emerged at a time of upper-class retreat. In that the English intelligentsia came substantially to adopt the aesthetics of the older elite, it is perhaps unsurprising that middle-class writers signed up to the aristocracy's freighted loathing of the new homes. Of course, the slippage between what was said and what was practiced must not be underestimated. Middle-class Victorians criticized the values of commercialism, but they built, bought, let, and sold their homes on an astonishing scale. Moreover, as we shall see in the next chapter, Victorian middle-class writers came increasingly to deploy the old stereotypes for some intriguing new purposes.

The indisputably commercial realities of suburban living inevitably complicated for the Victorians, and complicate for us, any notion of the space as separated from the practices and values of the public sphere. Sharon Marcus insists, in her study of Victorian apartment living, that we must "question the hegemony of separate spheres ideology not only because it applied to only one class, the bourgeoisie, but because it may not even have applied to that class."[44] Representations of suburbia as dull, deadening, confining, and arid may seem to *us* a reasonable response to a world of enforced domesticity and starkly separated roles—which is to say, to the vision of the Victorian domestic environment we continue to espouse. Yet as Marcus points out, gender roles may not have been as fixed or profoundly different as we like to think, and the spaces of home and city, city and suburb were only unevenly demarcated along the lines of separate spheres. Certainly, the literature discussed here shows just how profoundly involved suburbia was in the battles of industrial modernity—how particularly engaged suburbia was, and was felt to be, in the practices and discourses surrounding commercialism and the values of mass production. Indeed, the writers discussed in this chapter were not critiquing suburbia for the rigid separation it enforced between the domestic sphere and the place of work. On the contrary, they were responding to the fact that the boundaries between public and private, commercial and domestic were, in the suburban landscape, unsettlingly fluid.

CHAPTER 3

Plotting the Suburbs

POPULAR FICTION AND COMMON KNOWLEDGE, 1850s–1870s

Novels set in suburban locales represent a world in flux. Such narratives turn on lodging house meetings, partial boarders, moving days, new arrivals, abrupt departures, and hopeful landladies, of the sort painted by James Collinson.[1] Located by definition away from the city center, with larger gardens and loftier mantelpieces, Victorian suburban houses appeared to many a physical, architectural manifestation of the culture's desire for the separation of home life and commerce. In fact, suburban life was intensely commercial: daily encounters with potboys, meat delivery boys, potted plant vendors, and other raucous door-to-door salesmen reminded residents every hour that they were not living in Arcadia. Moreover, as we have seen, Victorians rented, rather than owned, their homes. "In a period without the present-day ideology of home-ownership," moving house required then, as now, navigating advertisements, finding and handling agents, hiring movers, buying and selling furnishings.[2] (Perhaps this explains why the Victorians, renowned for their "clutter," loved smaller furnishing items like occasional tables: they were easy to move.) Beneath the shifting sands of social mobility run thick strands of apparently common knowledge that reassure readers of continuity with the past and the existence of enduring values. These values—such as suspicion of suburban homes' commodity status, the charge of vulgar furnishing—undoubtedly express suspicion of the new masses. But they also form a means of fostering connections, shared perspectives, in a time of dizzying change.

5. *The Landlady,* 1856 (oil on canvas), James Collinson (1825–81). Sheffield Galleries and Museums Trust, U.K. / Bridgeman Images. The Landlady advertises "furnished apartments" in the window; note too the venetian blinds and geraniums, familiar signals of Victorian suburbanism.

In a sociopsychological analysis of community formation, Sandra Jovchelovitch argues: "Communities produce a common stock of knowledge that endures over time and gives community members the points of reference and the parameters against which individuals make sense of the world around them and are able to connect their individual stories with larger narratives of community life. The common knowledge produced by communities offers nodes of connection from which the experience of belonging emerges."[3]

Fictional narrative and storytelling play a key part in the identification and working out of this "common knowledge," Jovchelovitch observes. "It is by telling stories that social knowledge comes into life."[4] Narrative explicates problems of the moment, connects them with resolutions, hitches past to present, and thence to future, making sense out of disorder and finding commonalities over time. Popular fiction—fiction that aspires to speak to the interests and concerns of the masses—may especially seek to identify and narrativize common knowledge; moreover the very popularity of the fiction may help in the constitution of common knowledge, deepening its penetration through culture.[5]

As middle-class residents from all over the nation found themselves separated from birth networks, inhabiting an architectural landscape in which regular moving was a fact of life, where migrants from other classes, nations, and communities found themselves in close proximity, anything like a truly common knowledge was of course an impossibility.[6] Yet the experience of difference, variety, and heterogeneity only drives the desire to formulate connections, find groups, see patterns—as well as set boundaries, police borders, distinguish those like me from those not like me. Popular fictions worked with, explored, explicated what might provide, in a fast-paced, changing environment, rootedness, fixity, and belonging, the kinds of common knowledge that might work to provide anchorage. Fiction set in the suburbs identifies codes and cues for sense making and repeats them among texts, offering reassurance that some signals may be safely interpreted, that some values endure. To that end, the stereotypes of the suburbs identified in chapter 2 progressively evolved into plot arcs that both unpacked and tested familiar interpretations of the new suburbs.

Distinctive suburban plots may easily be traced. In one strand, dating back to Bulwer-Lytton, a male hero stumbles by accident into the suburbs, is ensnared by a woman, and must find his way out; Wilkie Collins's *Basil* (1852) is a key midpoint between *The Disowned* and later novels by George Gissing. Others begin, like Emily Eden's best seller *The Semi-Detached House* (1859) and Bertha Buxton's *Great Grenfell Gardens* (1879) with an advertisement placed in the *Times*'s "Houses to Let" section, where "semi-detached villas, at Clapham or Croydon," were puffed on a regular basis.[7] The *Times* advertisement is knowingly mocked by a narrator or protagonist; a stranger-hero (usually a hero, although sometimes a heroine) arrives to examine the property, the home's exterior and interior are compared with the advertisement, and the occupants and decorations are assessed in relation to the ad. The stranger's way of thinking, produced by the alien's own community, makes it difficult for the new arrival to interpret the new space at first, while the community struggles to interpret the stranger in turn; this plot device reflects a pattern that, social psychologists argue, precipitates self-assessment and boundary assessment in all kinds of communities. Whenever a stranger arrives in a new social group, he or she "asks awkward questions, behaves out of pattern," Jovchelovitch notes; "the absence of common knowledge linking up stranger and community reveals with great precision the fundamental social psychological role of common and shared knowledge in linking individual and community life and producing the experience of belonging."[8] In fictions centering on the arrival of male protagonists, the feeling of exclusion, the inability to interpret the new group, is rendered painful—sometimes literally, as we shall see. Fictions centering on female protagonists tend to work, by contrast, to open up connections and find shared points of contact that offer portals between worlds.

BASIL

The suburbs were a place that required narrative to help residents make sense of the startling newness of where they lived. At the heart of the problem, it seems, in text after text, is the complicated intertwining of the commercial with the domestic in a site whose architecture promised their separation, at a time when that separation was held key to national wellbeing. Not all suburban popular fictions give heroes access to the necessary knowledge to manage the imperative business of separating out worlds: as we saw in chapter 2, some heroes retire, vanquished. Wilkie Collins's *Basil,* the text that began to make the sensation writer's reputation, offers a particularly unnerving iteration of a narrative that was to become familiar at the end of the century, that of the man who stumbles into suburbia and finds himself ensnared in its commercial tentacles. Together with *The Disowned* and Whitehead's "Suburban Retreat," the novel presages fin de siècle Victorian texts that evoke suburbia as a dangerous wasteland, antithetical to elites (and men).[9] Yet Collins's narrative makes clear the tragedy could have been averted; access to a body of suburban common knowledge would have helped the hero navigate the landscape and its pitfalls. The knowledge Basil lacks is not elite taste, interestingly enough, but familiarity with suburban codes and the ability to puncture stereotypes—the kind of knowledge the reader is fully expected to possess.

Published some seven years before *The Woman in White* (1859–60), Collins's *Basil* is presented as a first-person account of a well-born man (who refuses to give his last name, so as to protect his family) and his downfall after a fateful omnibus ride into the alien suburbs. Bored, looking for adventure, Basil spots a beautiful girl and follows her; like a number of other suburban popular fictions, the novel narrates the arrival of a male visitor who, as he looks around, strives to interpret what he sees. He moves inside and repeats the business of looking, all the while being looked at carefully in turn. Margaret Sherwin turns out to be a linen draper's daughter, dominated by her vulgar father, who is in turn dominated by Mannion, a mysterious clerk. Basil is disturbed by the suburbanism of her home and the middle-class values of her family but seduced by her physical beauty; Collins's hero allows himself to be inveigled into a marriage that cannot be consummated for one year, at the end of which he discovers he has been cuckolded by the treacherous clerk. Mannion has been exploiting Basil's weakness—his desire for his wife and his inability to interpret suburbia—all along, in order to gain access to his wealth. In a particularly memorable scene, Basil hears the sounds of his wife and the clerk together through the thin partition wall of a cheap hotel near a train station; he lies in wait for the clerk and beats him, grinding his face into a newly macadamized road, thereby disfiguring him forever.

Basil has been read by Tamara Wagner as a critique of emerging suburbia as embodiment of "the promotion of bourgeois domesticity" and a "place of fraudulent economies."[10] It is certainly true that the elite young man's foray into suburbia involves an encounter with a virtual vampire, a looming, bloodsucking horror embodied in the cold-eyed Mannion whose strange smooth façade defies interpretation ("Never had I before seen any human face which baffled all enquiry like this. No mask could have been made expressionless enough to resemble it").[11] Just as Bram Stoker's *Dracula* (1897) was to render in monstrous form the meeting of Victorian man and geographically distant other through the auspices of trains, telegraphs, and steamships, so *Basil,* half a century earlier, offers a horrifying example of what may follow a meeting between social classes enabled by expanding omnibus routes. Mannion too seems one of the undead, a man with "delicately-formed lips . . . as changelessly still as if no breath of life ever passed them. There was not a wrinkle or line anywhere on his face."[12] Like the most Hollywood of monster's faces, the only time Mannion's face can be accurately read is during lightning storms: "A flash came, and seemed to pass right over his face. It gave such a hideously livid hue, such a spectral look of ghastliness and distortion to his features, that he absolutely seemed to be glaring and grinning on me like a fiend."[13] *Basil,* again like *Dracula,* shows readers the dark heart of their own fears in an age when network and infrastructure expansion brought together people from different social groups and communities.

Basil renders vivid the fear of the alien, of encountering Others. But it also offers a playbook for future meetings. For there is a third perceptual consciousness in play, beyond the reader and the suffering, ignorant Basil: a mature Basil describes events long after they have occurred. His problems could have been avoided if only he possessed the insight that the narrating eye possesses, the text suggests, so that rather than simply contrasting suburban malevolence with a visitor's innocence, the text prompts readers to interpret suburbia in a way the experiencing Basil does not. The narrator quickly signals that the desire Basil feels for the suburban Margaret is misplaced, for instance, so that the reader's desire and Basil the character's desires are *not* aligned; the reader's desire is, rather, connected to the older narrator's drive toward wholeness, the time in which the younger character will share the narrator's "mature" grasp of the world. In this way, *Basil* drives us on a journey to find the security of an ordered worldview. If narrative helps us make sense of and find order in life's traumas, as Peter Brooks suggests, *Basil* is shaped not merely to diagnose but also to assist in sense making, in an era of increased social mixing.

With meetings between classes and social groups comes the desire to manage the threats posed, potentially, by such encounters. F. S. Schwarzbach has argued that "the continuing Victorian obsession with the detection of crime is . . . connected to deeply rooted anxieties about identity in a modern urban society. The fear that in the new, socially heterogeneous milieu of the modern city it becomes nearly impossible to tell the true gentleman from the imposter is a feature of urban culture as early as the Elizabethan and Jacobean period. . . . [But] the modern urban social revolution intensified the need to find some way to mark visually the criminal element."[14]

Mannion is—if you can only find the right time to look at him, to spot his curious breathlessness—a man whose aspect is "fiendish." But how else, Collins's text asks tacitly, can the imposter be distinguished from the worthy man, especially in a world where new kinds of façades require new interpretive skills? Besides, what *is* gentlemanly or ladylike in an era of social mobility, when money and/or the possession of land no longer necessarily connect to a particular birth, breeding, education? These questions are especially pertinent in suburbia, a landscape of larger homes, generously sized plots, and interiors furnished with decorative objects, all markers that once (theoretically) provided visitors with legible signals of class and worth.[15] Collins's novel essentially asks its readers: What and who is worthy in the suburbs?

The sense-making operation begins in Collins's text with the suburban façade and even the streets near the Sherwins' North Villa. Descriptive terms are laden with foreboding: the exterior is a wasteland, "silent; desolately silent."[16] On the next visit, Basil sees the object of his affections carelessly tormenting a caged bird, framed in the window, like a play, and on the next he finds himself bribing a servant. Indeed, in every encounter Basil has on the streets outside North Villa, he is involved in duplicity or performance of some kind.

When he finally enters the house, the lowering sense of threat only increases, adjectives pointing out the danger: "Everything was oppressively new. The brilliantly-varnished door cracked with a report like a pistol when it was opened; the paper on the walls, with its gaudy pattern of birds, trellis-work, and flowers, in gold, red, and green on a white ground, looked hardly dry yet; the showy window-curtains of white and sky-blue, and the still showier carpet of red and yellow, seemed as if they had come out of the shop yesterday; the round rosewood table was in a painfully high state of polish; the morocco-bound picture books that lay on it, looked as if they had never been moved or opened since they had been bought."[17] The suburbanite Sherwins are guilty of nothing more than buying new furniture, new doors, and putting up new wallpaper thus far, but the narrator cues readers to associate these purchases with "oppression" and threat—even the door sounds like a pistol, while the polish produces a sensation of pain, so that the house seems to assault the guest as soon as he walks in the door. Brightness and color are designated "showy" and "gaudy," words associated with the kind of vulgar display that should provoke disgust in the right-thinking, right-feeling.[18] (Textiles owned over generations would most likely be faded, so that brightness and high polish is a signal of new purchase, consumption.) The use of natural images of birds and flowers on wallpaper and carpets was especially reviled by design reformers such as Henry Cole, and further points out the "poor taste" of the occupants, while the unopened books signal that the occupants buy for display rather than self-culture. Charges of vulgarity were increasingly deployed, Rosemary Jann has argued, to "keep in their places those who encroached on social boundaries"; a suburban house may look large and well furnished, but the environs and the objects and textiles within it could, if interpreted carefully, reveal the interloper, the arriviste. Jann argues that, as the century progressed, "a command over and deployment of particular types of knowledge, taste, and behavior—in short, cultural capital—often played a more powerful role than money in establishing status," and certainly *Basil* makes clear that the Sherwins, wealthy as they seem, are utterly lacking in the cultural capital that would render them members of a "real" elite. Their habitation looks rich, one might say, but their habitus, embodied in their aesthetic choices, is palpably far below Basil's.[19]

Basil makes clear that he was disgusted from the first moment of looking at the new suburbs: the "newness and desolateness of appearance revolted me, just then."[20] But he presses on, time and again fighting down the emotions of disgust that point to his social and cultural training, his higher-class habitus. Indeed, in a novel intensely conscious of the act of looking at what is new and different, the mature narrator uses a language of, not only disgust, but also pain to evoke the intensity of Basil's perceptual experience.[21] Pain is produced on hearing a door's opening, as we saw earlier, then, on entering, "the eye ached at looking round"; since "all surrounding objects seemed startlingly near the eye; much nearer than they really were," the narrator continues, "the room would have given a nervous man the headache, before he had been in it a quarter of an hour."[22] The mature Basil omits to say whether he, as a young man, experienced the headache; certainly, if he did, it did not prevent his return. He returns and returns. William Ian Miller, drawing on Freud, argues that disgust has two predominant forms: the first is an "initial prohibitional barrier," a disgust that joins with morality and shame, and the second is a disgust produced by surfeit, excess, overindulgence. The first can, paradoxically, incite, through prohibition, exactly what it is constructed to prevent; the second, where surfeit is connected with pain, may function more successfully to kill desire, punishing, rather than merely piquing. This captures the pattern of *Basil;* the young protagonist is initially repulsed, but his repulsion only serves to incite (it "augments, even helps create, the desire it wishes to prevent").[23] Pain (together with all the other alarm bells Collins sets ringing) progressively points out a transition toward surfeit and punishment—the time when Basil lies prone, an attempted murderer, a cuckolded husband and disinherited son, humiliated, suffering a "heavy trance of mental pain" in the later pages of the book.[24] Basil's desire for the common and the vulgar escapes, is even inflamed by, categories of taste. The hero's gaze locks onto the body of the linen draper's daughter, and he pursues what he knows to be forbidden until he is abject and humiliated, seeing disgust at his behavior in the eyes of those around him.

For Basil is not merely the looker, the perceiver; he is the object of observation. *Basil* represents the gaze to which the arriving hero is subject as obviously malign. The house and even the sidewalks look back at him as he looks around, "glaring" in a fashion reminiscent of film's "forbidden gaze," when the looked at looks back.[25] A print of the Queen glares, the narrator tells us, from the wall; it is presumably "good taste" to own a portrait of the queen only if you can claim to know her personally, or are at least rich enough to own a painting of her, so that the print copy in an elaborate frame (it is topped with a crown) points out the vast distance between the occupants/owners/purchasers and the Sovereign. At the same time, the bought print and frame signal the residents' ability to buy copies of what was once the preserve of the aristocrat, a new power rendered visible, ironically enough, in Victoria's own gaze. Indeed, the print Queen's face proceeds to color the description of the drawing room, so that the interior appears to stare with Victoria's eyes: "The paper, the curtains, the carpet glared on you; the books, the wax-flowers in glass cases, the chairs in flaring chintz-covers, the china plates on the door, the blue and pink glass vases and cups ranged on the chimney-piece, the over-ornamented chiffoniers with Tonbridge toys and long-necked smelling bottles on their upper shelves—all glared on you."[26] A queen should, at least in the imagination of the elite, glare at the unworthy, but here, in a dreadful volte face, an upside-down, Alice-in-Wonderland topsy-turveydom, the print queen and her cheap glass vases glare at the worthy. What anchors the reader in the face of these terrifying unsettlings of social and cultural hierarchies are the terms and references that continue to fix the room as "bad taste," terms that hint at lower-class excess ("flaring," "over-ornamented") and objects and organization that suggest women, newness, and amateur collections instead of men, tradition, aristocratic prestige. Wax flowers in glass cases were a popular bourgeois woman's handicraft at mid-century, for instance, and were often belittled in the popular press. Numerous decorative objects cheek by jowl suggest the new, uneducated collector deploying her spending power carelessly, while we are led to see a lack of functionality in their massing—china plates attached to the door will fall off and break, glass on the mantelpiece will take on the effects of smoke. Tonbridge toys, meanwhile, small objects "turned in holly, plum-tree, cherry-tree, sycamore, and various foreign woods," will not be played with—there are no small children in the home.[27] Lack of functionality was exactly what design reformers critiqued about the rococo revival aesthetic of the early Victorian years, so that Basil's mature perspective is colored by aesthetic reformism and ideas that will come to fruition in the Arts and Crafts movement.[28]

The world is new and strange, and power is moving inexorably into the hands of the masses (clerks whose history is unknown), but common knowledge of what is good taste and what is vulgar continues to provide a touchstone of enduring meaning—even as the book itself recognizes that bad taste allures, that the common, the vulgar, commands our fascinated attention. The story speaks, in the passages discussed, to a knowing reader, who recognizes the references to Tonbridge toys, wax flowers, floral carpets, and so forth, and knows they are codes for degraded taste. The novel is, in this way, very much a sensational modern novel, with most of the hallmarks of a genre that bridged popular print journalism and fiction (and, for that matter, the stage) to appeal to the interests of the masses. *Basil* offers, not so much loathing of suburbia writ large or a critique of bourgeois domestic life, as a means to articulate the vulgarity of *other people;* to distinguish the worthy, the knowing, the insightful from those who pretend, those who are unconscious of how they appear. The interior décor of the Sherwins' house glared on "you"—on *us,* the fiction-reading, periodical-reading masses. Collins is speaking to a community who want to think of themselves as *not* the Sherwins; those who feel themselves to be the deserving, rather than the undeserving, middle class, aspiring to connect with a common knowledge that is shared but *not* common; unifying, yet only open to some.[29]

RECASTING SUBURBAN STEREOTYPES: EDEN'S SEMI-DETACHED HOUSE

The association of the suburban domestic with the feminine became particularly familiar, and particularly significant, in the second half of the nineteenth century, as the world of suburban living was said to be dominated—in the daytime particularly—by women and women's work. As the rhythms and patterns of commuting apparently reinforced the feminization of suburbia, many authors built on Linden's, Rushworth's, and Basil's mistrust of suburban women. When the men go to work, the world of suburbia goes under "the unquestioned rule of woman," T. W. H. Crosland argued in *The Suburbans*—adding sourly, "which is not good" (Crosland hints that wives do nothing but laze around all day, until the hour before the master is due home).[30] A number of writers contended that suburbia, so carefully detached from the world of work and business, theoretically at least, was therefore both a scene of and a force in the separateness, anonymity, and isolation of humans in an age of machines and disrupted birth networks (Gissing argues in *The*

Whirlpool that commuting has produced a generation of men who know almost nothing of their supposed home).[31] Sir Walter Besant, walking the streets of suburbia at the beginning of the twentieth century, remarked that one of the most striking features of the suburban arrangement was the lack of human interaction, and damningly he maintained that this was true not just for men but also for women: "They lost all the London life—the shops, the animation of the streets, their old circle of friends; in its place they found all the exclusiveness and class feeling of London with none of the advantages of a country town. . . . In the new suburb of Stockwell there were no interests [in common]; the wife of the small wholesale merchant would not call on the wife of the retail dealer; the wife of the barrister would not call on either; there was no society, and so for fifty years the massive dulness of the London suburb continued."[32] In chapter 2 we saw the ways in which familiar tropes of suburban dullness may be traced back to early Victorian stereotypes that emerged in an effort to defuse the cultural and commercial power of the massed middle classes. Yet, as I've argued, those tropes of suburban dullness were not universally endorsed. Annette R. Federico, discussing Marie Corelli's late-century popular fiction, suggests that the privileging of the city at the fin de siècle by male writers was effectively a privileging of the male sphere of action, in which the denigration of suburbia was a trivializing of the world "associated with feminine domesticity, homogeneity, and the delights of nature (or at least of a small garden)."[33] This pertinent observation may fruitfully be applied to texts written much earlier too, for indeed, even in the early decades of suburbanization, women engaged suburbia in potentially surprising ways. Emily Eden's *Semi-Detached House,* from the 1850s, is a case in point: Eden evokes the domestic suburban space as a site that crucially facilitates and sustains new connections among women. Yet before these connections can take place, her characters first need to discover, and then overset, their stereotypes of suburbia. The critical significance of this process in the novel points not only to Eden's consciousness of the pervasiveness of the stereotypes but also to the gender assumptions that underpinned them.

Eden indicates that no resident can even think about living in an 1850s suburban home without navigating prejudices born of stereotype. The aristocratic heroine's ideas about suburbia are so shaped by what she has heard and read, she is hardly willing to move there at all. "I should hate my semi-detachment, or whatever the occupants of the other half of the house may call themselves," Lady Blanche Chester declares roguishly on the novel's first page, when the plan of residing in suburbia is first raised, and she repeatedly jokes about what her neighbors will look like ("fat") and wear ("thick, heavy mittens").[34] Recently married, Blanche is pregnant; her diplomat husband, Arthur, is about to embark on a vaguely outlined "special mission" to Berlin for three months. A semidetached house is chosen as the best housing option because her doctor wishes her to be out of unhealthy London during her husband's absence yet "within reach of [the doctor's] surveillance."[35] A home entitled "Pleasance" in dreadful-sounding Dulham is, her husband assures her, the natural choice (Balham and Fulham, both old settlements, became resolutely suburban areas in the nineteenth century); Eden begins, in other words, by raising and engaging the most familiar stereotypes of suburbia. If the house's moniker is, like Copperas Bower, a sign of middle-class pretensions to aristocratic elegance, the bathetic contrast offered by the suburb's name seems to point out the contrast between advertiser hype and deadening reality.

Indeed, the narrator explicitly draws attention to the inflated language used by those who deal in homes for commercial purposes. "Now it is a remarkable fact in natural history that in all the suburbs of London, consisting of detached houses, called by auctioneers 'small and elegant,' or on Terraces described as first-rate dwellings, there is always an invisible macaw, whose screaming keeps the hamlet or terrace in a constant state of irritation," she remarks early in the novel. The narrator goes on to present the undiscoverable but ever-present macaw as a comical symbol of all that is worst about suburbia:

> Nobody at Dulham owned to having one, and detection was impossible, for there, as at all the suburban villages, the inhabitants lived by, and for, and with London. The men went daily to their offices or counting-houses, and the women depended for society on long morning visits from London friends and relations; and they did not, as they observed with much pride, "visit at Dulham." So the macaw screeched on, and as his noise seemed to come from fifty houses at once, everybody suspected everybody of keeping this plumed atrocity. No. 3 sent to No. 5 to beg that the bird might be shut up for a few days, as No. 3's baby did nothing but start, and would not wean. No. 3's messenger met No. 5's maid-of-all-work, coming with a bold request that the macaw might be sent away, as "Missus's mother-in-law was subject to bad headaches, and was driv half mad." As neither of these parties owned even a linnet, in the way of bird, the nuisance was not abated by this negotiation.[36]

The macaw's incessant screech reminds us of the "stereotyped" home advertisements in the pages of the *Times,* or even the homes themselves—the endless, meaningless, repetitive rows that seemed not only a product but also a visual illustration of the mechanical processes of industry. At the same time the imported exotic bird, so miserably out of place in its caged suburban home it cannot stop shouting, figures as yet another suburban stereotype, representative of the dislocated suburbanite even as it reveals her ill-directed consumerist tendencies. Suburbia appears at this point in Eden's text to be Dulham indeed, a place remarkable for its lack of culture, taste, peace, or human interaction: the men all leave for work in the daytime, while the women who remain refuse to visit each other and simply twitch curtains.

Yet Blanche's middle-class neighbors resist her expectations in some surprising ways. Mrs. Hopkinson, the resident of the other half of the semidetached house, may be something of a curtain twitcher herself (she is first seen in a "commanding position in the window"); she is certainly obsessed with domestic detail, and she needs an aristocrat to point out to her the value and aesthetic of her own porcelain.[37] But the relationship that evolves between the two women is structured to deflate many of the aristocrat's stereotypes. Blanche is repeatedly forced to acknowledge and value the utility of the sturdiness and domestic practicality she initially disdained. After an evening lingering by the river at dusk, for instance, the nervy Blanche finds her health deteriorating: "Stretched on the sofa, pale and shrunk, with red eyes and hot hands, a feeble attempt at a cap at the very back of her head," she feels actually ill.[38] To add insult to injury, at this moment something goes "radically wrong with the kitchen flue," filling the place with smoke and expelling the home's residents into the garden.[39] The person who saves the day and revives her is the practical Mrs. Hopkinson, who, finding Blanche on a chilly bench, takes charge, inviting them into her side of the house before demonstrating her knowledge of the errant kitchen flue—for after all, her own is exactly the same. At last we see value in the repetitive architectural features of terraced and semidetached homes.[40] The relationship between the women proves more than just one of utility, or of middle-class facility with kitchens, for once the initial contact is made the two heroines come to realize they are in the same marital boat. Just as Blanche feels abandoned by her husband in pregnancy, so, Mrs. Hopkinson admits, she too has been left by her husband John for more than half of every year since their marriage, including after her confinements.[41] Cementing the connection, Eden goes on to reveal that the two husbands knew each other in the past: Mrs. Hopkinson's husband saved

Arthur's life by nursing him during a fever. The discovery increases the debt that the aristocratic pairing owes their solidly practical middle-class neighbors while reinforcing the novel's evolving commitment to bourgeois domestic skills. Aristocratic social isolation and romantic self-indulgence are shown to be dangerous: her endless fantasies about her health and the possibility her husband's love might wane leave Blanche prey to actual ill health. Mrs. Hopkinson's no-nonsense attitude, her knowledge of the workings of the suburban domestic interior, and her engagement in distinctively feminine networks (she quickly gets Blanche involved in the daily concerns of the people in her own life) all prove crucial, stabilizing Blanche psychologically and healing her physically while preparing her for happy, productive motherhood.

Mrs. Hopkinson's skills acquire particular significance when the redoubtable suburbanite assists Blanche in labor: indeed, the middle-class woman is ultimately given the credit for the continuity of the aristocratic family in a sequence of scenes in which the upper-class characters seem barely able to function in the face of a genuine, if everyday, crisis. With the family doctor and the hired nurse both away, and a newly returned Arthur reduced to wringing his hands in despair, one knock at the door stirs up Mrs. Hopkinson, who, declaring herself "as good a month nurse as any in the kingdom," springs into action.[42] Eden makes it quite clear that the replacement doctor corralled into attending the birth does more harm than good in the hours that follow, whispering "horrible surgical anecdote[s]" to an aghast Arthur; it is Mrs. Hopkinson, who has just time for a "brusque word or two," who seems actually to deliver the boy, a son and heir for the Chesters.[43] Her skills as midwife and nurse clearly outstrip those of the professionals Arthur engages, and her presence conveniently next door makes her far more useful, because more available, than they. The proximities of suburbia thus prove peculiarly advantageous to the young aristocratic family. Arthur and Blanche both view Mrs. Hopkinson as a lifesaver, and from now on she is described explicitly as a "friend."[44]

This is not, of course, a friendship of the streets or of the shops; it is a new kind of friendship that is specific to the suburban home arrangement. The friendship that grows within the semidetached house brings together women who would not ordinarily meet socially, and shows them through the very similarity of the homes they inhabit that they indeed have something in common. Discovering a shared chimney flue leads to a discovery of shared marital burdens and even an unlikely shared history; the parallels are reinforced daily through conversations about decorative objects, servants, room arrangement, children. And intriguingly, in this new friendship, the normative class hierarchy is unsettled as the aristocratic heroine comes to recognize the superior domestic management skills of her middle-class neighbor—a point made most obviously when the baby's safe arrival, and thus the continuation of the family name, is brought quite literally to Mrs. Hopkinson's door.[45] Women who know what to do with a smoky flue, women who understand basic obstetrics, women who can manage their own children, are the women who will prosper in suburbia, Eden's novel suggests. The stereotype of suburbia as a deadening space seems finally overturned in a novel that describes it as a place of friendship and new birth, for women and families especially.

Yet there is a price to pay for the friendship of Blanche and Mrs. Hopkinson: Eden's novel does not, as Monica Cohen has pointed out, paint an uncomplicated vision of interclass community. Cohen rightly observes that the aristocrats' attraction to their middle-class neighbors depends upon the fact that the latter "do not scrimp and save, start businesses or invest in industry. Although they have serious concerns about how to marry off their fortuneless daughters, they seem utterly uninterested in money."[46] Mrs. Hopkinson never asks for Blanche's friendship—is in fact deeply unwilling to thrust herself on Blanche socially because of Blanche's elevated position. And when social mobility happens late in the novel, it is through the auspices of the generous aristocrats, who confer (as in Bulwer-Lytton's novels) social advancement to those they admire. The relationship Blanche imagines with Mrs. Hopkinson going forward is one that looks dangerously feudal: "I should like her to be near baby, she understands him so thoroughly; and if she would take care of him, I could take care of her," the heroine observes.[47] Middle-class social mobility is therefore put squarely into the control of the upper classes, and the Hopkinsons' acceptance of this is a condition of the friendship that flourishes.

To ground the point, Eden includes another family in the novel that does *not* accept upper-class control of the social hierarchy; that family fails to achieve the Chesters' friendship and support and, after financial disaster strikes, must leave Dulham and the country. Eden's vicious portraits of the Jewish speculator Baron Samson and his thrusting wife are shaped by another set of contemporary stereotypes, ones that are emphatically not defused.[48] Patterns of immigration may have given extra impetus to anti-Semitism around the time Eden was writing: Geoffrey C. Field observes that "roughly speaking . . . the Jewish population in Britain grew from about 35,000 in 1850 to 243,000 in 1910."[49] Moreover, Jewish men were playing an increasingly prominent part in public and political life at the time, and Eden (an aristocrat and Whig hostess herself) makes explicit, bitter reference to the Jewish Disabilities Bill that had finally cleared the way for Jewish men to sit in the House of Commons the year before.[50] Struggling to achieve social position and wealth by any means—and repeatedly decried for their "yellow" skin and strange inability to look people squarely in the eye—the Samsons in their pushing behavior preclude the kind of friendship Eden valorizes between the compliant Mrs. Hopkinson and Blanche. Only the Samsons' much-put-upon niece Rachel, a victimized figure they attempt to exploit, is left in England at the end of the novel, when the couple abscond to escape criminal charges for the Baron's financial wrongdoings. Rachel's marriage to a relative of Mrs. Hopkinson plays out the possibility of Jewish acculturation and assimilation that was itself a stereotype in nineteenth-century literature.[51]

Eden's novel is perhaps best understood as an effort to siphon off pressure in the face of increasing social plurality. Her text works to create a type of suburbanite who is most consistent with traditional English aristocratic values and then marks her out carefully from the suburbanite who is *not.* If Bulwer-Lytton, Sala, and Whitehead center their attention on the commercialization of the suburban home, Eden's text seems more preoccupied by the question of how women can thrive in an era of increased social mixing. The aristocratic Blanche is willing to communicate and interact with a stout woman who is not well dressed and does not understand porcelain as long as she does not undermine upper-class social privileges—and is not Jewish. Pushing at the stereotype of suburbia as deadening Dulham, Eden challenges some of the most common preconceptions about the new areas, suggesting that women's experiences of suburbia may be especially full of life. But she does not dispense with stereotypes entirely; like her predecessors, Eden finds stereotyping a powerful tool for both expressing and managing the challenges and threats of modern suburban life.

THE DWELLERS OF GRENFELLIA

Eden's *Semi-Detached House* was far from the only mid-Victorian novel to acknowledge, only to overset, stereotypes of the suburb as deadening and dull. Women's suburban popular fictions are especially likely to evoke the new suburbs as places of productive meetings and supportive communities. Bertha Buxton's *Great Grenfell Gardens* (1879) is an intriguing case in point—the novel presents the shared garden in a suburban block as a fruitful meeting place where very different kinds of people find shared values, shared commitments, and new insights.[52] Beginning as usual with the arrival of a lodger, the action of Buxton's text leads to recognition of the heroine's personal integrity and the evolution of a block (if not a suburb) shaped by the idea that the twining of the commercial with the domestic in suburbia can, if properly approached, redound to the general good. Commercial exchanges that do not involve human closeness or emotion fail in the novel, while commercial interactions that do—renting out a home, most obviously—are valorized, and promise to unify the suburb's disparate groups. The vulgar, meanwhile, is cabined, identified, set off, and easily managed.

Strongly associated with those whose tastes are retrograde and driven by mass culture, the home in Wilkie Collins's *Basil* is at once a labyrinthine alien space and a repellent community whose values the mature narrator does not share. Collins's reader is left in no doubt that Margaret and her family are unworthy, the Sherwins' home is tasteless, Mannion a bloodsucker; in this way, even as Collins lays bare the potential threats of the suburb, he reassures the reader that she, by contrast, can read its cues, is party to a common knowledge that bonds her into an alternative suburban community, a different kind of habitus. She feels the disgust that marks her out as worthy; she possesses the kind of common knowledge that is not vulgar (a word that was, after all, for centuries, a synonym for "common"), but that nonetheless requires an intimate, even elaborate understanding of what vulgarity *is*.[53] Buxton's text concedes that worthiness is difficult to assess in the new suburbs, though Buxton again reassures readers that they can distinguish the worthy from the not-worthy. Still, her novel takes an interesting tack, suggesting that worthiness is something women are especially good at identifying in the complex, socially heterogeneous suburbs.

A number of different families and households rent homes backing onto a shared garden in Buxton's text. Chapter 1 (entitled "The Dwellers in Grenfellia," perhaps to hint at an aspirational connection to the fashionable central London areas Tyburnia and Belgravia) begins as usual by quoting an advertisement. The ad is placed, in this instance, by an "enterprising" firm of builders, and is for "a number of most desirable family residences, all detached, possessing every modern convenience." The overblown language of the ad is obviously designed to provoke the usual smile of recognition, the sense of reading a novel from a familiar literary community, although on this occasion the builders claim a "distinguishing attraction": a "spacious social recreation-ground."[54] Jovchelovitch argues that occupation of a public space is key in the development of community, for public sites are places "where community life becomes visible and known to the community . . . where social actors experiment with the openness and unpredictability that is intrinsic to the multiplicity of unique perspectives they encounter."[55] And indeed, this is a novel that brings together people and households from quite different backgrounds: while most residents of the Gardens are middle class, they include migrants and immigrants (Germans, Americans, Italians), people from different backgrounds and professions (a writer, a barrister, a retired colonial merchant), and others who are harder to place, including an adventurer and members of the arriviste aristocracy. What connects them all are the Gardens, "a subject of inexhaustible interest to all Grenfellians," a place where meetings are arranged, opinions are exchanged, communal identity is formed (all are "Grenfellians"), shared values reinforced.[56] For instance, on one occasion Estella, one of the novel's heroines, is tempted to pluck a particularly beautiful rose, "the pride and joy of most of the Grenfellians"; catching herself in time, she flushes at the thought that she has nearly "committed what she and all Grenfellians would certainly have considered a theft."[57] Estella may, on an individual level, struggle to like some of the residents, but she finds meaning in, and abides by, the community's rules for living.

On every page the reader is shown she is in a world she knows, a text whose visual and literary cues she recognizes. The first few pages of the novel engage timeworn images of the suburban: the homes' bow windows look like "two pairs of bulging eyes," while the doors "had the appearance of gaping mouths, which stood ready and waiting to swallow up all who gained admittance within."[58] Indeed, Buxton seems so steeped in the tradition of suburban popular fiction that for a moment the novel looks set to veer from the romantic into the sensational iteration (the backs of the houses offer "only a smooth brick surface," Mannion-like, "indented at intervals by small-paned windows, which appeared sightless except at the hour of sunset, when they shone with a luridly-reflected light").[59] The moment passes, but it is replaced by another, equally familiar scene. The final precipitating event in chapter 1 is that a good-natured German resident, Mrs. Braun, has placed an advertisement for boarders in the *Times,* to the mortification of her unmarried daughter, Theodosia: " 'To gentlemen engaged in business during the day a pleasant home is offered in No. 39, Great Grenfell Gardens, SW. Excellent references must be given. Cheerful musical society, and a bath.' "[60] In *A Room with a View* some thirty years later, Miss Bartlett finds herself, in the face of George Emerson's casual reference to his father's whereabouts, "unequal to the bath.

All her barbed civilities came forth wrong end first."[61] Buxton similarly enjoys herself at the expense of Theodosia, a character clinging to propriety on the precipice of respectability.

Indeed, as the plot of new meetings unfolds, and "social actors experiment with . . . openness and unpredictability," Buxton's novel continually pokes fun at those who attempt to apply "old" social rules to make sense of a more plural society. The lively Estella, her sister, Nettie, and Mary, the eldest daughter of the family, navigate their way successfully by evolving what are evoked as "new" and better mechanisms for assessing those they meet. Mary, in particular, dispenses with the idea that one must know the antecedents of social acquaintances: when her father, onetime colonial merchant, complains, "[I have] already regretted my weakness in yielding to this mad scheme of yours in giving this dinner party, and inviting a couple of men to my house of whom I know literally nothing," Mary is unimpressed, reminding him he has formed a good opinion of one by meeting him.[62] Later, her father's nervy willingness to jump to old conclusions about social cues almost costs Mary an advantageous marriage. The daughter's sifting strategies are invariably correct.

Personal judgment, based on in-person meetings, is set forth repeatedly as the means by which the worthy can be distinguished from the unworthy; feelings and emotions are valorized as mechanisms of truth telling and are the only ones on which women should rely. The impersonal practices of business are shown, time and again, to fail as means of distinguishing who is to be trusted from who is not. Mrs. Braun, a sympathetic if stereotyped character, uses business practices to aid her when she places an advertisement for a boarder in the *Times,* and Buxton shows up her mistake. The adventurer, Mr. Peregrine Latimer, is able to get good references from his bankers, on which the poor landlady mistakenly depends; the city, in the form of the anonymous and deceitful bankers, is an alien and unreliable world.[63] To be sure, the novel is not simply antagonistic to the world of business, and it defends those characters who must engage in it (Mrs. Braun herself has the narrator's support for renting out her house: "She had lately been snubbed and ridiculed by many of the Grenfellians, because she proved her good sense, and asserted her independence, by letting a portion of her enormous house").[64] Still, the novel indicates that the practice carries risk. These risks are to be combated, not through knowledge of history or shared birth networks or through the channels of business, but by building up personal networks that extend from and ultimately bond private and public: the city may be navigated, but only through the auspices of personal connections. Mary asks a trusted friend to implement "rigorous enquiries . . . in the city," for instance, and in this way, she is ultimately able to uncover Latimer's duplicity.[65] Within the Gardens themselves, gossip is given a place as a form of information that can, if appropriately interpreted, be revealing; one of the novel's heroes, Ronald Vivian, is gently criticized for not listening to Grenfellian chatter about how his mother had become engaged to/inveigled by Latimer.[66] Decorative objects certainly signal personal value in Buxton's text and participate in the potentially transformative power of looking (Nettie longs for beautiful pictures "and blue china and iridescent glass, and all those things which . . . 'unconsciously refine the mind through the eyes'").[67] But human relationships founded on emotion, trust, and regard for others function as the most important networks for the transmission of meaning in the commercially engaged suburbs.

In *Great Grenfell Gardens,* as in many other fictions shaped by suburban plot arcs, female protagonists who read residents and strangers accurately, who trust their own readings, are rewarded with marriage. Great Grenfell Gardens opens up to new opportunities and socially advantageous marriages, as does Camberwell in the fiction of Mary Elizabeth Braddon (as we shall see in chapter 6); the Gardens function as a type of Foucauldian heterotopia, a space of networks typically considered incompatible but functioning together in ways that complicate their conventional cultural distancing. They thus embody, as S. D. Bernstein puts it, "real and imperfect mirrors of an ideal reality."[68] Read in this way, the Gardens offer glimpses of an alternative suburb. Through a place of exchanges between worlds, of openings between classes, sexes, and communities, Buxton projects a socially heterogeneous suburban block in which commercial, business, and social networks are to become, in the end, virtual extensions of the family itself.

CONCLUSIONS

Popular fictions set in the suburbs are typically put in motion by meetings between aliens, people who are not connected by birth networks, so that H. G. Wells and Arthur Conan Doyle may be seen as drawing on a long-standing literary tradition in their fin de siècle tales of strange arrivals into, and dangerous invasions of, suburbia. Two main plotlines follow alien encounters. In one, disaster ensues; a male protagonist is unable to decipher an alien community and falls prey to its inhabitants. In the second, a heroine's ability to interpret and function in suburbia is rewarded and, by the end, she may be able to connect the seemingly disparate—even directly competitive—worlds of business and home. Both strands of fiction set off the vulgar from the tasteful, the commercial from the authentic, striving to make legible a landscape and an expanding set of cultural and aesthetic practices that defy easy categorization. The texts examined here recognize, even embody, the unlikeliness of anything like a true common knowledge in an increasingly plural society—the choice to read another novel that opens with yet another advertisement placed in the *Times* speaks to an ongoing need for legibility and rootedness in the face of urbanization and social change. Yet by returning to the same codes and clues, the same plot arcs and stereotypes, popular fictions helped create and render familiar a certain kind of common knowledge about the suburban house, its décor, its inhabitants, and its meanings among a community of middle-class readers. The reader might not be an aristocrat, might live in suburbia and let out her rooms to boarders, but worthiness remains attainable. In a world where fear of humiliation seems the most common fear of all, suburban popular fictions offer the reassurance that in this community at least we understand—and are understood.

CHAPTER 4

"Art at Home"

WOMEN AND THE SUBURBAN INTERIOR

> Most of us live in a "row," either of houses in a street, or of villas in a suburb. As regards our outward walls, the livery of sameness is donned by all, but there is scope for originality within doors, and surely our rooms should be made to suit our individual tastes and characters.[1]

In the second half of the nineteenth century, the new spending power of the middle classes, the increased availability of ready-made goods, and larger teams of servants in the home meant that domestic duties took up comparatively less of a woman's time.[2] Middle-class women, with fewer absolute responsibilities, turned to new ways of occupying their hours and days, and "decorative art," or interior decoration, became wildly popular from the 1870s on. Advice manuals responded to and helped drive the phenomenon; often addressed to suburban residents explicitly, to the experience of moving and setting up house, the aesthetic such texts develop is shaped by what is expressed to be the practical day-to-day realities of suburban life. The literature of interior decoration is a key resource for scholars of the Victorian suburbs, one that helps us identify what these spaces offered women. Such texts have been mined, to some extent, by art and social historians as interventions in aesthetic debates; they have rarely been examined for the light they shed on how women responded to, and narrativized, their lives in the suburbs.

The fashion for interior decoration, the rapidly expanding market of manuals and columns to feed and shape decorative practices and interests, allowed women to remain engaged in the home sphere, and to stage the family's modernity and affluence, at a time when domestic handicraft making was increasingly derided by an emerging Arts and Crafts culture.[3] Interior decoration advice manuals were, in many ways, exactly what Arts and Crafts practitioners disdained: writers addressed themselves to leisured, middle-class, female consumers—to amateurs, in other words, not craftsmen or trained connoisseurs. The texts' ideas about what should go where, what textiles should be chosen, and where they should be bought were expressed in relation to middle-class family life, and often to the practicalities of the suburban semi (rather than the museum-like Jacobin house). Writers regularly address suburbanites explicitly, suggesting their texts fill an important gap at a time when young couples regularly move to suburban areas, away from birth communities; Jane Ellen Panton opens the first of her many successful works by offering herself as a "good authority" on the margins of London to all young couples setting up home, for the first time, away from family and friends. (The loss of family advice was not always a bad thing, Panton observes: one advantage of living in a suburb is that at least mothers-in-law are not around to make unwanted "suggestions and comments on the new *ménage*.")[4] Writers do not assume that all readers live in suburbia, and their aesthetic advice can certainly be applied to town and rural living, but in that interior decoration texts address themselves to a mobile, middle-class population, their aesthetic is substantially generated by suburban architecture and ways of life (like commuting). John Ruskin famously argued, in a passage in "Modern Painters" that still resonated at the fin de siècle: "Art . . . is no recreation. It cannot be learned at spare moments, nor pursued when we have nothing to do. It is no handiwork for drawing-room tables, no relief for the ennui of boudoirs. . . . To advance it men's lives must be given."[5] The literature of interior decoration insisted that, on the contrary, the suburban drawing room, bedroom, hallway, and nursery were canvases ready for art and, moreover, that suburban women were ideal artists, capable of realizing art's highest goals of moral enlightenment and social regeneration "at home."

Some of the most important early interior decoration works include Rhoda and Agnes Garrett's *Suggestions for House Decoration in Painting, Woodwork and Furniture* (1876), Lucy Orrinsmith's *The Drawing Room; Its Decorations and Furniture* (1878), and Lady Barker's *The Bedroom and Boudoir* (1878), all part of Macmillan's Art at Home series, edited by W. J. Loftie. The many works by Panton, beginning with *From Kitchen to Garret* (1887), are also key: her first text, based on popular columns in the lively threepenny weekly *Lady's Pictorial*, went through seven editions in six years, and was in its eleventh edition ten years later. Her works, and those of her peers, are invariably critical of much suburban architecture—that is to say, of unvarying, uniform façades, poor building practices, cheap materials, and the sharp- or thief-like practices of what Panton called "the demon builder." Each of these texts presents interior decoration as a way of rescuing home life and, by extension, society and the nation, from the forces of capitalism and commodity culture, in ways that draw on, or at least resonate with, the drivers of the medieval revivalist as well as the Arts and Crafts movement. The difference is that, time and again, the suburban home is presented not as a sign of the problem but as the probable solution, so long as a reading, thinking, and vigorously practicing female interior decorator is present to work, decorate, and design. Tying a pursuit (home decoration) to a set of commonly agreed-upon problems (too-rapid urban development, suburban architectural uniformity, poor taste), interior design manuals take up Ruskinian arguments about architecture's social function, turning the pursuit into a cause, the pastime into virtuous labor, thereby dignifying women's domestic work and laying the stage for women to do yet more. Indeed, a surprising number of the texts I discuss in this chapter argue explicitly that for women's decorating to have its full moral and social regenerative effect, women need to become professional, paid interior designers. Interior decoration texts insist that decoration is necessary business, that suburban women are the laborers who will rescue the nation, that the suburban home is the crucible of change.

RUSKIN AND "NATIONAL CHARACTER": THE THREATS OF THE SUBURBAN HOUSE

Intense public debate raged about the architecture of the suburban landscape in the middle of the nineteenth century, about its uniformity, the quality of its building, and the rapidity with which new homes were laid out and constructed. To many Victorians, architecture was a signal of national character; John Ruskin and Augustus Pugin argued that architecture provided access to truths about a culture in material form. Buildings offered intimate glimpses of a past that was at once a nation's and a shared human heritage: "We may live without [Architecture], and worship without her, but we cannot remember without her," Ruskin argued in 1849. "How cold is all history, how lifeless all imagery, compared to that which the living nation writes, and the uncorrupted marble bears!"[6] The buildings of our moment, Ruskin believed, are thus not only how we are to be remembered but also how we *are*—a freighted idea for a nation fearful, in an age of evolutionary insight and scientific discovery, of what it was and might soon become.

Looking out across a rapidly suburbanizing landscape, Ruskin saw in poor building practices and hastily constructed homes signs of national disease and impending social disintegration. His near-apocalyptic vision of suburbia in *The Seven Lamps of Architecture* is worth quoting at length, for it helps frame what he felt was at stake:

> I cannot but think it an evil sign of a people when their houses are built to last for one generation only. There is a sanctity in a good man's house which cannot be renewed in every tenement that rises on its ruins: and I believe that good men would generally feel this . . . and that, far more, a good son, a noble descendant, would fear [destruction] . . . to his father's house. I say that if men lived like men indeed, their houses would be temples. . . . And I look upon those pitiful concretions of lime and clay which spring up in mildewed forwardness out of the kneaded fields about our capital—upon those thin, tottering, foundationless shells of splintered wood and imitated stone—upon those gloomy rows of formalised minuteness, alike without difference and without fellowship, as solitary as similar—not merely with the careless disgust of an offended eye, not merely with sorrow for a desecrated landscape, but with a painful foreboding that the roots of our national greatness must be deeply cankered when they are thus loosely struck in their native ground; that those comfortless and unhonored dwellings are the signs of a great and spreading spirit of popular discontent.[7]

Suburban homes rise from "kneaded fields" like something from a horror movie in Ruskin's text. Distinctly inhuman geological outgrowths, they seem to suggest the ground itself has risen up against its people in "pitiful concretions of lime and clay." Prefiguring the Martians of H. G. Wells, the houses are terrifying partly because they are emotionally and morally incomprehensible, "shells" without feeling or foundation. But they are also machine-like: the "gloomy rows of formalized minuteness" are not just the same, they are repeatedly and exactly the same in ways that point out their genesis through the auspices of an automaton.

Nicholas Daly argues, in *Literature, Technology, and Modernity, 1860–2000,* that the great anxiety at the heart of modernity is not simply the clash of machine and man but the fear that the difference between the two will be erased. Daly's formulation helps explain something of the terror that lurks within Ruskin's account, for the problem is not just the homes' poor or hasty construction but also the fact that Britons choose to live in them and embrace the impermanence they offer. Ruskin deeply fears the fact that his peers are seeking movement and motion in place of stillness, stability, rootedness: suburban homes "mark the time when every man's aim is to be in some more elevated sphere than his natural one, and every man's past life is his habitual scorn; when men build in the hope of leaving the places they have built, and live in the hope of forgetting the years that they have lived."[8] The Victorian desire for class mobility, and the new practice of moving out of birth communities, makes modern Britons, in Ruskin's vision at least, terribly like the homes in which they live—"alike without difference and without fellowship, as solitary as similar." The one time Ruskin references human feelings in this passage—fellowship, loneliness—is to point out the capacity brick-and-mortar dwellings, as well as people, evidently lack. The world of suburban building is so terrifying because people have begun to lose their emotional as well as geographical and temporal connections to place. If there is a new community, a new fellowship developing, Ruskin cannot see it; in suburbia, he sees only anonymity, wasteland.

Of course, Ruskin's views were far from universally accepted; indeed, his contemporaries often turned the force of their sarcasm on his "windy purple declamation" and "conviction that there is but one right way of doing things, and that all other ways are wrong."[9] Yet his view that building reflected national character was referenced by plenty in the period, Christina Crosby points out, noting that, after Ruskin, "the idea is a truism, a reference any writer on architecture could assume."[10] She quotes a passage from the *Builder* to support the point: "If the history of architecture is the history of the human mind, [an outside observer's] researches will indicate a very chaotic mental state of the present generation."[11] To be fair, T. Mellard Reade, the author of those words, was not exactly "any writer," for, as a geologist, architect, and civil engineer, he was a contributor in his own right to the fierce debate about architectural styles at mid-century.[12] Still, we find Ruskin's idea that building reflects character, and that stable, established homes are a signal of national health, lingering into the twentieth century—most memorably in Mrs. Wilcox's horrified, pathos-laden response to the news that Margaret and Helen Schlegel will have to move from their home in *Howards End:* "To be parted from your house, your father's house—it oughtn't to be allowed. It is worse than dying. I would rather die than—Oh, poor girls! Can what they call civilization be right, if people mayn't die in the room where they were born?"[13] Forster explicitly engages Ruskin in the novel, referencing and quoting from *The Stones of Venice,* Ruskin's warning about another great mercantile city's collapse. The narrator also observes that Oniton was the sort of place built in

England "while architecture was still an expression of national character."[14] Here, though, Forster wraps up the idea as a wry joke: if architecture is a reflection of national character, then it is; it can't stop reflecting, an epistemic reality elided in the subordinate conjunction ("while"). Forster, stepping into the mind-set of one of his novel's self-serving characters, implies through the speciousness of the slip that contemporaries have given up believing Ruskin's premise only because it reveals something so unpalatable about the character of their moment. Brief, pained admiration for Ruskin surfaces; the art critic was still able to hope and advocate for an architecture that reflected something admirable about his nation, the novelist suggests. Forster, writing about a "half-baked" generation of massed suburbanites fifty years later, gives himself the miserable task of dissecting its failures instead.[15]

INTERIOR DECORATION AS MORAL IMPERATIVE

Yet this is far from the only available vision of suburban architecture in the years between Ruskin and Forster, as we have already seen. It lingers, though, as a warning in the margins and in asides throughout women's works on home decoration, as a horror of which all contemporaries know how to speak. Lady Mary Anne Barker seems to align herself with Ruskin when she argues, with metaphorical head shaking, that, "as regards our outward walls, the livery of sameness is donned by all." But, Barker continues prosaically, "there is scope for originality within doors." Interior decoration literature aimed at a female audience typically presents the problems Ruskin identified as not so much a harbinger of national doom but a call to arms; an opportunity to help resolve some of the most pressing problems of modernity. Writers routinely present interior decoration in terms of moral imperative, drawing (with Ruskin, and others) on the culture's deep commitment to what Stefan Collini has called "the primacy of morality," in particular a near-obsessive valuing of altruism.[16] Treating interior decoration as an altruistic, other-regarding act ultimately helped ease women into professional labor (as we shall see presently).

The addressee is typically gendered female, in women-authored books at least: Jane Orrinsmith's book speaks to the "earnest decorator," an "anxious inquirer" who is specifically referred to as "she." Panton's *From Kitchen to Garret* is subtitled "Hints for Young Householders" and mostly concerns the problems of an imaginary "Angelina" setting up house, for the first time, in the suburbs. Here and in later works, Panton takes the tone of an experienced woman of the world addressing younger peers as they begin their married life, as does Barker in *The Bedroom and Boudoir.* Deeply alive to the possibilities of a newly global marketplace, littered with references to imported objects and styles, these books share themes that both connect them to and distinguish them from Wildean aesthetes of twenty years later, for here decorative art is emphatically a woman's affair, rather than the preserve of educated, affluent male connoisseurs.[17] It is also a moral proving ground, rather than *l'art pour l'art,* a way to improve social and national health and, on the individual level, test and stage a woman's character.

In *Household Gods: The British and Their Possessions,* Deborah Cohen traces in detail the ways in which the discourse of interior decoration became, from the middle of the century especially, invested with moral imperative.[18] "Wealth, no longer something to be hidden or given away, had become a sign of just rewards for a productive life," she argues, but the mere acquisition of goods and furnishings was not enough: in an era of mass production, the kinds of goods chosen, and how they were displayed, signaled levels of moral feeling, while bad taste was evoked—especially in the aftermath of the Great Exhibition of 1851—as related to real moral turpitude.[19] Moving away from the home handicrafter's affinity for the imitative arts, writers premised that any object that pretended to be what it was not was deceitful, and further contended that such small-scale deceits could rub off on residents. Grained paint, for instance—paint scored while still fresh so as to convey the appearance of wood—is excoriated by interior decoration advice writers of the 1870s: "It is always ugly, always inartistic, and, being an undoubted attempt to seem what it is not, I set my face against it always," Panton explains, and she repeats the point in nearly every home decoration book she writes.[20]

Religious writers like clergyman Andrew Boyd played a part in shaping the theory that furnishing choices had moral effects in the early 1860s: Boyd argued in a widely read essay, "Concerning the Moral Influences of the Dwelling" (1861), that "beauty and use go together; the prettiest house will be the healthiest, the most convenient, and the most comfortable. And I am persuaded that great moral results follow from people's houses being pretty as well as healthy."[21] A beautiful house—and to Boyd, the most beautiful house imaginable was a modern villa in the Gothic style—was filled with useful objects that inculcated good habits and thereby strengthened a man's character: "It makes an educated man domestic, it makes him a lover of neatness and accuracy, it makes him gentle and amiable . . . to give him a pretty home." Yet the domesticity Boyd admires is oriented not so much around the demands of a family as around a man's need for space and quiet: Boyd stresses that his own office is "in a comparatively remote part of the house . . . there is no sound of household life; no pattering of little feet; no voices of servants in discussion."[22] The office enables his act of writing, he argues, but he gives the credit for creativity not so much to the other occupants of the home, who labor away in silence, as to the furnishings in the room and its peaceful outlook—to the green textiles, the oak chairs, tables, and bookcases, and the tendrils of ivy that wind picturesquely around the window. His aesthetic vision is centered on the idea that actions are produced by physical environs ("we are all moral chameleons . . . we take the colour of the objects among which we are placed"), and to that end he makes a pointed contrast between suburban or rural and urban habitations: "Few people can look at a pretty tasteful villa, all gables, turrets, bay windows, twisted chimneys, verandahs, and balconies, set in a pleasant little expanse of shrubbery, with some fine forest-trees, a green bit of open lawn, and some winding walks through clumps of evergreens, without tacitly concluding that the people who live there must lead a very different life from that which is led in a dull smoky street, and a blackened, gardenless, grassless, treeless house in town."[23] Boyd's very sentence construction encourages readers to connect villa exteriors with middle-class values, with a taste for what one might call moderated plenty: in a long, positively evoked catalog of architectural and landscape features, we note that the pleasant shrubbery is "little," the open lawn a "bit," and that there are "some," but not too many, winding walks and trees. The urban home, meanwhile, is evoked in absences and negatives that suggest a life of loss and squeeze, the house thrust into the end of the sentence to evoke syntactically the cramped space of city streets. The moral chameleon living against a dull smoky backdrop will become dull himself, limited and constrained, we infer, while the man who lives in a suburban or rural house will become a man of steady principles, creative energy, and moderate, self-disciplined affluence, thereby living out and embodying a middle-class ideal.

Ruskin himself famously developed the idea, in his 1864 lecture "Of Queens' Gardens," that a restful home was necessary for the man forced to deal in the daytime with the rough-and-tumble of the marketplace. Ruskin, who became only more concerned as the years passed about the impact of modernity on men, argued: "The man, in his rough work in open world, must encounter all peril and trial . . . often he must be wounded, or subdued, often misled: and *always* hardened." The home serves as respite, as sanctuary, for the businessman—"a sacred place, a vestal temple, a temple of the hearth watched over by Household Gods." The high priestess of the temple-home was woman, or, more particularly, wife, for Ruskin had by 1864 shifted away from his belief that bricks and mortar anchored national character; women serve that function instead, and they are able to perform it no matter what their surroundings: "Wherever a true wife comes, this home is always round her. The stars only may be over her head; the glowworm in the night cold grass may be the only fire at her foot; but home is yet wherever she is."[24] Ruskin's interpretation of the temple-home as absolutely disconnected from architecture marks a critical step along his journey toward despair about the shape and values of the modern city. Ruskin, needless to say, did not agree with Boyd that the villa served as peaceful respite from and healthful alternative to urban problems, and he turned to women for social regeneration, evoking them in and through a language of medieval chivalry, thereby turning his back emphatically on the splintered edifices constructed by his colleagues.[25]

Women writing on interior decoration in the 1870s, meanwhile, endorsed the idea that occupation of a beautiful home acted as an important counterweight to the iniquities of the public sphere, and that beauty and good taste were both correlated to, and productive of, moral, self-denying, self-disciplined character. They drew on—and even referenced—Ruskin's vision of woman as particularly charged with the business of ameliorating the consequences of modernity, including the dangers of selfishness. But, unlike Ruskin, they rooted their vision of moral improvement in women's work in the brick-and-mortar reality of a suburban house, finding signals of moral uplift in wallpaper, curtains, and antimacassars, not grass and fireflies. A woman's ability to decorate—to learn key tenets of aesthetics and apply them to home furnishings—is evoked as a practice of urgent moral and social significance.

Ruskin denounced feminine art as small-scale and ephemeral, as we have seen, mere "handiwork for drawing-room tables . . . relief for the ennui of boudoirs." Writers of interior design manuals present decoration as a near-epic act: no idle pastime, it is conceived as highly challenging and conflictual, the relationship of built environment and woman shaped as one of struggle, difficulty, and obstacle. (The full title of Panton's 1896 book is *Suburban Residences and How to Circumvent Them.*) The house fights back: indeed, many writers present decorating suburban houses as akin to the pioneer or colonial experience, the house as alien space that resists or repels the woman who lives inside it. The act of layering on wallpaper and putting down rugs is regularly conceived as one of subjugation, civilization, control. This language may reflect the actual colonial experience of some of the writers who penned the texts—the author of *The Bedroom and Boudoir,* for instance, Lady Mary

Anne Barker (later Lady Broome), was born in Spanish Town, Jamaica, daughter of the Island Secretary, and lived in India with her first husband and in New Zealand and South Africa with her second. In *The Bedroom and Boudoir* she explicitly equates decorating a suburban home with the challenges of colonial life, and explains that the latter showed her how important it is to impose "beauty" on surroundings. "I have never found it necessary to endure, for more than the first few days of my sojourn, anything in the least ugly or uncomfortable," she opines; whether looking out "over the snowy peaks of the Himalayas" or the chimney pots of London, imposing her own aesthetic on her surroundings was a struggle that not only tested her mettle but also allowed her to imprint herself in material, tangible form on the landscape she was called to inhabit: "People cannot always create, as it were, the place in which they are obliged to live. One may find oneself placed in a habitation perfectly contrary to every principle of correct taste as well as opposed to one's individual preferences. But that is such an opportunity! out of unpromising materials and surroundings you have to make a room, whether bedroom, or boudoir, which will take the impression of your own state. As long as a woman possesses a pair of hands and her work-basket, a little hammer and a few tintacks, it is hard if she need live in a room which is actually ugly."[26] Ugliness is produced by the builder who constructed the home, possibly (the point is not quite put into words) the husband who compels you to accompany him. Beauty is produced by the woman who sets about the dwelling with her tools, who molds the surroundings to make them take the "impression" of her state. Ruskin's vision of women's artistic labor as idle pastime, a private, domestic, "merely" personal act, has been transformed into one that enacts and supports the mission of the nation to imprint itself, and its industrial economy, on the globe.

A scene of conflict and overcoming appears in most woman-authored interior decoration literature, and it is invariably located in the suburban home whose unworthy fire grates, ill-designed windows, or subterranean kitchens try the patience of the writer-decorator or architect. It is cheap fittings and the builder's cost-cutting practices and showy but flimsy attention-grabbing designs that test us, to be clear, not the uniformity of suburban façades. Besides, "that is such an opportunity!" as Barker put it; women writers call upon their readers to see the problems as a call to arms. The act of decorating the suburban house is rhetorically packaged as an act of subduing the forces of speculation and capitalist industry, of preventing them from invading family life, and of testing one's own resolve and self-discipline. (A similar tone of cheerful determination pervades Catharine Beecher and Harriet Beecher Stowe's co-written *American Women's Home,* though here the forces to be subdued are the wilderness, poverty, and the roughly hewn homes of new pioneers. Beecher and Stowe find remarkably inventive ways to make the house beautiful: a scooped-out carrot, we are told, filled with water, "will send out graceful shoots in rich profusion," while a sweet potato run through with knitting needles will in time make "a beautiful verdant ornament.")[27] A battle is particularly likely to be waged between the housewife and the "demon builder" or landlord in Panton's and Barker's texts—texts that excoriate such figures for their mistakes, their cost cutting, their need to maximize profit, and their failures of taste, which are all correlated. "The best which can be hoped from an ordinary modern builder is that he will put in harmless grates and mantelpieces, and abstain from showy designs," Barker snorts, while Panton agrees that grates are a particular area of failing: "Nowhere, I think, does the ordinary landlord or builder 'skimp' more than in this. Any grate is considered good enough for the ordinary suburban residence."[28] The builder is presented as a man animated by alien values, selfish, rooted in commerce and industry, a figure who cannot appreciate good taste or family need. Moreover, his choices cannot simply be uprooted, and his decisions have palpable impact on familial life. Yet he isn't physically present to complain, and Panton argues that part of living in a suburban house is a willingness to overturn his decisions in favor of a family's requirements.

For instance, the drawing room was typically signaled by the installation of the home's largest, and grandest, fireplace. But the dining room should be the sunniest, so that husband and wife can enjoy a warm breakfast before work. A pleasant breakfast—and a cool afternoon—help family life go better, thus occupants must realize "the builder's dictum is anything but a final one" and be prepared to switch rooms: "Allow the position of the sun at different times of the day to determine where the dining, drawing, and morning rooms are to be, and take nothing else whatever into consideration," Panton argues.[29] Her dictum that interior decoration decisions must be forged in response to the rhythms of domesticity are shared by virtually all woman writers of design texts; the builder, the landlord, the architect, and even the "boys" who come to deliver goods are identified as challenges to be managed and overcome. Delivery boys required significant thought, because their reaching hands and greasy hair could stain hall wallpaper while they were kept waiting by the cook; Panton recommends stretched and nailed oilcloth, chosen in colors to match the hall paint, in place of wallpaper, to provide a washable surface where it's needed.[30] Such interior decoration advice is evoked as not just the dissemination of feminine influence, the sanctification and sanitation of the home, but also a way of asserting domestic and family values in material form. The woman with an oversized dining room fireplace displayed that she valued pleasant breakfasts and her husband's good temper, while an oilcloth hallway not only spared wallpaper expense but visually signified thrift. Aesthetic maxims no doubt responded to real-world problems (smudgy walls, freezing drafts, grumpy husbands), but the moving of a room or the hanging of an oilcloth further signified a housewife who was aware of, and capable of doing battle with, the encroachments of the commercial world.

What strikes any modern reader of these advice texts is that the uniformity of suburban homes, their standardized hallways and sitting rooms and mantels, is presented, not in Ruskin's terms of horror, but as the bedrock of a shared female experience. "Choosing a House," the first chapter of *From Kitchen to Garret,* offers advice to a young middle-class married couple about where to live; Panton gives a detailed assessment of the possibilities and opportunities of the different suburbs around London for the middle class, and she offers her own views about which are most salubrious and well served by trains.[31] The author does not expect that the age of the home will be in question; she assumes the house will be modern, and from there the whole book follows, based on a shared understanding of the floor plan—from kitchen to garret—and of the shops and services that cater to such homes. Panton's cheerful attitude to the repeated floor plans and façades of suburban homes, the source of so much hand-wringing in the press, so terribly disdained by Ruskin, is common; authors note that repetitious architecture is a fact of modern life without rancor. Indeed, the aesthetic ideas articulated in the texts are remarkably repetitious in themselves and seem hardly likely to distinguish the homes or foster much-vaunted "originality": there is a surprising degree of agreement that one buys the best textiles at Liberty, loves the patterns of Mr. Morris, but hates disturbing wallpaper patterns that fail to join up or that "make faces at you" when you're ill. One uses potted palms, brass bowls, and china knickknacks for decoration and portieres (curtains covering doors) to keep out the outdoors (and all drafts), admires green-stained furniture, buys corner cabinets at Smee and Cobay and all sorts of remarkable odds and ends at Shoolbred's on Tottenham Court Road (founded in the 1820s, this department store began manufacturing furniture in the 1870s).[32] Aspinall's paint is best (and happens to be advertised in the book), Chippendale furniture admirable (if you can afford it), screens charming, antimacassars and dados essential, and all but the prettiest books must be covered up with curtains. Cosy Corners, a portable premade inglenook, can be installed to give any room a modern, Arts and Crafts look and feel—with the added charm that, when your lease is up, the Cosy Corner is "designed to be simply taken away with all other belongings at the end of a tenancy."[33] Anticipating likeness of homes and a mobile way of life, the texts not only expect but seek to foster a community of like-mindedness rendered visible in design.

Aesthetic principles are nested in shared values: readers may have different incomes and monthly spending capacities, but all can agree, the writers posit, that the suburbs are the best choice for a young couple seeking a home without "smuts and blacks" pouring through the windows, that the suburban "compromise" between urban energy and rural peace is the best choice for a young family, that shams and imitations are to be avoided at all costs.[34] Honesty, cleanliness, compromise, quiet, self-discipline, domestic primacy—these values run through every aesthetic recommendation like threads in a tapestry. The very sameness of the designs that result is, in the end, precisely the point,

6. Smee and Cobay used this design for a Panton drawing room in many of their advertisements. From Jane Ellen Panton, *Suburban Residences and How to Circumvent Them* (1896). Reproduced by kind permission of the Syndics of Cambridge University Library. Misc. 7.89.1028.

7. "Aspinall's Enamel." Panton rarely missed an opportunity to puff the brand. From Jane Ellen Panton, *Suburban Residences and How to Circumvent Them* (1896). Reproduced by kind permission of the Syndics of Cambridge University Library. Misc. 7.89.1028.

for this is a painstaking painting-by-numbers approach to interior decoration, one that shows readers how to put together the appearance of casual ease and middle-class design dado by dado. Mrs. Panton, for instance, explains to readers in all her books how to integrate a piano (which she considers "a very ugly piece of furniture") into a morning room: the back must be hung with a curtain suspended from "one of Shoolbred's plain piano rods," a writing table

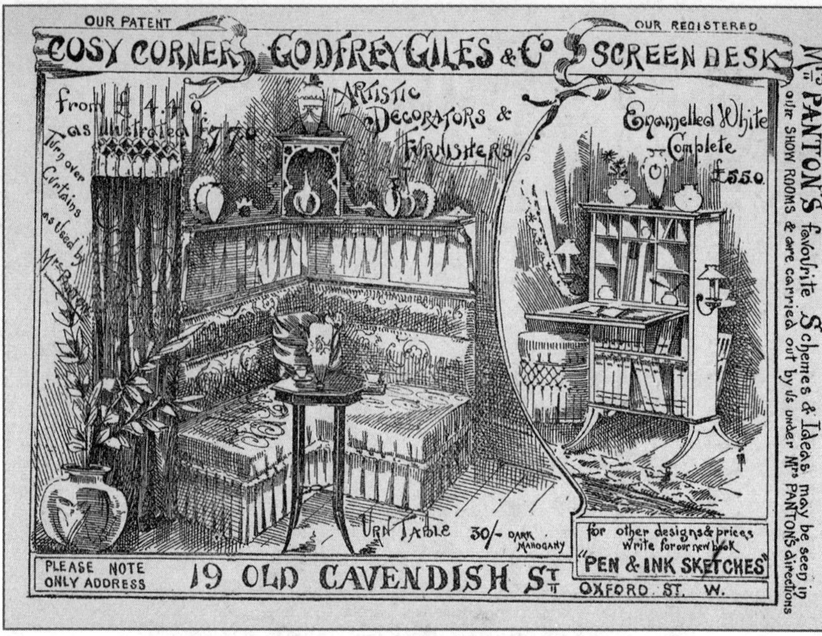

8. "Cosy Corner." Its charm was that it could be moved from house to house. From Jane Ellen Panton, *From Kitchen to Garret: Hints for Young Householders* (1887; revised edition 1893). © British Library Board General Reference Collection 07944.e.3.

should be set against it, a table and tall palm placed either near or at the bend to "disguise" the offending object, while "along the top can be placed a piece of serge, or felt or damask, or, what is better still, a piece of Eastern embroidery," which can serve as "an excellent shelf for odds and ends of china and bowls of flowers" (figure 9).[35] Readers new to the middle class, new to marriage, or who have moved away from their birth families and must learn to manage a household for themselves learn how to stage the scene to communicate modernity with a middle-class confidence they obviously did not feel.[36] Panton's advice is relentlessly detailed, although she gives slightly different options depending on whether the resident actually wants to use the piano or not, has an appropriate screen, or wishes to signal "a more careless arrangement" than can be achieved by a gathered curtain (in which case, "a large square of drapery can be arranged gracefully over the back, securing it with small tintacks on the inside of the lid"). In each design (and Panton modifies her piano arrangement slightly over the years), the thrown material signals affluence, stacked books on the fabric serve as weights, signifying literacy without bookishness, while the ubiquitous Victorian potted palm points the viewer to overseas territories and reminds of the industrial networks that facilitated the arrival and domestication of such exotics in England (not to mention the purchasing power that allowed occupants to buy and replace palms as needed), thereby connecting the scene to the energies of modernity. The reason Panton gives for her energetic efforts to conceal the piano is its "coffin-like" appearance; the author tells us proudly, in *From Kitchen to Garret,* "I have once or twice been asked if I have a piano, so little in evidence is this instrument."[37] In fact the desire to conceal the piano, to repurpose it as a decorative object, reminds us that pianos were losing their cultural cachet as hire-purchase programs and mass production made the instruments available to the lower-middle and even the working class. Advertisements for pianos nestled in the pages of *Lady's Pictorial* beside ads for cheap seaside days out, while an image of production-line assembly methods at Brinsmead's Piano Manufactory equates pianos with any other industrially produced object (figure 10). In Braddon's 1886 novel *One Thing Needful,* Lord Lashmar references the modern financial systems "on which needy people buy pianos": possession of the instrument was no longer necessarily a signal of affluence.[38] We note, though, that the offending piano, smothered in fabric, remained in Panton's morning room for decades, so that presumably part of what the writer is staging through her curtains and bowls and clutter of tables remains her ability to own the piano—the observant visitor surely saw it was there—combined with an elite's disdain for a commercially purchased object—signaled through her apparently studious efforts to conceal it. It is just visible in Panton's most expensively equipped version of the scene—a room in her imagined dream house—lurking behind an extremely large, and rather dangerous-looking, potted palm (figure 11).[39]

The great success of interior decoration books and of Panton's own columns suggests that women relished just this kind of prescriptive advice, which appeared to render clear-cut and straightforward something that was surely anything but easy. At a moment when cultural and aesthetic values were in flux, when middle-class spending power, new department stores, and new systems of store credit met and uneasily negotiated the tastes of the older elites, readers could figure out how to walk through a minefield by following Panton's, or Orrinsmith's, or Barker's detailed advice on how to drape a window, a toilet table, a piano, or a door (the bus was there to take you from Bayswater to Shoolbred's, after all). Readers presumably did not mind that their arrangement of plants and pots and pianos and curtains could be seen

FIG. 12.—A Draped Piano.

9. "A Draped Piano," from Jane Ellen Panton, *Nooks and Corners* (1889): "The top should always be arranged as shown in the sketch, for though these things may deaden the sound, and a good musician would, no doubt, rage about them, they can be removed in three seconds to a side table should music be the order of the day" (71–73). © British Library Board General Reference Collection 7817.e.6.

all around the neighborhood; indeed, if anything, readers were encouraged to see the reproduction of design choices and furniture arrangement as a heartening sign of community and shared values. Surely many suburbanites derived enormous comfort in learning, from someone titled "Lady Barker," that "there are perfectly simple, inoffensive wardrobes to be procured of varnished pine or even deal . . . which, if it can only be kept free from scratches, is at

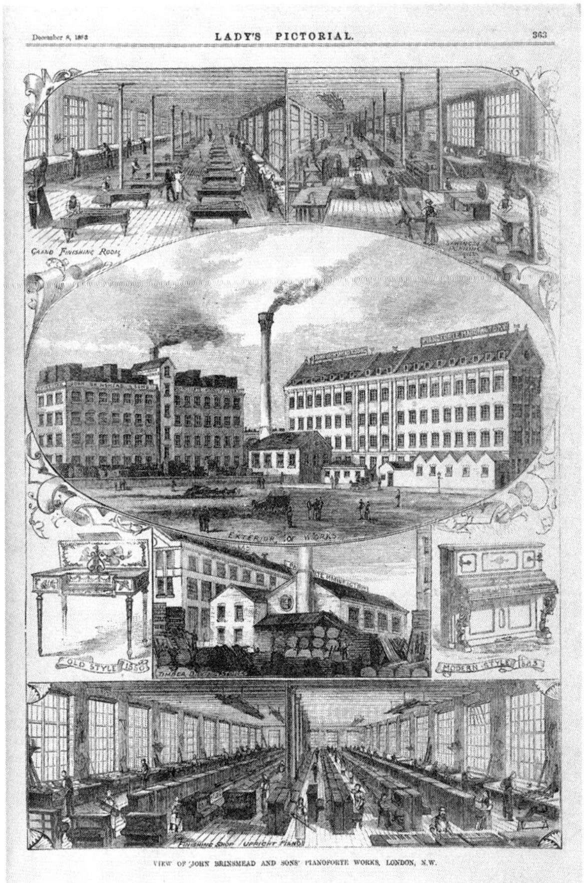

10. "View of John Brinsmead and Sons Pianoforte Works, London N.W." The scene celebrates the mass production of pianos. *Lady's Pictorial* (December 8, 1883). With thanks to the Alexander Turnbull Library, Wellington, New Zealand.

least in good taste," or, even more practically, that batiste should be used on a toilet table because it is so cheap and can be easily replaced (decorative choices, Barker adds delicately, should be "of so elastic a nature as to be capable of expansion under favourable circumstances").[40] Design texts appear enormously complex and hard to follow, but the woman hunting a brass pot to set beside her hire-purchase piano, an escritoire to put beside a cheaply made folding door, presumably experienced the comforting sense that she had met the challenges of the day head-on. At the same time, the business of

11. "A Charming Morning Room" or the well-hidden piano. Look for it to the left, lurking behind a potted palm. From Jane Ellen Panton, *A Gentlewoman's Home* (1896). © British Library Board General Reference Collection YA.1994.a.8396.

turning the home into a domesticated space, of repackaging industrially produced, commercially purchased objects as part of a domestic design aesthetic, could never end, both because so many objects needed domestication and because Victorians so regularly moved. (Curtains and cloths, occasional tables, pots, china bowls, plant tables, and so forth could be taken with you, perhaps easing anxieties about their expense.) This rendered interior decoration an engrossing and unceasing occupation—indubitably industry, of a sort.

For it was not only purchased objects that required decoration and thus domestication. Architectural features of the suburban home interior engaged particular energies on the part of the period's interior designers. Fireplaces were a deep source of angst; often plaster painted to look like marble, suburban fireplaces, the writers agreed, were ugly, tasteless, ill proportioned, and poorly functioning, chosen for show, not heat or family comfort. They showed smoke stains, they were hard to clean, "unduly prominent," dreadfully drafty, and above all fake, either because they aped the appearance of stone or because they pretended to the aesthetic of the Stately Home (possibly both). Panton spent pages on the marble or faux marble fireplace in all of her works; she recommended the purchase of a slow-combustion stove for the business of actually heating the room, but that was just the beginning of the labor. Next came "disguising" the "marble incubus" with yet more lengths of fabric.[41] For this, she recommended "the simplest drapery in the world," "known as the 'Gentlewoman,' after the paper of that name." The Gentlewoman could be made quite easily "by taking a plain strip of material 24 inches wide, and 24 inches longer than the mantelpiece itself. This is trimmed round the sides and front with ball fringe or cord. If cord is used, a bunch of pom-poms should hang from each of the front corners, and the corners are lined on the cross with thin silk or sateen the same colour as the material, and this is simply put on the shelf and drapes itself." Panton concedes "people cannot understand its virtues until they have seen it," but as soon as they do, she claims, "they understand at once what a valuable help it is to circumventing the ordinary marble mantelpiece of badly-designed houses."[42] It may well be hard for us to fathom the appeal of a long droopy cloth with pom-poms on the edge, but the charm of the Gentlewoman surely lies in the way it transforms an "incubus" selected for commercial reasons—an incubus is a mythological male demon that lies on sleeping women and rapes them—from a male threat into, again, a domesticated object. If the incubus lies on women, the Gentlewoman lies on the incubus, and smothers it in pom-poms. Design, in other words, renders palpable, visible, the woman's successful engagement with the world of industry and production, the containment of the incubus and all he represents—his power, his shifty tricks. The suburban exterior built to make money, the interior features purchased by landlord or builder—the mantelpiece as well as badly seasoned floorboards, ill-fitting sash windows, drafty doors and chimneys—are, through the women's decorative practice, her choice of furbelowed cloths, muslins, dados, cretonnes, and antimacassars, transformed, metamorphosed from objects that remind viewers of the values of the world of commerce into domestic objects that reassert triumphantly the values of women's work. As Talia Schaffer says of watches that were wrapped in layers of decoration in earlier decades: "It is precisely because the artifact is purchased that it requires to be literally enwrapped in signifiers of the home."[43] The fake marble fireplace was purchased and installed to signify a "desirable suburban residence," but, by covering the fireplace with the Gentlewoman or the mass-produced piano with an embroidered cloth, the decorator battled the commodification of the home.

12. The Gentlewoman draped on a mantle. From Jane Ellen Panton, *From Kitchen to Garret: Hints for Young Householders* (1887; revised edition 1893). © British Library Board General Reference Collection 07944.e.3.

Each aesthetic recommendation connects to a nested set of values; shared aesthetic principles serve to remind occupants and visitors that the home and its occupants are part of a community oriented around a shared commitment to thrift, self-discipline, altruism. Mrs. Panton takes her vision of a community of readers to such a degree that she shares the name and address of her own upholsterer in the text and explains the minutest, most practical details of the relationship: "Save in London, where she has married daughters she can stay with, she has to be put up," she explains, though Mrs. Panton reassures readers that the redoubtable Mrs. Bacon "is such an admirable worker and so quick and industrious . . . one saves her fare over and over again."[44] Passages like these have the feel of a letter, rather than a manual, as if Panton is sharing intimate secrets with a friend or family member. It is perfectly clear, however, perusing the advertisements at the start and end of Panton's texts, that the "community" she invited her readers to enter with her was shaped, dependent on, and supportive of many of the "sharp" practices she claims to overset. Whether or not the industrious Mrs. Bacon actually received money from the recommendation and passed it on to Mrs. Panton, it seems likely the famous decorator was in mutually beneficial relationships with many of the design shops, department stores, furniture makers, paint producers, and textile manufacturers recommended in her pages—who advertised prominently in her books. Readers, discovering in an advertisement for Jackson's Varnish Stains a few choice words from *Lady's Pictorial,* for example, or seeing Mrs. Panton's name scrawled in an image of the Cosy Corner, surely knew that Mrs. Panton herself both wrote for, and advertised books in, *Lady's Pictorial.* Shoolbred's advertisements appeared regularly in the front and back matter of manuals that recommended shopping at Shoolbred's. Every suburbanite knew to take advertisements with a grain of salt, to see money-making schemes behind the suburb's inflated claims. In Panton's column "Other Folks' Homes" for the *Gentlewoman,* the author lists the names and addresses of every shop she recommends, most of which we hear her hymn with wearying regularity, most of which reference her in their advertisements in turn; William Wallace and Co. is warmly recommended by Mrs. Panton, a firm of designers who, in their turn, sagely advise purchase of the "Panton" Indispensable Corner Wardrobe. The aesthetics recommended were inevitably navigations of, but never rejections of, industrial production and the values of consumer culture; after all, the objects recommended—the ball fringe, fabrics, potted plants, "Aspinall's oxidized paint," brass bowls, Liberty wallpapers, Shoolbred's piano rods, and of course the design manual or magazine itself—were purchased by the woman in the marketplace. And if you were unwilling to sew a Gentlewoman yourself, to cover your mantelpiece, you could simply buy one, ready-made, from J. Wilson at 159 New Bond Street.

The story of epic battle between home and commerce, private and public, that shapes interior design literature was, in other words, almost too obviously a fiction. This fiction was a familiar one in the later nineteenth century. Decades of Romantic Revival adventure stories in periodicals like the *Boy's Own Paper* and by the likes of Rider Haggard and Rudyard Kipling evoked the heroism of struggle and overcoming.[45] Aesthetes and modernists drew on this arc at the turn of the twentieth century in their own tale of breaking with the past and rejecting the Victorian bourgeois. (As Schaffer puts it, "The story of modernism is . . . a good old fashioned adventure story in which brave heroes finally triumph over the prudish public. If modernism were modernist, it would be a fragmentary tale of hesitations.")[46] Women writers of the 1870s engage a similar story of struggle and eventual triumph in their accounts of decorating halls and bedrooms. Barker's bracingly aphoristic "as long as a woman possesses a pair of hands . . ." could easily grace the pages of

13. "The 'Panton' Indispensable Corner Wardrobe" as advertised in the *Gentlewoman* magazine (September 8, 1894). © British Library Board General Reference Collection LOU.LON 257 [1894].

a fin de siècle adventure tale. But if this is a reflexively later Victorian or Edwardian rhetorical move, it nonetheless points to the anxieties that the narratives of success and triumph strive, repeatedly, to ease. Just as imperialist adventure stories reveal ambivalence as well as gung-ho energy about the business of dominating the globe, so Barker's account of decorating the home stages the suburban residence as a place that requires intervention, a problem of the modern age. The home was not chosen by the woman who lives in it; the woman does not control the landscape of her life. The demon builder and even the smudgy delivery boy surely stand in for all the figures whose values

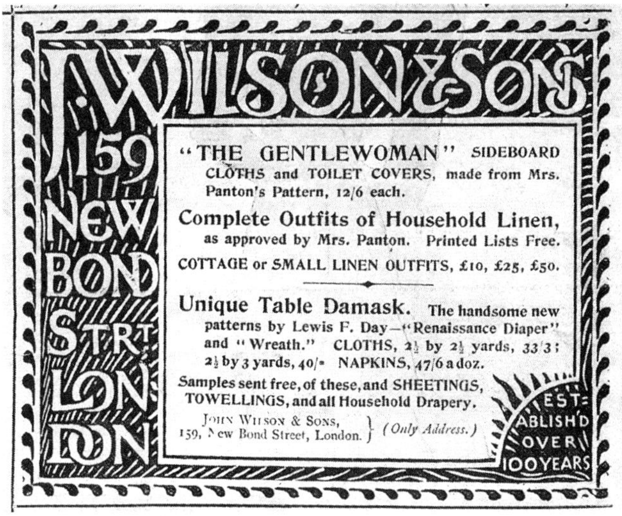

14. J. Wilson and Sons, "The Gentlewoman." If you couldn't make your own Gentlewoman, you could always buy one, as this advertisement suggests. The *Gentlewoman* (January 1893). © British Library Board General Reference Collection LOU.LON 310 [1893].

marked not only society, and the built environment, but also women's lives. Sickness could come at any point to destroy the peace and happiness of the home (most of the interior decoration books under discussion give significant attention, even whole chapters, to discussions of how serious illness should change the arrangement of the furnishings in a house). Read in this light, articulations of interior decoration as conflict and subjugation hint at a social and cultural dislocation that home decoration promises to ease, giving the occupant material stakes in the world she inhabits. Interior decoration holds out the alluring promise of battling the demon builder and his brothers—and winning. It sounds, on the face of it, like wish fulfillment, or (at best) a pole star toward which women could steer. But remarkably, women decorators did make significant inroads into the fields of interior decoration, and even architecture, in the period. (Note that in an advertisement for Jackson's Varnish Stains, a woman is varnishing the floor while her girls, equipped with brushes, help.) And although the values of 1890s aestheticism stood in a complicated relation to women's decorative work, one important movement was centrally concerned with women's values and with the suburban landscape from the

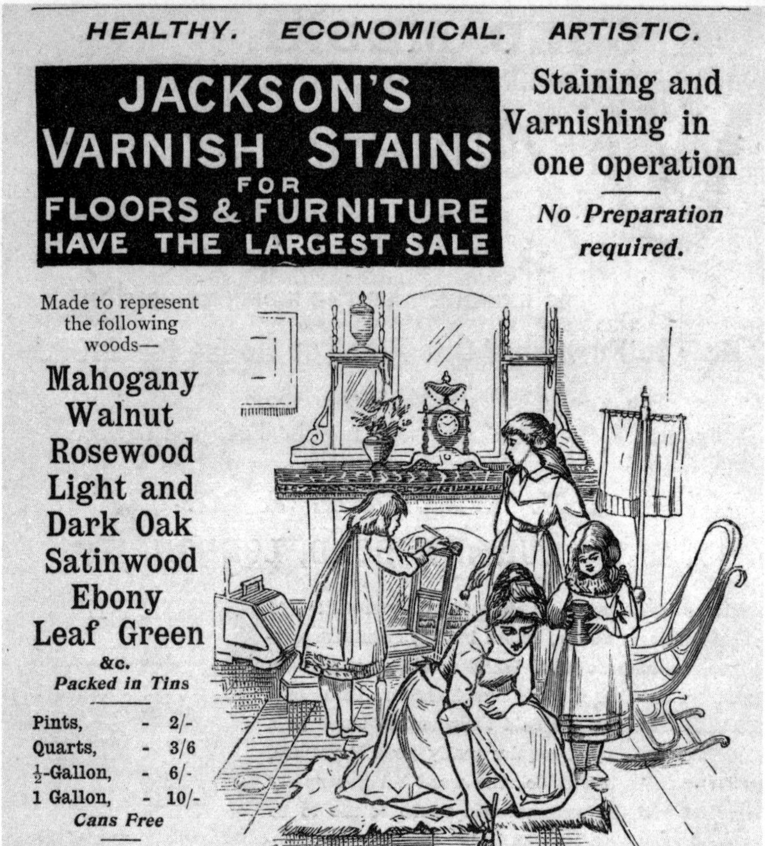

15. "Jackson's Varnish Stains." The advertisement anticipates that women (and their daughters) will be actively involved in making over their homes. From Jane Ellen Panton, *Suburban Residences and How to Circumvent Them* (1896). Reproduced by kind permission of the Syndics of Cambridge University Library. Misc. 7.89.1028.

1870s on: Queen Anne Revival style. Thus readers encouraged to see their aesthetic community as making a material difference in the world may well have known that, in some ways, it was.

QUEEN ANNE REVIVAL: SUBURBAN FASHIONING AND SELF-FASHIONING

Lady Barker advocates for the much-criticized Victorian clutter, or "litter," halfway through her book:

> I confess I like a room to look as if it were inhabited, and that is the only drawback that the rooms furnished in the seventeenth century style have in my eyes. You scarcely ever feel as if any one lived in them—there are seldom any signs of occupation, especially feminine occupation, lying about, no "litter," in fact. . . . I am told that litter is incongruous in a Queen Anne room, for that the women of those days had not the same modes of employment as ourselves. . . . I am always longing to overlay a little of the modish primness of the distant days we are now copying, with something of this busy nineteenth century's tokens of a love of art or literature. And in a room with any claim to a distinct individuality of its own, this would always be the case.[47]

The word "litter" first surfaces, according to the *OED,* in Jonathan Swift's 1730 satire "The Lady's Dressing Room," where it is tied specifically to women's accoutrements. Indeed, Swift's poem memorably evokes domestic objects as filthy clues to the truth behind the "haughty" Celia's projection of herself as "Goddess"; Strephon secretly rifles Celia's possessions, peeking under her bed, only to discover evidence of her disturbing physicality—"Disgusted *Strephon* stole away / Repeating in his amorous Fits, / Oh! *Celia, Celia, Celia* shits!"[48] Barker—whose vision of the seventeenth and early eighteenth centuries was of a time of "modish primness"—has a very different view from Swift of women's domestic objects; she presents them not as secrets to be hidden from public sight but as a means of staging a woman's labor and value for visitors. Barker here and throughout *The Bedroom and Boudoir* embraces clutter, busyness, and domestic industry, gently rebutting visions of the home as a place of temple-like calm and sanctifying peace. Feminine litter—homemade objects or cheaper, industrially produced purchased goods—was to be derided in the later decades of the century, in preference for antiques and rich imported *objets* whose value was assessed and guaranteed by experts and connoisseurs. In

Barker's text, the scattered objects remain tied to a discourse of middle-class personal responsibility—decoration as "work," domestic labor, busyness—and also stake out the value of a distinctively feminine aesthetic, in which a simple, unpretending interior integrates signs of women's work. Domestic objects are presented as not only appropriate in but also beautifiers of a home; the interior should not look, Barker argues, like a castle, a church, or a stately home but should express the interests and pastimes of the women who live in it.

Barker's text rebukes architects and designers of the period who, as Judith Neiswander puts it, "flaunted their wealth through a lavish display of expensive furnishings." Barker prefers "primness"—the sober, quiet, plain interior, or, as Loftie wrote, in *A Plea for Art in the Home,* a décor of "studied plainness."[49] Barker also battles those Ruskin-inspired, Gothic Revival aesthetes who felt women's crafts had no place in the beautiful home. Barker's design is, in the end, not so much a critique of Queen Anne Revival as an expression of it. An embrace of the domestic lay at the heart of the Queen Anne style, which rose to prominence in the 1870s: Loftie's 1876 text suggested that Queen Anne interiors could harmonize family life, bring back straying sons and brothers, elevate the tone of family discourse. Barker's affection for Queen Anne was widely shared by writers of interior decoration manuals in the 1870s and '80s (many of whom published volumes, with Barker and Loftie, in Macmillan's Art at Home series). Rhoda and Agnes Garrett's 1876 *Suggestions for House Decoration* was one of the first books to popularize the style whose architectural expression was practiced by the likes of John McKean Brydon—to whom the Garretts were themselves apprenticed—Norman Shaw, and John James Stephenson. Seen as a reaction against mid-Victorian heaviness, Queen Anne connoted to its proponents (Mark Girouard has argued) both art and enlightenment, Arnoldian "sweetness and light"; Queen Anne was reformist, secular, domestic, redbrick. It disdained the pretense to aristocratic gentility, celebrating, in essence, middle-classness; home and hearth (complete with embroidered drapery).

Queen Anne was, at the same time, hard to define; the term referenced and drew on the architecture not just of the reign of Anne but of a range of vernacular styles of the seventeenth and eighteenth centuries. It was, Deborah Weiner argues, a term that came ultimately to mean something of a mishmash, "an architecture of red brick and white sash windows which freely combined mid-seventeenth century gables, brick pilasters, brick pediments, and ribbed chimney stacks, wrought-iron railings, hipped roofs, wooden cupolas, external shutters, fanlights and brick aprons beneath the windows. Prominent

16. "Art at Home." This image, from Rhoda and Agnes Garrett, *Suggestions for House Decoration* (2nd edition, 1877) was used in all books in the Art at Home series published by Macmillan. © British Library Board General Reference Collection 07943.k.32/15.

roofs and chimney stacks were often decorated with the sunflower motif. It was an architecture of the façade. . . . The use of prominent gables . . . made the boundaries of one home distinct from those of its neighbor, in contrast to the image of the extended villa which the unity of white stucco had tried to convey."[50] Popularized architecturally by Shaw's Bedford Park development in

17. Rhoda and Agnes Garrett, "Drawing-Room Chimney Piece," from *Suggestions for House Decoration* (2nd edition, 1877). The Garretts agreed with Panton that a chimney piece should be covered with drapery, especially if the mantle was made of marble. © British Library Board General Reference Collection 07943.k.32/15.

London (1875–79), the world's first "garden suburb," the style was copied by speculative builders in suburbs across the capital and the nation, as gabled terraces no longer aped the stately house façade or extended villa but rather communicated to the world the existence of multiple, separate homes.[51] (Hospitals, schools, and women's colleges like Somerville at Oxford and Newnham at Cambridge were designed to look like clusters of redbrick houses, thereby hinting to residents the repose of a family home.) Queen Anne Revival spoke, Stephenson suggested, to a population in love with the novels of Thackeray, to country doctors and lawyers rather than medieval knights and ladies, banquets and jousts.[52] It looked for influence to an age of "cheerful red brick fronts among the green, the windows with their broad white frames and small window panes twinkling in the light," that "suggest all the pleasant associations of an English home."[53] Brydon made a similar point when he celebrated

18. F. Hamilton Jackson, *Bedford Park.* Jackson celebrates the beauty of the new Queen Anne–style suburb and its gardens. © Geffrye Museum, London.

Queen Anne as the successful expression of a newly flowering domestic national culture in physical, architectural form: "The home is a peculiarly English institution, and certainly no houses, be they stately or be they humble, express the feelings of homeliness more truly than those of England."[54]

Queen Anne offered a new way of not only building but speaking of suburbia. Queen Anne was not used for suburban homes alone, of course, but in that it was a style that embraced and celebrated the lives of the bourgeois—the small family grouping, the vernacular—it attracted writers discussing suburban interiors because its drivers dignified the middle class. To generations reared on Gothic Revival, generations that viewed the world through the lenses of Ruskin and Pugin, the redbrick homes were to be spoken of as horrifying excrescences, as modern armies moving across the landscape, invading it, pushing their secular, irreligious tentacles deep into the heart of England. The discourse of Queen Anne Revival, by contrast, rendered suburban building sympathetic, harmonious, English, at once modern and connected to the past. After all, Queen Anne's reign was another era of brick buildings and wood staircases, the Garretts point out, drawing a connection between Queen Anne–era brick and the bricks used by modern builders—brick and wood is and has long been the building material of "*ordinary* English houses," they stress.[55] Queen Anne style is thus presented as quasi-democratic as well as quintessentially English: it used what Loftie called, in his short introduction to the Garretts' book, "our native red brick." Stone and Gothicism the Garretts associate with castles, palaces, the rich; their business is with a collective that "has been too long overlooked"—the middle class. The bourgeois aesthetic the Garretts celebrate is one available to those "able to enjoy leisure, refinement and luxury *in moderation,*" the same people who presumably enjoyed Boyd's "bit" of grass, or who use batiste for their toilet tables while awaiting more "favourable circumstances."[56] The Garretts' final chapter is entitled, pragmatically, "What Will It Cost?"

Interestingly, even as Queen Anne was associated with the middle class through its red brick, wood staircases, and mishmash vernacular façades, it was also correlated and intimately connected to the contemporary women's movement. Some of the earliest and most important Queen Anne buildings were constructed through what Annmarie Adams has called a "feminist network": key figures in the Queen Anne architects' movement were either active in the contemporary women's movement or related to important feminist figures of the day. Agnes and Rhoda Garrett's younger sister was Millicent Garrett Fawcett, president of the National Union of Women's Suffrage Societies from 1897 to 1918, when women gained the vote. Both Rhoda and Agnes were active in the National Society for Women's Suffrage, and they spoke regularly at meetings. Brydon, who apprenticed Rhoda and Agnes, also served as assistant to Stevenson, whose sisters were active in the women's movement in Scotland; a close friend of Stevenson's married Elizabeth Garrett, another of Rhoda and Agnes's sisters, who became Britain's first woman doctor, the first woman dean of a British medical school, and (among many other firsts) the first woman mayor and magistrate in Britain. Brydon helped design the New Hospital for Women on Euston Road, which ultimately became the Elizabeth Garrett Anderson hospital, a commission that Adams argues "probably came to Brydon through personal and professional connections with the Garretts."[57]

The intimate relation between Queen Anne Revival and the women's movement, not to mention the democratic underpinnings of the style, may partly explain why women interior design writers embraced the aesthetic with such enthusiasm. Even Panton, who did not see eye to eye with Queen Anne advocates on the matter of simplicity, spoke of the revival (for the most part) approvingly; she drew on its wellsprings, fully agreeing that a house's architecture should be responsive to the needs of a middle-class family and not merely ape an upper-class stately home. There is a clear difference between Panton's designs and, say, the mid-century suburban designs discussed in my introduction: *The Builder's Practical Director,* remember, made little reference to family life and mentioned domestic storage only to indicate that a home's china cabinets could be used to accommodate wine. Panton's aesthetic and design choices are fully responsive to the needs of women and its younger occupants: the curtains in the nursery should be dark serge, for instance, "so that all light may be excluded, thus enabling the sense of darkness and quiet . . . so very necessary for a small child." A nursery must have a sofa not only for rest during illnesses but also because "it is a never-failing source of inspiration for regularly good games: it is a fortress, a whole city, a ship at sea, an elephant. . . . The broad square cushions are rafts to put off to sea in which the ship itself is destroyed." Panton's comic, confidential, friendly tone is disrupted only when she breaks into rage at the architects who do not take family needs into consideration when designing houses—her fury at the demon builder's willful ignorance of the need for nurseries on the same floor as the parent's bedroom is expressed in a litany of fiery questions: "Why won't they recollect that one or two rooms should lead out of each other? Why won't they remember nurseries are wanted in most houses, and why will they not arrange their plans with a remembrance of some of the most common events of domestic life?"[58] Panton argues that these and many other architecturally produced problems of her moment—the wrong fireplaces, the poor-quality fire grates, the house that must be reconfigured when illness strikes—are unnecessary, and could be averted, if only women were professional architects.

Indeed, Panton becomes strikingly polemical as she advocates for the entrance of women into the professions of architecture and interior design, in ways that connect this oddball writer (who is discussed in more detail in chapter 7) with her more famous activist sisters:

> Houses cannot be worse planned than they are when male architects are exclusively employed; they would be much improved were women

> trained to the profession, who comprehend that a bed should not stand between door and windows, nor in such a manner that the moment a door opens the occupant of the bed has a full view of the landing or passage; that deep recesses with shelves would spare us infinite expense and money; and that the fireplaces should be where we can sit by them and become warm. . . .
>
> And then, too, how sadly [the male architect] sins in the matter of windows! He either gives us so many and such large ones that we are ruined at the start by the expense we are put to for curtains or muslins, or else the tiny dull casement opens outwards and admits neither light nor air.[59]

Panton's later *Gentlewoman's Home,* culled from articles first published in the *Gentlewoman,* explains in detail the design of a house she would build, were she a professional architect—the nurseries would be on the bedroom floor, of course, and a day room for play would be complemented with a separate room for children's sleep.[60] Panton suggests that women's lives and family life generally will be improved when women become architects, that the suburbs will be happier places if people are pleased with the homes in which they live, that the fields of architecture and interior design will benefit from women's keen eyes and insights. Her voice was one in an increasingly loud chorus; her argument underpins many interior decoration texts of the period. So many of the problems in contemporary architecture and domestic life had, the writers argued, an easy solution. Suburban quirks and Queen Anne insights, braided with the idea of interior decoration as moral imperative, prepared the foundation for women's entrance, by the end of the century, into the arena of professional labor.

WOMEN AND THE PROFESSIONS

W. J. Reader argued that "the professions as we know them are very much a Victorian creation." From the beginning, the professions were identified in relation to what they were *not,* and what they were not was lower-class or open to women.[61] Commentators distinguished *trade* from *professional work:* trade to the Victorian, was, as Linda Peterson puts it, a "business that manufactures or sells some object or commodity," while professional work was vocational and required the application of intensive training and education.[62] The identity of the professional was built on the distance between mind work and physical work, and on vocation as a calling versus "mere" work for cash.

Advanced training and education were consequently central to the identity of the professional, in ways that set the professionals apart from amateurs and dilettantes as well as tradesmen and laborers: "Professionals, the new sociologists of professionalism opined, had special bodies of knowledge, acquired through extensive study, which defined them as highly educated experts; they accepted fees for particular work, rather than hourly or weekly wages; many had been 'called' to their profession and believed that their work constituted service to clients whom they agreed to serve, rather than customers whom they had not chosen."[63] As the century progressed, professional groups increasingly firmed up the boundary lines between what they were and what others were, to such a degree that, in time, the very existence of "professional organizations" setting norms and standards of training, education, fee taking, and so forth was itself a defining feature of a profession: "Professionals had organizations to define pertinent bodies of knowledge and appropriately ethical practices. Through these organizations they attempted to control recruitment to their professional groups."[64] The business of building organizations to formulate ethical principles and training goals, of defining professional life as substantially vocational, of working out fee structures and client terms, dignified the everyday labor of lawyers, doctors, businessmen, and so forth partly by limiting who could gain access to the group (above all, women and Jewish people).

Consequently women's entry into the professions, Kyriaki Hadjiafxendi and Patricia Zakreski argue in *Crafting the Woman Professional in the Long Nineteenth Century*, has been cast as a story of struggle and tussle. This imagines "the professions in the nineteenth century as enclaves that exist outside the spheres in which women tend to move, as walls they need to breach or boundaries they need to cross."[65] Such a reading treats the professional as a world set apart from the domestic, one to which women had to force access. Virginia Woolf's *Three Guineas* articulated this position most persuasively, and from the vanguard: the 1938 epistolary text, framed as a response to the question "How should war be prevented?" is substantially a reflection on whether the Sex Disqualification Act of 1919 had facilitated the entrance of women into professional work (thereby giving them access to the business of debating and running the country in times of strife). Woolf answers in the negative, indicating that, indeed, the professions remained a world to which women were given only limited access; moreover, she presents professional labor as structured by the very practices and ideals—the celebration of rituals, the policing of boundaries to separate insiders from outsiders, the reinforcing of hierarchies to distinguish the lowly from the elite—that animate fascism. Two unappealing systems, embodied in two spaces, structure a woman's choices: "Behind us lies the patriarchal system; the private house, with its nullity, its immorality, its hypocrisy, its servility. Before us lies the public world, the professional system, with its possessiveness, its jealousy, its pugnacity, its greed."[66]

Yet a number of more recent critics, including Linda Peterson and Monica Cohen, have started to contest this vision of women's entry into the professions. Accepting that the language of Victorian professionalism was, on the face of it, antithetical to women, such critics point out that the two spaces Woolf identified (the private house, the public/professional world) were not as distinct as they appeared to her, standing on "the threshold of the private house."[67] The separation of labor from vocational work, so central to the ways Victorian professionals conceived of what they did to earn money, in fact nudged open the door, since women too could argue "vocation" and purpose. Indeed, women justified their entrance into professional life by framing what they were doing *outside* the home as an extension of what they had formerly done *in* it: the industrious amateur also did what she did for love, not money, after all. In this way, women could argue that they were bringing the sanctifying influence they had formerly exerted through crafts and other domestic activities from hearthside to office.[68] This became a powerful means of rhetorically managing the business of expanding women's sphere, giving monetary employment the sheen of virtuousness while also implying continuity with the past, rather than fracture. Women presented what they were doing as an extension of something that they had always done: if the industrious amateur was what the professional was *not,* she was also a means of becoming it.[69]

Yet, as Panton's work shows, the relationship between the amateur housewife and the professional was more than a deft rhetorical managing. There was a deep affinity between many traditional "women's accomplishments and commercial enterprise." Women had been developing and honing decorative skills in their houses for decades, so that "the work of the amateur . . . offered opportunities for women to develop and refine the skills that were needed to participate in commercial enterprises and the public world of work."[70] Training in interior decoration could be deployed for money; practice in (say) textile selection and garden design gave women usable and adaptable skills. And here, the very standardization of house floor plans in suburbia helped, for the suburban home's duplicated interiors and floor plans and even problems allowed for the kind of standardized training and equilibrated skills that drove Victorian professional life outside the house. Repeated house designs both produced and required shared bodies of specialized knowledge (for example, that brand-new floorboards gap in the winter). The woman who had decorated an interior or garden plot in Camberwell was ready for Lewisham or Chiswick, so that the practice of decorating and managing multiple houses was a preliminary toward professional work outside, yet related to, the home. It was a small step from ameliorating architectural problems (by running up a pom-pom Gentlewoman) to thinking of how to stop them (by redesigning mantelpieces, navigating new relationships with construction workers, designing new homes). Panton suggests that women are not only well prepared to become architects, they are especially skilled at professions with direct application to women's daily lives and activities. Women architects, that is, know what women and families need. Victorian suburbia, a landscape of row terracing and duplicated semidetached houses, was a landscape whose very architecture facilitated the advance of women into professional life.

What was still needed was education and training, for "the 'professional ideal' of post-industrial Britain stressed human capital as it emerges in a meritocracy after training and certification have been completed."[71] This training was increasingly provided by nonfiction works, together with periodicals like *Lady's Pictorial* and the *Gentlewoman,* which in turn advertised schools and training facilities. Advice texts aimed at suburban housewives both aped professional manuals and shaded into them; letters provided mentoring on home decoration and home management, so that in and through the texts suburban women could not only imagine themselves as, but become, effective professionals. Notably, some of the first professions women listed on their census returns were in areas related to the home, even if the language they chose to describe their employment implied dilettantism. W. J. Reader hypothesizes, in his study of women's entrance into the professions, that the fight to gain entrance to the medical establishment left women with "little to spare for any other battle," because in the 1911 census he found no women lawyers or engineers and only a scattering of accountants. In fact, the Misses Garrett listed themselves as "house decorators" as early as 1881.[72]

The Garretts were apprenticed to Brydon by the mid-1870s, and may have been the first professional women interior designers, even some of the first businesswomen, in the country. (Ethel Smyth remembered them in her 1919 autobiography, *Impressions that Remained,* as "among the first women in England to start business [sic] on their own account.")[73] The Garretts' book, like Panton's, makes an argument for women's entrance into the profession of architect, again expressing frustration with male architects and designers for failing to shape designs in response to family life. The aesthetic of home furnishings has for too long aped grand, public, and religious buildings, they argue, and great buildings have guided public notions of "taste." "It is only within the last few years that architects and other competent designers have again begun to think the subject of domestic furniture and decoration worthy of their serious attention. The only designs that had any pretensions to artistic merit were executed solely for ecclesiastic purposes," they point out, before arguing that Queen Anne style reformists are responding to the problem: "Much has lately been done by the architects and designers of the Queen Anne school to improve the public taste in this direction, and to encourage manufacturers to introduce better designs into this branch of household art." Yet they do not present their vision of suburban interiors as avant-garde, or connect it to New Womanhood, but rather stress a reconnection with the craftsmen and values of the past in ways that point out their affinity with Ruskin, as well as the emerging Arts and Crafts movement. Celebrating Chippendales, for instance, the Garretts note: "These old pieces of furniture were designed and made by men (and often designed and made by the same man) who were thorough masters of their work and understood the construction of every part of it. Nowadays, however, it is no uncommon thing for the designer of a piece of furniture to know little or nothing of its construction." Returning handmade craftsmen-produced objects to the house, and "wholesome" materials like varnished wood in place of grained paint, "Houses as They Might Be" offers another polite nod to Ruskin when it suggests that, if the drawing room is really to serve as "a true index of the mind of the owner," he had better educate himself in "the principles of domestic art."[74]

The Garretts' adjuration to the reader is slipped in, quietly, halfway through the book. But insofar as it is addressed not only to a female but also a male reader—a connoisseur, moreover, who can "travel hundreds of miles to see the treasures of art in other countries"—it is a startling moment of claiming not only the right to decorate the house, and to shape principles of aesthetic value, but also to expect the men and women of the nation to learn, internalize, and enact principles of a fundamentally *domestic* art. The Garretts conclude their book, not only by positioning women as ideal architects, but also by presenting architecture as a profession that needs women to reshape it. Ruskin viewed suburban homes as "shells" inhabited by a restless population, signals of inexorable national and cultural decline, but the Garretts implicitly refute his thesis even as they accept his claim that architecture is intimately connected to the health of the nation. Education in the Queen Anne Revival style, appreciation of "domestic art" centered around family need, is what is really needed, they argue, to improve the mind, the character, and society at large. Queen Anne Revival emerges as an aesthetic that men and women must *together* embrace if they are to fill their homes with beauty and good taste and regenerate the nation.

CONCLUSIONS: WOMEN AND THE PROFESSION OF INTERIOR DESIGNER

Women writers championed the aesthetic of Queen Anne—another era of redbrick houses and wooden staircases—and, as they did so, countered narratives of the suburbs as places of terrible newness, vulgarity, and dullness. The redbrick suburban house—if viewed as a descendent of an architecture a century old—claimed tradition, inheritance, legitimacy. Insofar as interest in suburban decoration—"Art at Home"—was what male aesthetes disdained in the 1890s, seeking to overset the female decorative artist with the figure of the male connoisseur, the suburban redbrick house stands tacitly as the debased alternative to the museum-like Jacobean or Elizabethan home of the aesthete. Yet suburbanism was not just what aestheticism rejected. For, just as the woman aesthete was the shadowy rival of her masculine counterpart at the fin de siècle, in dialog with his tenets, so the suburban home shadows and implicitly debates the aesthetic interior. It was, after all, in and through the suburban residence that a generation came to see decorative art as a powerful form of self-expression and, ultimately, self-fashioning.

Along with gardeners like Gertrude Jekyll, as we shall see presently, Agnes and Rhoda Garrett made the jump from amateur to professional via the conduit of the suburban home, finding in an aesthetically conscious and affluent population a market for their services.[75] Jane Ellen Panton was a paid design consultant as well as a columnist and, together with her peers, "played an influential part in the eventual establishment" of design as "a new career for middle-class women," Judith Neiswander argues. Deploying the era's vocabulary of responsibility and moral purpose, Panton helped bring about a transition in the understanding of women's paid work, contesting views of professional labor as cheating families to celebrating it as duty, a national and social responsibility. In this way she and her peers claimed to ease the shape, rhythms, and experiences of family life.

Suburbia was a portal into the professions because the suburban house formed a bedrock of shared experience. Its very sameness helped facilitate the growth of shared practices, shared values, shared aesthetic principles. Education, through interior design texts, helped train a generation in articulating, developing, and putting those principles into practice. It must have been stultifying to many—no doubt many women loathed running up another Gentlewoman, fitting another portiere. And yet, given that standardization is at the core of our modern understanding of professional labor—professional work provides standardized services, and entrants into a profession must undergo standardized training—the suburban home enabled women's entry into the late Victorian professional arena by providing an opportunity not just to experiment, but to experiment in an area of specialization: suburbia.[76] Every woman who lived in a suburban home, who learned to want wallpaper from Liberty, to buy piano rods at Shoolbred's and upholstery from Mrs. Bacon, who knew to cover her gaping floorboards with parquet (if the budget allowed) or cocoa matting (if it did not) was receiving training in decorating not just her own but all suburban homes, and when her family moved, she gained the ability to apply her skills and learn more, so that suburban housewifery gained much of the shape and constitutive elements of a professional role.[77] Interior design books provided the educational voice, the aesthetic principles, the support network to readers whose daily lives became a kind of professional apprenticeship; suburbia provided studio-like conditions of opportunity and limitation, the space to experiment in an area of specialization, that the professional apprentice needs. The woman trained by such books—who managed her budget, regulated her staff, and applied aesthetic principles and practices as advised—was in the process of becoming a professional. The woman who wrote about suburbia for money, or who took money to advise others, or who set up her own business or own shop, followed the training process to its next, logical step.

"Against the backdrop of the parliamentary crusades, the right to make a home became a feminist rallying cry," Deborah Cohen points out in *Household Gods:* "This was a new domesticity, a more militant domesticity." She continues: "In Britain's most famous suffrage families, the women's cause and the business of home decoration became mutually sustaining enterprises—intertwined aims best understood within the context of a new domesticity."[78] It may seem hard to believe that middle-class interior decoration emerged in tandem with the emerging feminist movement, but Cohen points out that Emmeline Pankhurst had a furnishing obsession and a furnishing shop, first in Hampstead Road, later on Berners Street, then Regent Street, and finally in Manchester. The meeting between women's rights and interior decoration is a historical fact and occurs at three main points: mission, self-expression, and professional labor. The generations after Panton, Orrinsmith, Barker, and the Garretts saw and built on the promise of the works analyzed in this chapter, and by the end of the century almost every woman's paper had a design column and an art adviser, while in the trade press we find the names of a host of women decorators who plied their trade.[79] They have been forgotten, as was for decades women's deep engagement in aesthetics in the later nineteenth century, the pejorative firmly connected to women's decorative practices as "litter." Still, what enabled a broad-spectrum interest in design in the later Victorian period and, ultimately, women's professional labor in the field was the suburban home. Through shared experience, through the very repetitions and peripatetic movings and gaping floorboards and drafty mantelpieces that concerned so many social observers, women gained experience of not only aesthetic debate but also the rhythms and demands of the professional life that increasingly structured the modern world.[80]

CHAPTER 5

Women and the Suburban Garden

> How often it is that Fate places us amongst people whose characters, pursuits, and tastes we do not know! We hesitate how best to melt that barrier of icy reserve and shyness behind which we English remain frozen. How can we speedily break through the reserve . . .? There is at least one subject of conversation which usually calls forth a response—it is gardening.[1]

Suburban architecture, furnishings, and design were, as we saw in the last chapter, at the heart of an increasingly energetic conversation from the middle of the century as suburban inhabitants began to wrestle with, and stake out positions in, matters of taste. As the middle classes took a bigger role in defining what was beautiful, their aesthetic values and ideas about design were intimately related to the suburban homes in which they lived and worked. The suburban garden was, together with the interior, a key space for conversation and experimentation, a shared point of contact for an increasingly heterogeneous population and a canvas on which Victorians put into effect ideas about color, harmony, arrangement.[2] To that end, a host of gardening advice texts were published, in the wake of John Claudius Loudon, that sought to inform taste and shape practices. In the garden, as in the interior, women took on key roles, so that by the 1880s and '90s, Loudon's vision of women's limited suburban duties had become functionally irrelevant. Women gardeners were far from worrying about the state of their skirts in a damp garden. They were professionally employed in designing the suburban landscape and in shaping, through words, suburbia's aesthetic and function and their own relationship to it.

QUEENS OF THE GARDEN: WOMEN'S GARDENING PRACTICES

The nineteenth century was an era of enormous changes in garden design and garden possibilities. A wealth of new and exotic plants, located and shipped home by adventurous British plant hunters from southern Europe and other, warmer continents, changed the look and character of the garden beyond recognition. The repeal of the glass tax and advances in iron and glass production helped initiate the craze of the glass house.[3] "Bedding out" became popular, a system in which delicate plants grown under glass could be planted straight outside in warmer months, producing instant color and ending the frustrating months of bare beds during which gardeners waited for native perennials to bloom.[4] And there were many other important technological advances to ease the lot of the Victorian gardener, such as the patenting of the first lawn mower in 1830 and improvements in tool design.[5] Moreover, huge advances in printing press technology and distribution helped make gardening manuals available to the masses. Technology facilitated participation in gardening and influenced, particularly in the early years of the century, what gardeners put into the earth.[6]

Alongside these well-documented shifts another, less well-known development was taking place—the rise of the professional woman gardener. Gertrude Jekyll at the end of the century was perhaps the era's best-known female practitioner. In partnership with Edwin Lutyens, she produced many of the era's most important landscape designs and wrote numerous successful books and articles on gardening. But long before Jekyll, women were making serious contributions to gardening as amateur practitioners and theorists. For practical purposes women's gardening writing can be divided into two main phases, from the publication of Jane Loudon's successful works in the early 1840s until the early 1880s, then from the mid-1880s to the turn of the century. The earlier garden texts tend to be pragmatic advice to an amateur imagined to be taking up the spade for the first time; later Victorian garden writing is indebted to New Woman and aesthetic prose and presents the garden as a varied scene of both energetic activity and dreamy, languorous contemplation. Another strand of later Victorian and Edwardian garden prose, penned by professional women gardeners, synthesizes the practical bent of the earlier works with the era's intense aesthetic consciousness. All phases of the tradition are energized by what Michael Waters has called, in Ruskinian language, "the Queen of the Garden role" in Victorian culture.

Ruskin argues in his lecture "Of Queens' Gardens" that women must extend their "benignant power" "over all within their sphere," something that he never precisely defines but that seems to mean society in general, possibly even England itself: "The whole country is but a little garden." This broad sphere, "the territories over which each [woman] . . . reigned," Ruskin characterizes as "Queens' gardens."[7] Waters argues that, like the Angel in the House described by Coventry Patmore, the Queen of the Garden functioned to legitimize contemporary stereotypes of women as "guiding" rather than "determining" agents, contained within the private sphere and consequently able to provide moral bolster to the inhabitants of the world of commerce.[8] The garden has particular resonance in this ideological project because of its "peculiarly appropriate associations . . . with love, beauty, nature, and leisure," and thus, Waters remarks, expanding his analysis to include fiction and poetry, "Victorian garden writers (of both sexes) never tire of asserting that women have an 'instinctive' love of gardens and a 'native' affinity with the plants they nurture." He claims that Victorian imaginative literature tends, consequently, to show women in one of three main activities in the garden, all of which sanction and seek to further high-conservative ideals of woman's limited social role: as light gardener (cutting, tying back roses); as matronly garden supervisor, involved in Ruskin's "sweet ordering, arrangement, and decision"; or as ornament or decorative spectacle.[9]

More recently, feminist critics have noted the possibilities of Ruskin's vision of the garden, in particular the ways in which it pushes at the separation of public and private spheres. Accepting Ruskin's distaste for emerging New Womanhood, for substantive reordering of women's and men's political and economic relations to one another, such critics have pointed to the ways in which Ruskin's ideal nonetheless contests and undermines Patmore's. The Angel was, after all, confined to her house, yet, as Sharon Aronofsky Weltman argues, Ruskin's garden was both home and not-home; it was England, it was society, it was the world. Women's occupation of the garden thus invites broad and potentially challenging interpretations: Ruskin finally, Weltman contends, "urges women not to immure themselves behind their garden walls, but rather to redefine those gardens to include all of England, Victoria's demiparadise and sceptered isle." Ruskin emerges in Weltman's essay as one who offers an "intoxicating" vision of "power and a wide venue in which to apply it" to "those to whom the radical possibilities proffered by women's rights were out of the question."[10]

Prose advice texts aimed at the woman gardener furthered the Ruskinian vision of the suburban garden as not-home, as a broader and even public realm for women's activity, in a variety of interesting ways. Suburban gardens were located in a place that was, as we have seen throughout this book, a site of tension, a problem that urgently needed to be solved. The long rows of duplicated houses, poor building practices, and anonymous neighbors were major problems of the age, signals (to many) of national and cultural disintegration. If gardening could be the glue that brought disparate peoples together, as Frances Wolseley imagines in the epigraph to this chapter, could women also help heal the problems of the suburbs through garden cultivation? To many, the answer was an obvious yes. Implicitly, at times even explicitly, drawing upon Ruskin, writers argued that, indeed, the garden was not merely a spot of ground outside the home but an opportunity for women to take on national problems and grow their "power" in the process. Furthering that end, authors expanded considerably upon the kinds of duties Ruskin imagines women embarking upon in a garden, including advice on the rougher aspects of gardening, such as digging, manuring, and soil cultivation; on design, layout, and construction; and on the duties and responsibilities of an active, fully engaged garden manager.[11] Authorizing women to engage in physical labor, aesthetic debate, and technological innovation, texts build toward a new vision of the social arrangement in which *flowers* sanctify and *women* act. Indeed, as we shall see, it is no accident that many of the later Victorian gardening texts by women were structurally innovative and politically radical.

LADIES' COMPANIONS: THE LITERATURE OF THE VILLA GARDEN (1840–1880)

If eighteenth-century gardening was shaped by the rolling acres of the great country house, nineteenth-century gardening aesthetics and practice were shaped by the plots of land at the front and back of the semidetached or terraced Victorian villa. In 1903, Mrs. F. A. Bardswell remarked on the similarity of such gardens—the duplicated shape of the suburban plot, across classes, even as she noted the differences. She ranged suburban gardens on a spectrum, with a nod to Tennyson:

> Suburban gardens are of many kinds; there are all manner of notes in the scale. The squalid ones—alas! some are squalid—we see in London's shabbiest borderlands. They often belong to houses filled with many different families, and are a kind of no man's land. Hardly can we call them gardens; little enough is grown in them. . . . Then there

> are the tidy patches of the fairly well-to-do workman; some made hideous by mounds of shells and grottoes, others filled with useful and pretty plants. So we go upwards, step by step, to the good-sized strip or more ambitious villa garden. Wonders are done in these. Many a busy City man, whose garden is not far from the Marble Arch, knows all about Roses, and might give lessons on Grape-growing and Orchid-forcing to his relations in the real country.[12]

In an era of nostalgia for an agrarian way of life, the villa garden was a little oasis in the midst of industry, a hint at an Eden that was apparently lost. As Bardswell mused, even those who loved the city and city living delighted in the presence of gardens in the midst of the smoke and pollution created by industry: "Nor is it altogether unpleasing to have a garden near the busy haunts of men; the roar and rattle of the streets, that sound like the humming of innumerable bees, the strange glow of lights in the distance, the pealing of bells and the striking of many clocks, the thunder and whistle of the trains that link us with friends far off, the stir and throb of human life, that chimes in, not inharmoniously with the calmer life of Nature—all these things combine in making up the unexpressed enjoyments of the dwellers in gardens that lie close to the heart of towns."[13] Of course, Bardswell draws here on centuries-old associations of gardens with lost paradise, of pastoral gardens as alternatives to modern human industry, yet she refuses to perpetuate the morally freighted binary of country and city. In her account, the city is not morally bankrupt, its inhabitants spiritually bereft; indeed, she stresses that the city dweller in Marble Arch knows a thing or two about nature, and the hum of city life, rather than oppressing her, reminds her of the tranquil hum of insects. For, she argues, the energy of the city, its "throb," harmonizes with "the calmer life of Nature"; they are notes in the same chord, to use Bardswell's modish phrase. The author's approach is common in nineteenth-century gardening writing, which regularly celebrates the villa garden as a space that undermines the traditional country/city distinction. Today, garden writers pointed out, the delights of nature and cultivation are routinely found inside the city limits, and people across the nation are united in the pleasures of plant cultivation. The owner of a cottage garden and the City merchant buy the same publications, the same tools, and the same seed catalogues, and spend their evenings tending the same cultivars.

Women and men were united in thinking and writing about gardening from the very earliest years of the Victorian period. The marriage of John

Claudius Loudon and Jane Loudon is the most obvious example of a supportive gardening partnership, founded on John Loudon's identification of the suburban garden as fertile territory for literary text. Jane Loudon's *Ladies' Companion to the Flower Garden* sold more than twenty thousand copies; the *Dictionary of National Biography* notes that by 1879 it was in its ninth edition.[14] Addressing "amateur florists," the "possessors of small gardens," and regularly referencing her husband's *Suburban Gardener,* Jane Loudon recognized the existence of literate, leisured women with small plots and limited means, keen for instruction and advice on everything from soil culture to garden design.[15] A number of similar books sprang up around the same time, all of which conceived themselves as much-needed support for the struggling middle-class amateur, "the industrious and economical," as Louisa Johnson subtitled *Every Lady Her Own Flower Gardener.* "Books intended for professional gardeners . . . are seldom suitable to the wants of amateurs," Jane Loudon mourned in *Practical Instructions in Gardening for Ladies.* "It is so very difficult for a person who has been acquainted with a subject all his life, to imagine the state of ignorance in which a person is who knows nothing of it, that adepts often find it impossible to communicate the knowledge they possess."[16] Gardening is conceived in these texts as a hobby that women come to in later life, when family members are unlikely to be around to offer help, and thus, as with the interior decoration advice texts discussed in chapter 4, their advice is applicable to a wide range of housing types and generated in reaction to the suburbanizing population. The developing market of the how-to text put lone suburban women gardeners in touch with one another and created a sense of community spanning geographical regions and, to some degree at least, economic groups; if women, separated from family networks, gained knowledge of interior design from Panton, Orrinsmith, and Barker, they gained knowledge of gardening from Jane Loudon and her peers.

Writers share their experiences of failure as well as their successes in such texts; they invariably narrate their own evolution in a preface or introduction, for these are texts about gaining competence, becoming a woman of expertise. "When I married Mr. Loudon, it is scarcely possible to imagine any person more completely ignorant than I was," Jane Loudon begins sorrowfully in *Practical Instructions.* "I was soon heartily ashamed of my ignorance."[17] Her numerous and detailed books attest to the author's transformation into a woman with mastery over theory and practice alike, who has found a niche for herself in both Bayswater (the suburban marital home) and the literary marketplace. Loudon may well exaggerate her lack of competence at the beginning of her married career, in the service of the genre of the how-to text; her account of a triumphant upward trajectory recalls the ringing tones of the interior decoration texts considered in chapter 4.

The early garden books interestingly authorize active physical labor for women. Although Jane Loudon admits that "digging appears at first sight, a very laborious employment," she insists that "by a little attention to the principles of mechanics and the laws of motion, the labour may be much simplified and rendered comparatively easy." Pruning too she claims as an appropriate occupation for a woman: though it may look "a most laborious and unfeminine occupation . . . yet perhaps there is no operation of gardening which a lady may more easily accomplish" when armed with a good pair of shears. J. B. Whiting's *Manual of Flower Gardening for Ladies* similarly insists that spadework is possible for a woman when she is well equipped: "A little practice makes it comparatively easy, so that in a moderate degree it might be done with facility by a female."[18] Texts advocate the use of tools for women in the garden relatively early, in the 1840s; we remember that Barker suggested women pick up hammers and toolboxes in 1878. Conscious at all times of conservative ideas about women's physical delicacy in what was still the early Victorian period, authors suggest that heavy gardening is compatible with femininity because of modern advances in technology and industry, which has created better, more efficient tools, or through scientific thinking, which outlines "the principles of mechanics, the laws of motion."[19] To that end, texts work to disseminate necessary scientific and horticultural information to their readers; they then openly discuss aspects of gardening one might expect a prudish Victorian to shiver at—the sex and propagation of plants, for example, and the possibilities and uses of manure (chapter II of *Practical Instructions* focuses in great detail on "manuring the soil and making hotbeds"). The garden is not simply a site of repose in these texts, then, a scene for a woman to beautify. It is an opportunity for women to share in and experience what technology has to offer in ways that recall John Claudius Loudon's first edition of *The Suburban Gardener, and Villa Companion.*

Gardening should not just involve pottering picturesquely among the flowers, such works suggest. It is an opportunity both to act and to think: as Johnson remarked, "It compels the reason to act, and the judgment to observe."[20] At times gardening is even represented as a positive engagement in national public debates, as writers locate their discussions of garden design in a wider social and political context. Texts reference, for instance, the conflicts about color and design that were raging in "mainstream" gardening publications.[21] These include the debate between "wild" or "natural" and "formal" modes of gardening that was to smolder across the decades before flaming into open conflict in the century's last quarter.[22] Loudon's short-lived periodical the *Ladies Magazine of Gardening* alludes to the controversy over "complementary colour" sparked by Michel-Eugène Chevreul—any woman with strengths in dressmaking understands color well enough, Loudon sniffs—and issues a call to arms about the lack of species variety in suburban gardens.[23] "Bedding out" certainly had its advantages, but many worried that contemporary gardeners were becoming *over*dependent on scarlet geraniums (pelargoniums), blue lobelia, yellow feverfew, and calceolarias—that is to say, on showy annuals and semihardy perennials grown for maximum color and maximum effect. Limited plant choice also frustrated those gardeners conscious of the new wealth of plants introduced into Britain and the new advances in cultivating and rearing those plants. Women gardeners like Loudon were as interested in these kinds of conversations as contemporary publications aimed primarily at men, and, in response, they introduced their readers to a range of new exotic plants and explained how best to grow them.[24] The books thus not only introduce readers to political and aesthetic questions of the day but also encourage women to participate themselves through careful plant choice and garden design, turning the performance of gardening as well as the experience of reading and writing about it into self-consciously political acts.

Politically engaged does not, of course, necessarily mean politically radical; the early texts are far from straightforwardly innovative in their attitudes to the sexes' responsibilities or, indeed, to the garden. Like much British literature of the garden, early Victorian women's gardening texts at times idealize gardens as spaces outside culture, as *a*political realms beyond or outside public discourse.[25] As Anne Helmreich puts it, the garden, "seemingly without politics," "behaves as a myth, holding forth promises of harmony with nature."[26] The myth of garden as unconstructed space, garden as Nature, certainly operates when writers like Jane Loudon evoke their gardens as a sort of heaven on earth, an ideal world in which the promise of balance and order is fulfilled. She displays a touching faith in the stability of ecosystems that is difficult for a modern gardener to entertain: a particular pest, the lackey caterpillar, rarely overwhelms the garden, she claims, because "with that beautiful arrangement by which all the works of our Great Creator are balanced equally with each other, and none allowed to predominate, these insects are such favourite food for birds, that not a hundredth part of them are suffered to reach maturity."[27] Louisa Johnson stresses that to garden is to come close to God: observing the operation of Nature inculcates a deep appreciation for One "who created such pure and simple blessings for his creatures," she argues.[28] Unorthodox female behavior—sweating, debating, self-making—becomes possible in the garden because it is (apparently) a space outside culture, and thus nonconformist activities avoid acquiring normative social meanings. The garden's claim to "natural" status works to depoliticize the activities of the women who operate in it.[29]

Yet discursive passages celebrating the transcendent harmony of nature are invariably succeeded by more practical accounts of the "skill and ingenuity" a woman gardener needs to display if she is to control the unruly forces in her garden.[30] Of course, gardening advice texts by their very existence constitute a recognition that a garden is, in fact, no utopia, and while gardening may be about appreciating the harmonious operation of Nature it is also about wresting control for oneself, about stepping in and imposing human ideals of order and aestheticism.[31] Early Victorian writers tend to be particularly attuned to the constructedness of the aesthetic sense because of the prevailing idea that the garden, once viewed as ideally a reflection of nature, was and must be "the child of art."[32] The artificiality of the garden is especially apparent in the suburbs, where public spaces and amenities may easily be seen, where close-set walls and hedges mark out very visible boundary lines. But any flower garden "is essentially artificial," Jane Loudon tells her readers, its design and layout a matter of taste shaped and reacting to constraints; her texts give plans for different types of flower gardens and offer advice on different styles of structuring and planting gardens large, medium, and small.[33]

This attention to the garden's artifice constantly threatens to disrupt the texts' "naturalizing" project, repoliticizing the garden and women's activities in it. The woman gardener, adjudicating between designs and aesthetic styles, pondering debates about color and plant choice, assessing whether her plot is large enough for geometric arrangements, is no mere observer of God's great plan; these pragmatic texts are too conscious of the planning, labor, and challenges of a modern garden to idealize it consistently as a pastoral idyll. The texts' vision of the garden as a transhistorical mythic space never dominates, therefore, but rather coexists with a view of gardening as an occupation that benefits from access to the offerings of the market and modern innovations—tools and design books, gardening publications, scientific treatises, forced bulbs, and imported annuals. The representation of the woman gardener herself involves a similar tension. Evoked as essentially "feminine," she is also celebrated as the beneficiary of technological advances and market products that allow her to overcome her frailty and the challenges of gardening.

The tensions in these positions are a product of authors' complicated visions of women's proper role and of the garden's position in Victorian culture. As we have already seen, the garden unsettles the public/private binary so central to the Victorian social arrangement: it is reserved, private, an extension of the domestic sphere, yet it is necessarily outside the home. The suburban garden is especially challenging to situate, both outside and within contemporary discourses of the suburb, which, as we've already seen, itself unsettled ideological distinctions between public and private through its insistent commercialism. One might expect to see woman's role in the suburban garden articulated from the first as battler of commerce, but instead early texts offer the commercial opportunities of the suburb as a way for women to do more, gain more—as long as they have disposable income. Rather than spending hours and hours growing half-hardy plants from seed, Loudon tells her readers, "the readiest way for the inhabitants of a suburban villa" to achieve a superb "display for a whole summer" is to buy ready-grown plants from a nurseryman.[34] The suburban garden is celebrated as a place of joyous consumerism, artistic experimentation, and intellectual and physical activity for those women fortunate enough to have leisure time and money to spend on it.

It is easy to respond that consumerism is not something to be celebrated, of course, that the marketplace seduces; that women shopping for bright annuals—or Gentlewomen, or Panton's corner cupboards, for that matter—were being talked into parting with their money by an entrepreneurial culture that co-opted an emerging language of bourgeois female independence for its own, capitalist purposes. Indeed, some critics fear that to celebrate commerce at all is to ignore the disempowerment of women in consumer societies. Others have pointed out that this line of argument risks replicating a certain strand of Victorian thinking, in which women consumers are cast as passive and seduced victims of male aggression. I follow Erika Diane Rappaport in suggesting that women's shopping acquires particular meaning when set against "shifting definitions of the public and the private": occupation of the streets by women was, until deep into the century, a transgressive act in a culture uncomfortable with women's public display. "When Victorian and Edwardian women shopped," Rappaport argues, "they were central actors in the English economy; they altered the city" because "shopping allowed them to occupy and construct urban space." Suburban women's purchases of seeds or spades required journeying into the city, or shopping on the suburban high street, or using print catalogs and the post office, all activities that helped map out the suburbs as, from the first, places of women's leisure and pleasure as well as public movement. Suburban consumption patterns thereby fundamentally complicated, even refused, the cultural and architectural separation of public and private: "Shoppers blatantly disregarded the vision of society neatly divided into separate spheres," Rappaport adds, and the increasingly networked suburb evolved substantially to service the leisure practices of women, not just those of male commuters. The familiar image of the quiet suburban street would, in reality, have rung with the noise of rumbling omnibuses and trams, the whistle, by the end of the century, of trains; the Loudons' suburb of Bayswater was especially well serviced, sending more than fifty vehicles a day into the City by the late 1830s (including to central shopping areas).[35] If women's commercial engagement helped shape the evolving suburbs, commerce also offered women, in immediate and practical ways, opportunities to conceive of themselves as connected to the modern world, not shut out of it. Jane Loudon's celebration of the purchase of a ready-grown annual acquires particular meaning in the context of her effort to authorize women's gardening at a time when it remained, to some, a suspiciously physical act, a sweaty spectacle.

WILD GARDENS: FANTASIES AND FRUSTRATIONS IN THE 1880s AND '90s

The woman *is* the home, Ruskin famously remarked: "The stars only may be over her head; the glowworm in the night-cold grass may be the only fire at her foot; but home is yet wherever she is."[36] The woman is *not,* however, the garden, with all its attendant implications in Victorian culture of the artificial and (within Ruskin's scheme) the public. Moreover a woman's occupation of the garden is self-evidently a more complicated activity than Ruskin suggests: as soon as a woman begins to garden she gives the lie to Ruskin's ideal, for little gets done in a garden if she simply walks about the grass. ("She should revive; the harebells should bloom, not stoop, as she passes. You think I am rushing into wild hyperbole! Pardon me, not a whit—I mean what I say in calm English, spoken in resolute truth.")[37] Early gardening advice texts celebrate the energy, labor, intellectual drive, aesthetic decision making, and consumption involved in the creation of a successful garden. In the process Ruskin's vision of the garden as, in fact, a public space receives an intriguingly literal presentation. Less a reserved pastoral idyll, it becomes a scene of energetic action, modern innovation, political debate, commercial engagement, and finally professional labor.

Some New Women embraced the possibilities of interior decoration, as we saw in the last chapter, and a strong sympathy for New Womanhood emerges in a number of later Victorian gardening texts. Such texts include Theresa Earle's *Pot-Pourri from a Surrey Garden* (1896) and its successors, Eleanor Vere Boyle's *Garden of Pleasure* (1895) and *Seven Gardens and a Palace* (1900), Alice Dew-Smith's *Confidences of an Amateur Gardener* (1897), Elizabeth von Arnim's *Elizabeth and the German Garden* (1898), and Maud Maryon's *How the Garden Grew* (1900). Garden prose today—just as in the Victorian period—has a whiff of the conservative about it, seemingly bespeaking a nostalgia for a more peaceful way of life, a premodern, preindustrial existence.[38] Feminist politics, one might think, are likely to sit ill with the garden buff, yet long before Vita Sackville-West yoked her particular brand of feminism with glorious garden making at Sissinghurst in the second quarter of the twentieth century, Victorian women writers were turning the garden into a scene of creative aesthetics and creative politics. Authors compared women's competence in the garden with their limited opportunities for advancement in the public sphere, and they lauded women's entrance into the field of professional gardening. The garden is represented in such texts as a battleground not only between competing aesthetic styles but also between men and women over cultural representations of women and women's responsibilities in public and private life.

The tone and style of garden books began to change dramatically in the 1880s, becoming increasingly politically engaged and stylistically avant-garde. H. M. Batson summarized the shift in 1900: "The garden book of this present century was . . . until lately entirely instructive; it cared not to amuse; its aim was gardening and nothing more. In the eighties there were indications of an approaching change in the purpose of garden literature, and the last half-dozen years have seen this change stereotyped into its present features—less instructive, perhaps, but certainly more entertaining than the old."[39] One of the first books to herald the change in style, form, and function was *Days and Hours in a Garden* by Eleanor Vere Boyle ("E.V.B."), a book that describes the author's experiences of gardening at Huntercome Manor in Buckinghamshire in the early 1880s. Boyle draws inspiration for her middle-class readership from the grander, elite gardens of the past, using archaic language to evoke a space that is, unlike the modern suburban home, old, even timeless: "The garden's story," Boyle begins, as if on a sigh. "It is only eleven years old, though the place itself is an old place—an old place without a history, for scarce a record remains of it anywhere that we have ever found."[40] At a time when the newness of the suburban landscape was a constant source of complaint, Huntercome Manor offers the reassurance of English stability and the continuity of traditions. In later work, Boyle explains that old aristocratic designs are applicable to middle-class gardens, and she encourages readers to be inspired by them, even for "the tiniest plot": "The very best plan for a modern garden will still be that which most nearly embodies the idea of some delicious pleasaunce of old time."[41]

The casual style of her early prose reflects the character of her gardening: in the middle of Huntercome's grounds there is what she calls a "Fantasie" where "all my most favourite flowers grow in wild profusion."[42] Not for Boyle the hothouse geranium, the cultivated orchid from South America. And certainly not annuals arranged, like children of art, in geometric patterns. The Fantasie, Boyle's wood, is filled with native plants "for the birds to build in, and with room for half-a-dozen wild Hyacinths and a dozen Primroses under the trees; with moss, Wood Sorrel, and white and puce coloured Periwinkles, and many a wild thing, meant to encourage the delusion of a savage wild! . . . This 'fantasie' was a dream of delight during the past summer—from April, when a nightingale possessed in song the half-hidden entrance under low embowering Elm branches and Syringa—through all the fairy days and months, up to quite lately."[43] Boyle's rhetoric of the Fantasie reminds us of the use of the term in works by fin de siècle aesthetes who used such language to signal "that the story was adrift in time and space."[44] Huntercome was a real place, but Boyle's account transforms it into a lavishly entrancing realm, a dream of floral perfection, a fairy tale. How could the suburbanite conjure up a fantasie, a wood? There is always, of course, a space between a garden and a writer's account of the garden, a linguistic, conceptual, temporal, and geographic gap that drawings, plans, and photographs typically attempt to conceal.[45] But these texts were not only trucking in an unachievable aesthetic. One of the biggest shifts in approach toward the end of the century is the increasingly self-conscious exploitation of the gap between garden and rhetorical presentation as highly ornate aesthetic texts, like *Days and Hours in a Garden,* that were designed as ends in themselves; as flashes of the color that, Boyle argues, we all long for but do not often get to see in our busy working lives.[46] Jane Loudon's manuals were how-to texts written to assist the gardener, practically, in her garden; Boyle's books, and a score of woman-authored books that succeeded them, are designed to pass on advice, certainly, and tips for the modern garden, but also to give a woman reader pleasure while reading on a suburban chaise. As Maryon put it, "These other books, this literature on gardening! They are generally better than the garden itself. Practical they are not, but why ask it of them? . . . Through rockeries, ferneries, nut-groves, copses we wander as in a fairy dream."[47]

The dream is not completely detached from the moment, however; like all dreams, texts dwell on, unpick threads of real-world conflict, if sometimes in displaced or disguised forms. Texts turn and turn again to the contemporary battle between "formal" and "natural" gardening styles, so that part of what the texts offer is access to an up-to-the-minute debate. The major combatants in the conflict tended, as many critics and scholars have noted, to talk past one another; they were not as different as they liked to imagine themselves, both viewing themselves as defenders of "old-fashioned" gardening, both turning against garish color schemes and specimen-style planting.[48] But the realities of the other side's position or indeed of garden practice seem rarely to have troubled the adversaries. William Robinson, author of the enormously successful *Wild Garden* (1870) and arch proponent of the "natural" style, worked hard to perpetuate the myth that the bedding system (a feature of many formal gardens, which often included box parterres planted with single-color annuals) had all but wiped out native plants and the mixed herbaceous border. They could, however, still be found, he indicated romantically, in humble cottage gardens, and so a key feature of the late Victorian gardening aesthetic was born: the image of the simple dwelling, surrounded by hollyhocks, roses, and lavender, untouched and authentic, a repository of all that was threatened by modern life with its love of "forcing" and of hothouses, of instant gardens filled with blazing color.[49]

Women gardeners were almost uniformly ranged on the side of Robinson and later Gertrude Jekyll, who achieved a harmonious synthesis of the two ideals—house and garden were planned in relation to one another, as the formalists insisted, but in Jekyll's schemes the garden was organized not by an architect but rather by a sympathetic gardener committed to the charms of the herbaceous border and to massing and naturalizing, thereby softening the effects of architectural lines.[50] Women garden writers hymned the cottage idyll, the "return" of native plants, and advocated naturalized planting, suggesting that gardening was a means of taking on the inauthenticity of modern culture. Access to exotic cultivars, to pots of annuals, and to brand-new spades was no longer celebrated as a way of participating in the modern age. Now writers advocated taking a stand on the era's consumerist tendencies through plant choice and garden design.[51]

Moreover, the texts under discussion tend to present the conflict between early/mid and late Victorian gardening as a conflict between men and women, where a "demon-builder" equivalent must be overcome; many texts enact scenes between the heroine/speaker and a gardener or a nurseryman in which the latter stubbornly refuses to plant in masses and uses his position as a man—and thus the planter, sometimes the seller—to shore up his aesthetic. Occasionally the conflict figure is a family member or even a spouse: von Arnim's "Man of Wrath," for instance, is a painfully dominating spouse who undermines the narrator's gardening. Here especially, the conflict between wild and formal gardening, framed as a debate between oppressive man and rebellious woman, shapes the garden "plot" along New Woman lines.

Women defended the naturalizing style of planting and criticized formal rows and hothouse forcing as part of a broad claim that the latter took gardening away from the realm of the domestic and the private, rather as interior decoration writers suggested architects and builders intruded into the family's space. Hothouse growth is, texts suggest, beloved by men alone: formal bedding is practiced only by those who love public display, ostentation, the artificial. Women amateurs positioned themselves as those who prefer to watch and nurture the gradual, seasonal unfolding of native plants.[52] The plot may be small and edged with brick, the local nurseryman may insist on stocking lobelia and pelargoniums, but by cultivating roses and lavender, the woman gardener asserts in material form her adherence to a different set of values, to the past. Maryon's *How the Garden Grew* is typical in this regard, waging war on formal designs, on bedding out, on greenhouse-reared annuals.[53] Her fictionalized protagonist, Mary, who has been given five pounds for a year's garden cultivation by her father—"His Reverence" as she terms him playfully, in homage to the Man of Wrath—searches local gardens for inspiration and is horrified by the formally laid-out grounds of a well-to-do neighbor: "One grand garden filled me with anything but envy. It was so terribly trim, such rows of variegated geraniums, big calceolarias, featherfew and lobelia. I determined never to treat any bed or border to edgings; to mass even lobelia together and only break it with taller plants, such as geraniums, of the pure good colours quite possible I found, or salvias or fuschias. Here was line after line, pattern after pattern."[54] The repeated lines of the annuals suggest the lines of a factory or the rows of suburban housing. Mary is disgusted by such displays, which too strongly suggest the gardener's hands at work: "Grand beds of coleus and begonias there were, but these were beyond me, savouring too much of the greenhouse, and all the flowers in the rooms spoke of gardeners and hot-houses."[55] Mary sees her neighbor's garden with a moral as well as an aesthetic eye: color should be pure, not brash or vulgar, plants should not be too large (calceolarias are invariably criticized in late Victorian texts as having "no natural grace or refinement," as Gertrude Jekyll put it in *Home and Garden* in 1901), and grand instant display should be eschewed in favor of organic growth. Mary, not surprisingly, adores perennials: "The thought of their permanence delighted me. Dear, nice things! they would not need sowing year by year, but would yearly grow more and more 'in favour with God and man.' So I hoped, even as a mother hopes it for her children."[56]

Mary's adoption of the maternal role is significant, and characteristic of later Victorian women's gardening texts, which often cast the mother-gardener as the ideal antithesis to the professional male gardener—the kind to be found managing "grand" aristocratic landscapes or jobbing through the suburban landscape.[57] Male gardeners aim for display, size, the unusual, and so forth; they love greenhouses, and they insist on rows and order. Throughout the text Mary struggles to get Griggs, the gardener, to stop planting in lines and to eschew his modern geraniums in favor of "old-fashioned" plants like stocks and sweet peas. Women amateurs, by contrast, she suggests, prefer simple, naturally reared plants and act in harmonious consort with them, nursing them rather than forcing them: as she pats down the soil around her sweet pea seeds, she remarks, "I felt like a mother who tucks her child in bed. Surely the pat did good!"[58] Von Arnim's Elizabeth, a mother of three romping children, depicts herself similarly as the protector of her plants, defending them from the cold and rigid treatment of the gardener who, like Mary's Griggs, constructs "borders of beautiful exactitude and [arranges] the poor plants like soldiers at a review."[59] Elizabeth, again like Mary, finds the use of greenhouses troubling: "I don't use it for growing anything, because I don't love things that will only bear the garden for three or four months in the year and require coaxing and petting for the rest of it. Give me a garden full of strong, healthy creatures, able to stand roughness and cold without dismally giving in and dying. . . . No doubt there are many lovely flowers to be had by heat and constant coaxing, but then for each of these there are fifty others still lovelier that will gratefully grow in God's wholesome air."[60] Talia Schaffer reads this passage as a submerged comment on women who falter and droop in uncongenial circumstances and unhappy marriages. Yet von Arnim is also privileging an aesthetic that both she and Maryon conceive as essentially feminine—for plants that require patience and attentiveness rather than professional skill, plants that (theoretically) can be grown by any woman in any home with a spot of ground. Jekyll, enormously skilled gardener though she was, also placed great emphasis on domestic moral virtues in gardening: she argued that a good gardener must display "constant restraint and constant sacrifice."[61]

Not only were these virtues the preserve of women, authors suggested, women were especially likely, as mothers and wives, to be well trained in them. Indeed, authors routinely hinted that women were constitutionally best suited to gardening and had been doing it for a long time, both indirectly (by practicing the necessary skills in family life) and actually (as amateur gardeners and herbologists). Many reminded readers of the richness and longevity of the tradition they inherited, adjuring all to find and read the texts of authors like the Loudons and Louisa Johnson. "The lady-gardener is, emphatically, a modern product," Edith L. Chamberlain and Fanny Douglas concede, "but as the seed of every modern idea was laid far back in the centuries, so was this, and we seem to see it in the pleasant old still-room practices [of former centuries]."[62] By contrast the professional or jobbing gardener, with his modern preferences for plants grown using technological innovations, is evoked as a fly-by-night, nouveau presence in the garden. In *Pot-Pourri* Theresa Earle interweaves discussion of centuries of gardening books throughout her text, by men and women. Schaffer investigates how women aesthetes "resisted the connoisseurs' demonization of amateur women by constructing a new genealogy" of eighteenth-century skilled women; the development of a genealogy of gardening writers, in which women play an important part, constitutes a similar process.[63]

Emphasizing connection with the past rather than new beginnings, continuity rather than fracture, the aesthetic privileged in many of the texts discussed here—especially Boyle's works and von Arnim's *Elizabeth and Her German Garden*—is also yoked to the values and possessions of an older elite. To that end, the ground actually landscaped in many works is a large country estate, not a suburban semi. Grounds are ample, woods and copses abound, silver rivers leap with fish, and homes are old-timbered and stately. While some of the authors certainly lived in such houses, most of the books' readers did not—Earle, a suburban dweller but also sister to the Countess of Lytton, gently critiqued writers who did not add information "that will practically help people who live in cottages and small villas."[64] It is a central tenet of the statelier group of books that the upper and middle classes share more than divides them, that the *real* dividing line is between middle- and working-class people (the rougher, heavier men who must be kept in line); to that end, the act of garden beautification is presented as one the "higher" classes work on cooperatively in the teeth of working-class misunderstandings. Von Arnim and Maryon draw on stereotypes of laborers as culturally unaware and constitutionally blind to "higher" aesthetic delights; Earle celebrates the advent of the women gardeners precisely because, she says, "in suburban districts the dullness of the small plots in front of the houses is entirely owing to the want of education in the neighboring nurserymen."[65] Mary, Maryon's protagonist, is deeply condescending in her relationship with the hapless Griggs: she expects us to cheer her on as she learns to become more authoritarian in the garden, informing him he cannot return home to his family one day because she needs him to water her plants: " 'Griggs'—and my voice held dignified rebuke—'you are gardener *here,* and these flowers are your first duty.' "[66] Von Arnim's gardener becomes so frustrated by his mistress's many requests (for changes in garden design and plant culture) he takes to wandering around with a pistol, and is finally committed to an asylum. These scenes are clearly designed to elicit a Victorian reader's sympathies for the protagonist based on shared ideas about how the working classes do not have access to taste, but the middle and upper classes do; that how a great lady gardens, the problems she faces, and the choices she makes are fundamentally the same as those of a suburban dweller.

The texts' putatively collective vision of social hierarchies provides an apparently safe platform on which to stage riskier gender conflicts; the battles between gardener and mistress are routinely conceived as battles between one imagined to act freely and one who is hampered by social constructions of her gender. "If I could only dig and plant myself!" Elizabeth remarks wistfully at the beginning of von Arnim's text as she watches her gardener plant in rows, and then again later: "I wish with all my heart I were a man, for of course the first thing I should do would be to buy a spade and go and garden, and then I should have the delight of doing everything for my flowers with my own hands and need not waste time explaining what I want done to somebody else. It is dull work giving orders and trying to describe the bright visions of one's brain to a person who has no visions and no brain, and who thinks a yellow bed should be calceolarias edged with blue."[67] Class, gender, and aesthetics intersect in this passage, bolstering one another; the reader is expected to share the author's class viewpoint (the frustration of resigning control to one who has "no visions and no brain"), together with her aesthetic sense (who could think of planting calceolarias in this day and age!), and is thus led by the nose to agree that modern women should be able to take up their spades and plant themselves. "And why not?" Elizabeth asks disarmingly. "It is not graceful, and it makes one hot; but it is a blessed sort of work, and if Eve had had a spade in Paradise and known what to do with it, we should not have had all that sad business of the apple."[68] Of course, Elizabeth's humor is a sop to the reader here, who is in fact being presented with a challenge: if women are not given the spade soon, they will cause modern-day Adams as much trouble as Eve once gave her mate.

AESTHETICS AND THE PROFESSIONAL WOMAN GARDENER AT THE FIN DE SIÈCLE

Women had been describing their experiences of gardening in the literary marketplace for decades by the 1890s. At the fin de siècle, women like Gertrude Jekyll took on the role of professional, paid gardener and worked to educate other women in the practice through books and in professional schools.[69] The first female students were admitted to Swanley Horticultural College in the 1890s; the Glynde School for Lady Gardeners in Sussex was founded in 1906, though Frances Wolseley had been teaching students at the Ragged Lands property since 1901. Women nursery owners accepted female apprentices and trained them in the skills of market gardening; the Women's London Gardening Association, founded in 1891, advised on urban and suburban gardening, provided floral arrangements, and took in pupils and apprentices ("Pupils are expected to be ready to do anything required, and are not allowed to pick and choose their work," its advertisement stated).[70] A young woman named Annie Gulvin was the first woman ever to sign the work register at Kew; she had received her training at Swanley.[71]

Women gardeners did not provide services to suburbanites alone, needless to say—indeed, many of Jekyll's most influential designs were for properties far up the social scale. (Cultural cachet was embodied in the phrase "a Lutyens house with a Jekyll garden" in the early decades of the new century, referencing Jekyll's partnership with the great Arts and Crafts architect Edwin Lutyens.)[72] Jekyll's success—she is one of the earliest examples of a woman entering a man's profession and quickly becoming one of its foremost exponents—certainly depended on the existence of affluent and rural populations, not just middle-class suburbanites. But Jekyll's aesthetic was tremendously influential on suburban gardens, as we shall see, in part because she grasped how small-scale features, like paths and ponds and walls, could be sites for gardening. Moreover, the rise of the woman gardener was intimately connected to the growth of a body of leisured women with gardens and to the broader cultural argument that women were especially called to ameliorate suburban problems. In a range of ways, then, Jekyll's professional success was intimately related to the architecture and cultural forces of the suburbs.

The suburbs were places of floral cliché, or so late-century gardeners and aesthetic commentators claimed. Many blamed suburban residents squarely for this. "The indolent person who places himself in the hands of a nurseryman or a jobbing gardener will invariably have some hackneyed arrangement of calceolarias edged with blue lobelia, and scarlet geraniums edged with golden-feather," observes Edith Chamberlain, in *Town and Home Gardening* (Chamberlain headed the Women's London Gardening Association). "I was told by a clever lady gardener at Hampstead that one nurseryman 'did' all the gardens along a certain road down which she passed every day; the above combination was seen in every one of them, so that the monotony of a vista of similar houses was increased by the family likeness of the gardens."[73] Others attributed aesthetic dullness, more sympathetically, to suburbanites' long work hours: Theresa Earle argued that suburban dwellers "have little time to attend to the garden themselves."[74] Either way, the problem of identikit houses was "increased" by identikit gardens front and back; Chamberlain sees in planting practices the same kinds of thoughtless, mechanical duplications so many of her peers identified in bay windows and railings, cacti, macaws, and so forth.

The suburbs had long been placed, as we've seen, on the frontlines of a larger battle between those who defined themselves as people of taste and the masses—the aesthetically blind, the dull yet vulgar; the masses of calceolarias, geraniums, and lobelia were surely mentioned so often in gardening texts because they were floral stand-ins for "the masses." Brightly colored (hence "vulgar"), their flourishing was premised, not on slow and steady growth, but on rapid hothouse forcing. As "mere" annuals, they were unfit for their habitation, plucked from their "natural" location and transplanted, bought for cash. Geraniums and the like became, in this way, symbols of transplanted suburban dwellers themselves, also massed in groups. Geraniums were at once everything an anxious population feared, then, and a far more solvable problem than the rise of the thoughtless masses. Plants could be dug up, gardens redesigned.

In this way, women gardeners (of means, with access to the literary marketplace) laid out their claims to professional status. Frances Wolseley argued tirelessly that women gardeners were unusually well placed to step into the role because of their superior taste in color ("more developed with the majority of women than with men"), their girlhood training in aesthetics (gained, for example, through dressmaking and flower arranging), plus patience, humility, and long years of learning how to handle men (studying "the employer's pleasure" and managing "men . . . with firmness and strict fairness," she contends, are key components of the gardener's job).[75] Suburban gardens need thoughtful, hard-working, aesthetically conscious professionals to solve their problems—women who know "how preferable is the natural arrangement of well-grown tea-roses in one [villa], to the star-shaped beds of stiff geraniums in another." These kinds of arguments deftly turn women's professional labor into an act of social commitment, driven by the desire to be useful, to supply a nationally felt need. If the suburbs are, again, the problem, women are, again, the solution; a well-prepared, well-trained body that can bring the necessary skills to the landscape—and transform it. Distinguishing women's gardening from "mere" spadework, writers worked to render their occupation of the garden consistent with the discourse of the professions; Jekyll's credo presents it as necessitating "study," brainwork, and reading, while Wolseley characterized women gardeners as "directing heads to plan out work and guide others" ("we have plenty of fine, strong, hulking men" to do "spade-work," she adds).[76]

But what about woman's essential "charm . . . her softness and gentleness," Wolseley inquires. "Must we not preserve this above all else?"[77] The author is keen to stress that, on the contrary, far from detracting from femininity, gardening advances it. Indeed, Wolseley, together with a number of gardening writers, turns to Ruskin to make her claims, a move that points out just how powerful "Of Queens' Gardens" remained well into the twentieth century. Earle remarks that "Mr. Ruskin's teaching" has opened up girls' minds to the potential of aesthetics; Wolseley starts by quoting adjuration from Ruskin to " 'secure for [a girl] such physical training and exercise as may confirm her health, and perfect her beauty' " and his recommendation to " 'fill and temper [a girl's] mind with all knowledge and thoughts which tend to confirm its natural instincts of justice and refine its natural taste for love.' "[78] Wolseley turns then to the reader: "I ask what can more readily lead to the fulfillment of this ideal than a life of quiet, peaceful interests in the company of the pure and lovable companionship of flowers? . . . What can give greater intellectual and artistic pleasure and scope for imagination than planning the herbaceous border . . .? . . . Then, too, there is the interest of arranging work for others, marshaling the men at your command and apportioning the work to their different characters and temperaments. It is indeed no monotonous, unintellectual life."[79] Wolseley begins with an image that might well have attracted Ruskin, of a girl exerting "power" through quiet acts of love and peace; she ends with a head gardener whose power she evokes in military terms, "marshaling the men at [her] command." It is hard to believe Ruskin would have approved the shift, but to Wolseley it is a logical step: the author, in other words, grasped that Ruskin's garden was, as Sharon Aronofsky Weltman put it, "a wide venue in which to apply" influence and power.

For indeed, if suburban gardens needed women, women needed suburban gardens in turn-of-the-century texts. Very human problems are solved when women become professional gardeners and set their sights on the plots of suburban villas. Wolseley argues that the smaller scale of the typical suburban garden makes it perfect for women's work because "the size of the piece of ground is not too much for her to look after, the work is not too arduous." At the same time, suburban gardens are quite big enough to give the gardener exercise and satisfaction: "To plan successful combinations of colour really brings happiness." The suburban garden is not too big and not too small, in other words, for a woman who wishes to work through, but not smash, cultural expectations of her gender. Still, Wolseley hints at opportunities for even the more ambitious in the suburbs: if "jobbing gardening" is unsatisfying, women can "start a small nursery garden, and not only supply labour for these villa gardens, but also sell plants to them." Thus while she recognizes parental anxieties about a daughter's ambitions and advocates a trip to the doctor before embarking on the career of professional gardener, she also stresses that women will gain purpose, exercise, and happiness from the job, so that becoming professionals will give direction to many "aimless and useless existences."[80] Earle, meanwhile, points out that "single ladies" in "large villas" will likely prefer to employ a "woman head-gardener with a man under her to do the rougher and heavier work," so that women can support and aid one another through and in gardening work.[81]

Gertrude Jekyll reached the very pinnacle of the profession. Although she made fewer references to the suburbs and its problems in her writing, she became "one of the most important influences on the suburban garden" in the twentieth century.[82] Her designs typically synthesized formal layouts with more informal means of showing off plants—on brick walls, for instance, along paths, on arbors, or in ponds. This, a generation realized, could easily be pulled off in small plots of ground, and over the next decades a "variety of features and furniture . . . became popular in middle-class gardens, such as containers, sundials, rose gardens, winding paths, statues, pergolas, trellis work, garden arches, and rockeries."[83] Drawing on William Robinson, Jekyll made the herbaceous border of hardy perennials an important feature of the garden, which again "was particularly compatible with the new domestic-style suburban housing of the early garden city settlements." In these ways she helped birth the suburban garden into what it was to become: "carefully ordered and compact; it was decorative, and above all it was designed for family leisure in a private setting."[84]

Jekyll's aesthetic credo was articulated first in "The Idea of a Garden" (1896):

> [The best gardening] teaches us to form and respect large quiet spaces of lawn, unbroken by flower beds or any encumbrance; it teaches the simple grouping of noble types of hardy vegetation, whether their beauty be that of flower or foliage or general aspect. It insists on the importance of putting the right thing in the right place, a matter which involves both technical knowledge and artistic ability; it teaches us restraint and proportion in the matter of numbers of quantity, to use enough and not too much of any one thing at a time; to group plants in sequences of good colouring and with due regard to their form and stature and season of blooming, or of autumnal beauty of foliage. It teaches us to study the best means of treatment of different sites; to see how to join house to garden and garden to woodland.[85]

Jekyll's ideal garden design is (as many critics and scholars have noted) a harmonious synthesis of what both the formalists and the advocates of the wild garden admired: it combines the peace of the seventeenth-century landscape garden with the hardy plants of the cottage garden; it uses hothouses and greenhouses sparingly, structuring the garden around seasonal growth patterns. Indeed, the passage appears as part of an intervention into the formal/wild garden debate: "The Idea of a Garden" summarizes the positions taken by the major participants, outlining the strengths and weaknesses of both and ultimately championing the latter. Jekyll here and elsewhere applauds Robinson's success in saving the herbaceous border from the meretricious bedding system, and she disdains the idea that architects should take responsibility for garden design, as some formalists suggested.

Yet we must also note that, in Jekyll's scheme, the garden begins to take over many of the duties conventionally ascribed to women. Private and quiet, beautiful but restrained, separate from the bustle of modern life, the garden purifies those who come into contact with it. As Jekyll remarks in *Wood and Garden,* a beautiful garden "gives the delightful feeling of repose, and refreshment, and purest enjoyment of beauty," causing the owner "to lift up the heart in a spirit of praise and thankfulness."[86] "I venture to repeat that I hold the firm belief that the purpose of a garden is to give happiness and repose of mind," she adds in the 1901 *Wall and Water Gardens.*[87] The conception of the garden as a private, sanctifying space for the family is not, of course, new or unusual, and it might have escaped critical comment were it not for the fact that, in the context of the tradition of gardening writing examined here, it constitutes a change. For we have seen that, by contrast, early authors celebrated the garden as a *public* space, a scene of technology and modern advance, an opportunity for women to enter into political life and commerce. This is not to say that the early writers never celebrated the garden's peace and spirituality or that later writers never championed technology and public debate, but that the balance of the literature shifts; references to the possibilities of technological advance surface in later writing only to be submerged beneath discussions of the transformative qualities of the garden, the moral improvement it allows, and the pleasures of being cocooned from modern bustle. Such discussions take on particular meaning in literature written by women who were, like Jekyll, professionals themselves, who interacted with men in business and managed their own economic affairs. Jekyll's insistence on the garden's positive, morally uplifting effects is surely a product of a desire to shift the responsibility for improving society's morals away from her as a woman, liberating her and her peers to occupy the garden as professionals.[88]

CONCLUSION: QUEENS OF THE SUBURBS

The meaning of "queenship" was renegotiated throughout Victoria's reign. Victoria herself—both in private life and in popular cultural representations—oscillated between victorious, all-powerful Empress and self-abnegating, subservient wife, between aristocratic monarch and homely middle-class mother. Ruskin's vision of queenship in "Of Queens' Gardens" is, appropriate to its time, similarly complex, insisting on women's self-renunciation while conferring considerable economic and political influence on the gender. As Weltman puts it, Ruskin's lecture turns housewives into "rhetorically empowered queens . . . [stretching] the boundaries of domestic ideology and . . . [exploring] newly defined possibilities for women within Victorian culture."[89]

The vision Ruskin conjures is ultimately a mythic portrait: his queen is a "queen of the air," a "Pole-star" by which women steered.[90] Gardening advice texts, by contrast, are earthbound in every sense of the phrase, shaped by and responsive to the realities of brick and mortar. The woman gardener of these books is no mythological queen but an active laborer, an aesthetically informed designer, a participant in the marketplace, and, toward the end of the century, a professional business partner. Ruskin's garden of public influence becomes a space of work. Reframing women's relationship to the garden—and to society itself—across the course of Victoria's reign, the texts examined here do not just imagine feminine power, they hand power over to reading and gardening women. Suburban gardens become, together with the suburban interior, spaces of aesthetic experimentation, apprenticeship, and finally professional practice.

The last two chapters have shown how advice texts responded to, and reframed, what suburbia could offer women—how the very problems of the suburbs gave women purpose, how the repeated floor plans and gardens allowed for shared conversations about modern life. The work done by amateurs in the home also laid the foundations for professional work—the amateur who had grown her own herbaceous border could turn her skills to neighbors' gardens, just as the woman who had whipped up a Gentlewoman for her mantelpiece could run up more for clients; a discourse of vocation justified the leap. But what about later nineteenth-century fiction, written as decorative arts and gardening advice texts began to explore these exciting possibilities? We shall see, in the final chapters, that women novelists continued to find that the suburbs, with their new houses, their new plots of ground, required narrative to help make sense of them; fictions that spliced the suburbs into traditional romance forms worked to dignify the new areas, showing them to be consistent and harmonious with traditional values. As we have seen, the suburbs were already packaged in popular culture as terrible, stereotyped productions of a modern industrial and commercialized era. Women writers acknowledged that concern. But they also voiced alternative visions of suburban life, building new associative connections for the suburbs and finding in suburban villas the alluring possibility of new lives.

CHAPTER 6

Suburban Opportunity in Mary Elizabeth Braddon's Fiction

In the second half of the century, the suburbs increasingly found their way into fiction. Some of the novels that deal with suburban problems we know well—by George Gissing, H. G. Wells, Arthur Conan Doyle, and Arnold Bennett, for instance, and such texts have received sustained critical attention. Novels by these writers tend to share a fairly common sense of suburban problems, evoking the new areas as bastions of the lower middle class, spaces that are not only dull but fake and false, where residents ape a gentility they do not possess and that does not make them happy. Forster's *Howards End* is an obvious example, a novel that takes a far bleaker view of the new areas than *A Room with a View.* Leonard Bast's Camelia Road and the "accreting suburbs" are places of miserable restlessness and futile striving in the text, suburban development itself a terrible blight on the national landscape and the human spirit.[1]

But other articulations of the suburbs did exist: other ways of speaking of suburbia formed part of a lively conversation about what the new houses represented, offered, and might mean. We have seen, in the last two chapters, that nonfiction offers us ready access to some of the other voices in that conversation, women writers working out what the new topography presented them and how to make the most of it. To writers of gardening advice and interior design how-to books, the suburbs were opportunities, for women especially, for action and self-cultivation, evolving into apprenticeship spaces that served as virtual springboards into professional work.

A turn back to fiction in this chapter will show that women novelists also drew on circulating conversations about the meanings of suburbia, imaginatively laying out how the suburbs might open up new life courses, new avenues of human experience. There are many suburban-engaged novelists we might examine in pursuit of this: Charlotte Eliza Riddell, for instance, depicts suburban problems overcome by newly arrived strangers in novels including *City and Suburb* (1861) and *The Mystery in Palace Gardens* (1880). In Riddell's ghost stories, meanwhile, the just-arrived protagonist encounters, not a spider-woman landlady, but a spirit whose hauntings point to misdoings in the past. In stories like "Mrs. Jones," "Walnut Tree House," and "The Old House in Vauxhall Walk," a happy suburban life depends on unearthing crimes motivated (often) by financial greed; protagonists learn that suburban peace is possible, though only for the worthy, the altruistic. Rosa Nouchette Carey's *Heriot's Choice* (1879) agrees that worthiness is necessary for suburban happiness, but the narrative develops a slightly different metric for ascertaining worth—aesthetic insight, which is framed as appreciation of the "modest" suburbs. When the fresh arrival, a fourteen-year-old girl, scoffs at the dullness of Clapham Common, her host, Mildred, advises her to look more closely, to see the richness of the "pictures" of human and animal life in a suburb where farm and urban life continue to coexist.[2] Carey's narrator lingers lovingly on the "trimly cut lawn and clump of sweet-scented lilac and yellow drooping laburnum, stretching out long fingers of gold in the sunshine" at Laurel Cottage, Mildred's Clapham home, showing us that the older woman is committed to massing plants, to the "quiet spaces of lawn, unbroken by flower beds or any encumbrance . . . the simple grouping of noble types of hardy vegetation" Jekyll was to advocate.[3] The children's fiction of E. Nesbit also explores the possibilities of the suburban domestic: child protagonists in her turn-of-the-century fiction find that suburban areas offer ample opportunities for adventure, freedom, and imagination, not to mention class advance.

Numerous examples exist, then, of novelists whose treatments of the suburb complicate or even overset stereotypes of suburban dullness or monstrosity. I focus in this chapter, however, on the work of a single writer, Mary Elizabeth Braddon, in order to show that attention to the suburbs can help us reframe the oeuvre of a comparatively well-known author, one who finds her way onto university syllabi today. Braddon will serve to some degree as a case study of a novelist who lived and worked in the suburbs, who was deeply engaged by suburban promises, possibilities, and threats, and who employed detailed knowledge of suburban landscapes and common practices to shape—and open up—her stories of domestic experience. Similar studies could certainly be offered of other writers: Riddell lived in Tottenham and Sunbury-on-Thames near Staines, Nouchette Carey in Hackney, Hendon, and Putney, while Nesbit moved all over Lewisham. But Braddon is distinctive both for her literary prominence in her lifetime and for the remarkably long span of her professional career. She wrote about the suburbs from the 1850s well into the twentieth century, so that analysis of her work reminds us, once again, that suburban themes were emphatically not a topic for the fin de siècle only. I offer sustained readings of her fiction here to show that the suburbs, differences between individual suburbs, debates about the suburbs, and the changing character of suburbs remained a vibrant, evolving imaginative resource for this best-selling writer for a full fifty years.

Braddon was the progenitor—with Wilkie Collins—of Sensation Fiction in the 1850s and '60s. She knew virtually everyone in literary and artistic Victorian London: close friend to Bulwer-Lytton, admired by Thackeray, Dickens, Tennyson, Gladstone, Hardy, and Henry James, Braddon had her portrait painted by William Powell Frith and was celebrated by Ford Madox Ford as a consummate professional "who took her work more seriously than herself."[4] She lived in and moved around the suburbs often over the course of her life and made the tastes, interests, and practices of a suburban and lower-middle-class readership the subject of many popular fictions.[5] But she was no cheerleader for the suburbs, no spokeswoman for their charms; on the contrary, she was often their fiercest critic, identifying, even as she capitalized on, suburban pretensions with distaste. *Belgravia,* the journal she edited, was so named, she remarked to Bulwer-Lytton, because " 'Belgravia' is the best bait for the shillings of Brixton and Bow."[6] Lower-class and middle-class aspirations are held up to ridicule in her work, and whenever the term "suburban" is used in her writing, it connects to old, familiar associations of tastelessness and vulgarity, dullness and monstrosity. Braddon did not critique only the lower suburban classes. She mercilessly poked fun at what she presented as suburban "fads" like interior decoration; in *One Thing Needful* (1887), a foolish Mrs. Jellyby–like character lauds interior decoration as socially regenerative, declaiming: "I am a member of the Dado Society, and I think I have made many a humble home happy by the introduction of an artistic wall-papering and sage-green delft jar here and there on a bracket." Mrs. Mulciber's "dado-istic" musings make the exasperated hero "feel murderous."[7]

Yet the jokes Braddon makes at the expense of the people reading her novels, the interests they shared, the ambitions they nursed, are scattered across pages in which the suburbs function narratively as places of movement, opportunity, and change. The suburbs may not always appeal to the eye, and fools and criminals walk their pavements, but they are nevertheless places where new paths can be forged, where young women especially may choose and map out new lives, including, by the turn of the century, professional careers. Some of the most dangerous, thrusting characters Braddon depicts are, without question, suburbanites; the world of her novels is full of suspect aliens and transplants coexisting with too-bright paint and the deathly aroma of brick dust. But she deploys the plot arc of the suburban popular novel—discussed in chapter 3—turning on home advertisements, alien arrivals, and thrifty landladies, to lift worthy heroines out of the lives into which they were born. We saw in chapter 3 that the suburbs generated new plotlines for fiction shaped around the new landscape and its inhabitants, a fiction that strove to identify shared values and meeting places among mobile populations and socially heterogeneous groups. Suburban popular fiction also tends to privilege feeling and emotion, suggesting that these are more successful methods of finding out the truth in the commercially engaged suburbs—certainly in the business of renting out a house or a room—than the arm's-length practices typically deployed in the world of business. A number of Braddon's fictions fit broadly into this scheme, yet Braddon is a particularly interesting figure because she so loudly critiques the world of the "suburbans" as a world of fakery and posturing. It is only by focusing our attention on the suburban areas in which Braddon herself lived—especially Camberwell, Richmond, and other areas spread along the banks of the Thames—that we access a counternarrative, where the suburbs generate life-changing opportunities for women who enter them with a vocation to work.

FROM "TILBURY CRESCENT" TO CAMBERWELL

Braddon's 1868 novel, *Dead-Sea Fruit,* draws on many contemporary complaints about the lower-class suburbs in its evocation of "Tilbury Crescent," an imaginary neighborhood. It is at once too quiet and too loud, like Charles Whitehead's "Suburban Retreat." Smelly, labyrinthine, the whole area is painfully unfinished, full of what Dickens calls, in *Dombey and Son,* "a hundred thousand shapes and substances of incompleteness": "The sulphurous odours of a brickfield," Braddon writes, "pervade the atmosphere. . . . The din of a distant high-road, the roar of many wheels, and the clamour of excited costermongers, float in occasional gusts of sound upon the dismal stillness of the neighbourhood, where the shrill voices of children, playing hopscotch in an adjacent street, are painfully audible."[8] Braddon highlights the potential for slippage between suburb and slum in an age of poor building practices, where buildings are constructed for financial gain rather than to foster human connections: "Decent poverty has set a seal upon this little labyrinth of streets and squares and crescents and terraces, before the builder's men have left the newest of the houses, while there are still roofless skeletons at every corner, waiting till the speculator who began them shall have raised enough money to finish them."[9] Similar descriptive passages can be found throughout Braddon's oeuvre, particularly in suburbs she has made up. "Brigsome's Terrace" in *Lady Audley's Secret,* perhaps her most famous novel, again uses the image of empty houses as skeletons:

> Mr. Maldon had established his slovenly household gods in one of those dreary thoroughfares which speculative builders love to raise upon some miserable fragment of waste ground hanging to the skirts of a prosperous town. Brigsome's Terrace was perhaps one of the most dismal blocks of building that was ever composed of brick and mortar since the first mason plied his trowel and the first architect drew his plan. The builder who had speculated in the ten dreary eight-roomed prison-houses had hung himself behind the parlour door of an adjacent tavern while the carcases were yet unfinished. The man who had bought the brick and mortar skeletons had gone through the Bankruptcy Court while the paper-hangers were still busy.[10]

Braddon sounds like Bulwer-Lytton, her mentor and friend, or Dickens, in these passages, lamenting the destruction of the English landscape, critiquing the developments of lower-class suburbs especially as miserable stepchildren clinging to a town's "skirts."[11] But it is not only the slum-like lower-class suburbs she holds up to criticism: middle-class suburbanites' aspirations to gentility range from foolish to dangerous, from the frippery of the Dado Society to Braddon's most (in)famous creation, the murderous Lady Audley.

When Braddon references real neighborhoods she knew well, particularly Camberwell and Richmond, the language she uses is quite different; the homes of these suburbs are neither "dismal," nor dangerous, nor "dado-istic." Like many of her contemporaries, Braddon moved often: she was born at number 2 Frith Street, Soho Square, in the 1830s—"prim and respectable" at the time—but her family fell apart when her mother discovered that her solicitor father was not only disastrous with money but unfaithful. (As Robert

Wolff points out, Braddon was to narrate his perfidy and personal weakness numerous times in the course of her writing career, in plots of mothers and daughters struggling on after a father's betrayal and failure.)[12] After a restorative stint in St. Leonard's-on-Sea in Sussex, Mary and her mother returned to live in London, first in Hampstead and Hammersmith, then Camberwell. Later, once Mary was old enough to help participate in the business of righting the family ship, she lived at 26 Mecklenburgh Square in Bloomsbury, purchasing in 1865, with the money she'd earned, a small suburban home in Twickenham to rent out. She settled at a property far up the suburban scale, Lichfield House in Richmond, a year later, in an expansive home she renovated with her partner (later husband), John Maxwell. She lived in Richmond until her death in 1915, bearing six children and step-mothering a further five, Maxwell's surviving offspring from his first marriage, all the while weathering a series of scandals surrounding their unorthodox relationship. Maxwell, a publisher, was also a property developer, deeply engaged in the politics surrounding the building and development of Richmond; he served as chairman of the Lock Committee of the Richmond Vestry at a time when the extremely low levels of the Thames in Richmond, caused by damming at London Bridge, was a matter of urgent local significance.[13] A number of streets in Richmond are named after characters in Braddon's novels because of Maxwell's part in the growth of the area: if suburbia left its mark on Braddon, she also left her mark on it.[14] Affluent Richmond, as we shall see, appears in Braddon's fiction as a place of ease, an endpoint for the worthy. Camberwell, a mixed-class, rapidly changing suburb, is a place of striving and difficulty. It is a site that tests resolve and endurance, separating the women who deserve happiness and a greater sphere of action from those who do not.

Camberwell appears remarkably often in Victorian literature. *Did You Ever Send Your Wife to Camberwell?* inquired the title of a one-act farce by Joseph Stirling Coyne, first performed at the Adelphi in 1846 and still in theaters in the 1890s.[15] Full of all the misunderstandings one would expect from a Victorian farce, the play shows Mr. Honeybun, urban dweller in a cheap apartment near the Strand, sending his wife on a time-consuming errand to then-genteel Camberwell so he can conduct an amour in her absence. The audience who saw the play at the turn of the century must have found it a quaint period piece, for by then Camberwell was emphatically urban, well-connected to the London center by trains. (It is the setting of Gissing's *In The Year of Jubilee,* and despised by many of its inhabitants.) In Coyne's drama, Camberwell is a countryfied spot accessible only by horse-drawn omnibus, set apart from London's smoky cityscape. Mr. Honeybun puns to his wife that, given their lack of money, his only "prospects" are "six church steeples, and no end of chimney pots"; urban life is prey to encroaching modernity, the mania for machinery and newness. Mr. Honeybun's hapless neighbor Mr. Crank is an inventor who, four days before the action begins, left the job he had for twenty-five years as clock maker in the rural village of Stoke Poges to finesse a garbled patent for a "hydro-galvanic locomotive steam engine on a new principle." The slow-paced, time-rich world of Stoke Poges (the satirically evoked "romantic pump—the gothic ruins of the market-house—the ancient pound") contrast sharply with the world of the Strand, in which the need to move fast, to "[strike] while the iron's hot," to rush for the omnibus, are mentioned repeatedly. Meanwhile, in a hint at the suburb Camberwell was in the process of becoming, the wealthy aunt owns "a green parrot and a ring-tailed monkey," enduring signals of consumerist suburbanites.[16] The farce proceeds to stage a collision between the worlds of Camberwell, countryside, and London, for it turns out Mr. Honeybun's Aunt Jewell has used the omnibus to travel into the city to visit her nephew, while Mr. Crank's wife has chased him on the train. The resulting confusions, failed meetings, and near misses lead to arguments, threats of disinheritance, the destruction of not one but two marriages, and the possible squashing of a baby beneath a chest of drawers. The attempt by Mr. Honeybun to send his wife to Camberwell fails ultimately because, for all his up-to-date references, he's unable to grasp the shape of industrial modernity: seeking to exploit the transportation network, he (like Mr. Crank) has forgotten it not only takes Londoners *out* but brings outsiders *in.* The joke at the heart of *Did You Ever Send Your Wife to Camberwell?* is that you'll need to send her a lot farther than Camberwell if you want to get her out of your way because, like it or not, London and its environs are as inextricably bound as the Honeybuns themselves.

The young Braddon and her family moved to Camberwell around 1848. Her parents separated, family fortunes at a nadir, Camberwell was the choice of a single mother forced to economize. Braddon, who was to take the socially risky step of becoming a professional actress to help support her family, knew Coyne's play well—she referred to it in one of her most celebrated texts, *Aurora Floyd* (1863), and performed in another of Coyne's dramas, *The Man of Many Friends,* in 1855. (A wry reference to *Did You Ever Send Your Wife to Camberwell?* surfaces in *A Lost Eden,* Braddon's 1904 novel, when a playwright hopes for professional success by penning a new farce, *Go To Putney.* It includes a baby dropped—"or supposed to be dropped"—from the window.)[17]

Braddon left the stage to write in 1860, yet in a long career as author, journalist, editor, and trenchant skewerer of middle-class anxieties, she never forgot Camberwell. Coyne unapologetically addressed his play, from its very title, to a masculine, city-dwelling interlocutor; Braddon journeys to domestic interiors in novels like *The Doctor's Wife* (1864), *Lost for Love* (1874), *The Story of Barbara* (1880), and *A Lost Eden* to show readers a Camberwell that is a place of struggle but also growth and hope. Parrot-owning suburbanite Aunt Jewell is replaced by mothers, daughters, and sisters who are in the suburb to start again; gardens are weedy and overgrown, homes are dirty, the skies are smoky, but it is the very challenges of part-rural, part-urban Camberwell that test the women who live there. Those who are passive, those who allow Camberwell to decline around them, set off on a downward trajectory. Those who work to clean the houses of pollution, prune the gnarled trees, and clear the weedy paths are those whose character is proved: the reward for fixing suburban problems is moving on, as Braddon did, to the Eden of Richmond. Braddon represents Camberwell as a staging post in a Pilgrim's Progress through not only urban areas but also the classes.

CAMBERWELL IN THE NINETEENTH CENTURY

H. J. Dyos's pioneering *Victorian Suburb* put South London Camberwell under a microscope to show how urbanization occurred in the nineteenth century, examining both the macroscopic social and cultural shifts that enabled growth and the on-the-ground agreements, arrangements, and relationships between developers, speculators, investors, and builders that turned plans into brick and mortar.[18] More recent historians and literary critics have been drawn back to the suburb, examining it as at once a remarkable example and a case study of more general, widespread phenomena. Camberwell was in some ways distinctive: it expanded 31 percent between 1851 and 1861, while the rest of the city grew 19 percent, and, judging from the occupations Camberwell residents reported in the census, the suburb was substantially middle class. In 1861, it had an unusually low percentage of laborers (5.5 percent) and transport workers (7.5 percent) and a higher percentage of professionals than the rest of London (10.5 percent of employed males, as compared with 6.9 percent outside the suburb). Indeed, men in middle-class occupations made up 35 percent of the total population in 1861, as compared to 19 percent for the city as a whole. Five percent of men were involved in agriculture, as compared with 2 percent in London as a whole, suggesting that Camberwell retained its rural character for some time. Census data on women indicate "Camberwell attracted an unusual number of female home owners (probably artisanal house keepers), dressmakers, laundresses and the like," and a "substantial one-servant class" (households with just one servant), Patricia Branca notes.[19] Braddon's own home in Camberwell was headed by a woman, and *The Story of Barbara* centers on an all-women household. Braddon's decision to situate her female characters in the suburb may reflect not just personal experience, then, but a broader Camberwellian phenomenon.

Still, Camberwell defies easy generalizations. Middle-class but with an unusually high percentage of female home owners, unusually professional but also unusually agricultural, growing very quickly but managing to retain its rural character, by the end of the century it was also home to Sultan Street, one of London's most notorious slums. A local historian named Douglas Allport offers insight into life in Camberwell in the 1840s, when Coyne's drama was first played: Allport, taking up his pen in 1841, presented Camberwell as still the leafy spot celebrated by the great botanist Dr. John Lettsom in the 1790s. Writing just a few years before Braddon's family took up residence, Allport lingers over the pleasant situation and the good air of Camberwell (neighboring Peckham too, Allport notes, "is strongly recommended for invalids"). The writer sees social stability, at least among the more affluent classes: "The character of the wealthier inhabitants remains much the same as in Dr. Lettsom's time, when they were described as consisting of respectable merchants and tradesmen, and of those holding eligible situations in the public offices."[20] Yet Allport, like Coyne, sees changes afoot. "In 1789, the number of houses in the entire parish did not exceed 800," he remarks, before tallying "a surprising increase in the population" housed in some 7,233 homes. The total number of residents in 1801 was 7,059, a figure that had risen to 39,662 by 1841. And, even though the book is replete with bucolic etchings and historical scenes, the author admits: "In many parts of the parish gravel is worked to some extent; and there are numerous brick-fields in those places where the plastic clay offers the necessary material for that manufacture. Extensive gas-works are established on the canal near the Kent-road, and silk-spinning is actively carried on in New Peckham. The hills . . . offer, for the most part, very eligible sites for building."[21] Allport presents only a few tantalizing glimpses of urbanization and industrialization in action, preferring to concentrate on the suburb's rural past. Still, contemporary reviewers clearly understood that Camberwell was on the edge of a massive takeover. As *Chambers's Edinburgh Journal* observed, employing a typical image of suburbia-as-embracing-monster: "Camberwell . . .

is a village to the south of London, now nearly involved in the wide-spreading limbs of the ever-growing city."[22]

Camberwell's rapid growth may be attributed partly to its ideal location for clerks, a particularly fast-growing new social group. Located one and a half to two miles from the City, Camberwell's expansion began before the advent of the rail in the 1860s partly because meagerly salaried clerks could live there and walk to work; by 1901, one in eight of all London's clerks lived in Camberwell.[23] Journeys into the city in Braddon's day—the omnibus Mrs. Honeybun was to take—took the form of a horse-drawn coach service, but since fares were high and journeys long, this mode of transport was not much used by commuters.[24] The mere fact that omnibus routes existed, however, had an effect on house and street design, since homes no longer needed space outdoors for coach houses and mews or indoors for male grooms. Female domestics alone were required by the Braddon family, as for the Aunt Jewells of Camberwell, which constituted a considerable saving. The development of horse-drawn omnibus routes had a significant, and early, effect on the shape of the new streets and the size of the homes: the terraced streets that offer residents today little space for parking were built because the original tenants expected to use public, not private, modes of transport; they were able to afford their homes precisely because they no longer had to pay for the upkeep of a stable of hungry horses.[25] Camberwell's older homes were soon surrounded by newer terraces, the open ground sold both for building and for industrial concerns.

The problems of rapid change and building were nowhere more evident than in Sultan Street. Colored dark blue with a thick black line by Charles Booth in the 1890s (dark blue indicated "chronic want," black the "vicious, semi-criminal"), this street of seventy-six houses on three floors was built on a plot of cow pasture between 1868 and 1871, stuck in between older cottages, villas, and the back gardens of a terrace, dominated by the noise and pollution of a railway line. It has been described as one of the prime "settlement tanks for submerged Londoners," and H. J. Dyos and D. A. Reeder's evocative description contrasts painfully with Allport's account of healthful Camberwell airs: "Cowsheds and piggeries squeezed up with the surrounding houses, and a glue factory, a linoleum factory, a brewery, haddock-smokers, tallow-melters, costermongers keeping their good stuff indoors with them while leaving rotting cabbage-stalks, bad oranges, and the like on the street, created between them an atmosphere which, mingled with household odours, kept all but the locals at bay."[26] When Braddon wrote *The Story of Barbara* in 1880, this horror was unfolding—Dyos and Reeder date Sultan Street's period of most significant decline, and its demographic departure from the rest of Camberwell, to the decade between 1871 and 1881. Braddon's novel contains references to the "wealthy drysalters and millionaire soap-boilers floating on the surface of Camberwell society," suggesting a consciousness of Camberwell's change.[27] During the 1890s, the rest of Camberwell began to decline too, new slums developing on the north of the suburb, setting in motion a social shift downward for the area as a whole, so that Booth's poverty map of the area has plenty of light and dark blue areas, indicating the residences of lower classes (although the areas around St. Giles', Allport's church, remain comfortably red). Camberwell declined toward the fin de siècle, like many another suburb "on the original frontier of London's expansion," as the areas that accommodated the first waves of growth turned into slums and "the tide of middle-class settlement . . . rolled on." Mary Elizabeth Braddon was one of those who rode the tide away from Camberwell—to Richmond.[28]

BRADDON'S CAMBERWELL: A LOST EDEN

Braddon's fictional Camberwell is, in many ways, consonant with the Camberwell sketched above—a home for the socially mobile, with a rural past, where industrial development has produced slums. Elements of Brigsome's Terrace and Tilbury Crescent surface for, like Coyne, Braddon positions Camberwell as a battleground in the collision between tradition and modernity, one in which innocence is at risk, where "old" time meets "new" time and the rural meets the machine. Yet she tends to depict Camberwell in the 1850s, the decade she lived there with her family, as quite different: in that era, she suggests, signs of industrial modernity were only just beginning to encroach. Camberwell was, in those days, virtually Edenic: "The Walworth Road, with its frequent interruptions and cheap shops, was not much more than a mile distant," the narrator observes in *A Lost Eden,* "but here there was no sound of traffic nor canopy of smoke."[29] Gardens were, apparently, huge and lavish. Indeed, Braddon re-creates within the suburb of Camberwell a kind of Huntercome: the garden was stocked by a previous tenant fifty years ago and is full of all the kinds of plants so beloved by Boyle, Maryon, von Arnim, and Jekyll, discussed in chapter 4. Here there are no annuals arranged as children of art, just "a kingdom of roses and syringas and lilacs and laburnums"; long borders are "crammed with peony and iris, lupin and columbine, marigold and nasturtium, scabious and white pink, all the friendly perennials which ask so little of the gardener."[30] Camberwell in the 1850s was, according to Braddon, everything the "wild" garden enthusiasts advocated, not an enclave of the artificial and transplanted but a home of native flowers.

Braddon's 1904 narrator argues that this floral dream has now vanished: "Such a garden today would be described as 'residential estate, ripe for building.' Indeed, the dear old lawns and herbaceous borders, the rose-walk and the hazel hedge, have long ago given place to closely packed houses, and the rural lane that Marion loved has been engulfed in the Metropolitan Immensities."[31] Braddon's point seems clear: with the loss of native plants, the suburb has lost its claims to Eden; Camberwell *was* Paradise, but urbanization destroyed it. The Trevornock family in *The Story of Barbara* also occupies a "semi-detached cottage . . . as clean and pure as a homestead far away in a pastoral land, remote from the smoke of cities" —a home that sounds, at first, like the lush wild gardens of *A Lost Eden.*[32] Yet in the 1880 text, whose action again is set in the 1850s, the narrator admits the appearance of purity and rural remoteness is *already* an illusion: the home must be energetically and regularly cleaned by its suburban resident to preserve the look of pastoral idyll. "Mrs. Trevornock's existence was a perpetual warfare against 'the blacks,' " the narrator concedes, "not an oppressed negro race, but those wandering atoms of solidified smoke which came floating on the wings of the wind from the tall chimneys of Lambeth and Bermondsey." Progress is already on the march, embodied in the housing; suburban growth is figured as an army of "infantry" in "serried ranks" moving through the landscape. Indeed, given the date and the repeated references to the Crimea, Mrs. Trevornock's efforts against "floating" specks and "wandering atoms" appear at once heroic and foolhardy, a sort of domestic Charge of the Light Brigade. As the plot develops, and war breaks out, the novel suggests that, while "every eye in England was turned to the Crimea, every thought was of the news from the seat of war," every eye should have been turned closer to home.[33] The 1904 *A Lost Eden* repines for a Camberwell that the 1880 *The Story of Barbara* admits was not quite such an idyll.

The Story of Barbara begins, like many another suburban-set fiction, with an advertisement placed by a struggling mother in the *Times* for a lodger to help bolster the family's income. Braddon immediately goes behind the text of the advertisement. Acknowledging the puffery it contains, she examines the motivations that prompt claims of exaggerated size:

> " 'Having a house larger than they require'—you must say that, mother . . . It's the correct thing."

> "Only sixty words allowed for five shillings," said Mrs. Trevornock, looking up distractedly from an original composition, which she was indicting with the assistance of her two daughters.
>
> "But you really ought to put it, mother," cried Flossie, on her knees beside the table. "It's the only thing that takes the edge off the humiliation."[34]

The sympathetically evoked daughters Barbara and Flossie here term the deception so regularly excoriated, for "desirable suburban residences," "the correct thing": the lies in the advertisement are not only acknowledged lies, they are lies the women feel the wider community endorses, indeed positively requires. It is "the correct thing," from society's perspective, to shroud their family's need. Yet if it is, as Barbara suggests, the commonly acknowledged "correct thing" to lie, no one will believe their house unduly spacious—so what, exactly, does the lie achieve? Flossie suggests the best they can hope for is to take the "edge" off their humiliation, for the ad's purpose is a navigation of their place in the community. It is a way to retrieve dignity, for we feel humiliation in seeing disgust at our behavior in the eyes of others, William Miller contends.[35] By telling the lie that their home is too big for them, the Trevornocks demonstrate that, though poor, they know the middle-class game so intimately they can deploy its codes and ward off disgust. Lacking economic capital, they possess social capital—and seek a lodger for their house who shares what Pierre Bourdieu termed their class habitus, "the internalized form of class condition and of the conditioning it entails."[36] Knowledge of "the correct thing" is the "common knowledge" a culture reached for in order to glue social groups together, protecting and clinging to a retreating vision of what constituted cultural capital—large houses and leisure.

But the business of placing an exaggerated ad in the paper also suggests that the Trevornocks understand the role of home advertiser, not just home dweller; they navigate the demands of the marketplace. They do this with discomfort, unhappily aware of the slippage between what they know to be true and what they feel they must do to let a house on the market. Their unease over the decision to puff the house is not uncommon, of course, and historians and critics have tended to read such expressions as hypocrisy, mere pretenses playacted to conceal the drive to exploit others for selfish economic gain. More recent scholars have examined such articulations in more sympathetic ways, pointing out that the culture placed a very high value on ethical behavior even as it advocated striving for economic advancement. Read in this light, the awkward consciousness the Trevornocks have of what the business of advertising requires—the alienation the characters feel playing a role shaped by the demands of a market economy—is not necessarily a signal of their hypocrisy or a hint of their unfitness, as women, for professional life. It perhaps records their virtue at a time when Victorians were trying hard to manage the thorny problem of how to work out the self-conception of the new professional.

The Victorians, as Stefan Collini in particular has argued, highly valued morally exemplary actions, especially service to others and personal self-discipline. Religious and quasi-religious rhetoric framed altruism as not only preferable but necessary if one was to conceive of oneself as a good person. Doing one's duty required doing service to others, and the decline of Christianity only reinforced for many the absolute imperative of maintaining moral obligations to others so that older moral codes could continue to provide anchorage. Victorian moralists, Collini observes, even "exhibited an obsessive antipathy to selfishness, and consequently their reflections were structured by a sharp and sometimes exhaustive polarity between egoism and altruism"; this put professionals in a quandary.[37] As Susan E. Colón summarizes, "The Victorian moral vocabulary often required morally exemplary actions to be counter to economic self-interest . . . acting against one's economic interest for the sake of a larger social good was regarded as an imperative duty by Victorians of all political and religious persuasions."[38] In an account that integrates the insights of Collini and Jennifer Ruth, on the ways in which fiction helped work out the tensions in the emerging professional ideal, Colón continues: "An awareness of a tension between the market and the aesthetic economies was built into the Victorian professional self-conception," which therefore needed "to theorize a kind of labor that was both economic and transcendent, that both acquiesced to and resisted market logic."[39] Braddon's fiction offers, hesitantly, a theory of how women might manage this elaborate dance.

Braddon's *Story of Barbara* shows women engaging, hesitantly, in professional work and working out, among themselves, how to acquiesce in and also resist market logic. What is moral, what is required, are much discussed in the early pages of the novel, so that women provide a strongly ethical context for their decision making. This moral context forces business participants to be constantly aware of the consequences of what they do; the family network prevents agents from acting in dangerous isolation of others. Furthermore, the trust that builds in the family and the knowledge women gain about community members from conversations are shown repeatedly in *The Story of Barbara* (as in earlier novels, like Buxton's *Great Grenfell Gardens,* discussed in chapter 3) to provide the only reliable foundation for sound decision making. Bankers and other written references are, again, shown to be open to manipulation; arm's-length transactions cannot be trusted. In Braddon's novel, as in Eden's *Semi-Detached House* or Buxton's *Great Grenfell Gardens,* women's market-related activities, set in and around the home, lead to positive outcomes, as if the home circle exerts a kind of massive magnetic moral pull, keeping selfishness at bay, enforcing the primacy of emotion, helping characters rightly sort and read their instincts (based on knowledge of other people). Men's professional activities, by contrast, unfolding in the City, away from the home, veer into dangerous speculations and crashes, for antiheroes like Eden's Baron Sampson or Buxton's Peregrine Latimer are shown to be isolated, hence more easily tempted, more liable to forget the dictates of moral behavior. Even heroes, the novel's worthy men, are more likely to depend on rules and standardized practices over moral principles and instincts, which lead them into quicksand, causing them to trust the unworthy. Capital relations thrive best in Braddon's fiction when they are conducted and managed in and around the home.

The Story of Barbara rewards women who handle "the sordid question of terms" in the home, who play on a level playing field with professional men, who see the tensions endemic to professional life and determine to steer as much as possible by moral precepts with a large dose of feminine "instinct." Indeed, Braddon hints that the best place for professional labor, the place that can most plausibly help manage the divisions in the culture of the professional, may in fact be the home, by the hearthside. The Trevornocks' approach is, certainly, rewarded. Crucially, the hero understands the behavior of the Trevornocks, reading their professional role-playing as, without question, "the correct thing": Captain Leland, the Trevornock's prospective boarder, interprets cues adroitly, in the way that (say) Collins's Basil does not. Leland is able successfully to decode both his landlady's habitus and the landlady's subject position. He ignores the size of the bedroom (it was advertised as "large and airy"; it isn't). He does not care that out of the window lies not so much the promised rural locale as "half an acre of flower and vegetable garden, a canal, a stretch of open ground, and a conglomeration of roofs, melting away into the thickness of London smoke." Nor does he mind that the extensive gardens dwindle into a couple of tight gravel paths: "It was a large garden for Camberwell, as Mrs. Trevornock had remarked, but scarcely large enough for stateliness. The neat gravel walks were narrow. People walking two and two were obliged to be rather near together." The Trevornocks' property is the kind so mocked in "Houses to Let," but Leland sees that engaging in the market does not preclude worth; on the contrary, he sees that his new landlady and her family have balanced out meeting economic demands with ethical practice. Their very objects display this: "The old-fashioned furniture was well worn, but not shabby," Braddon's narrator explains. "The open piano and bookshelves, the spring flowers and modest array of old china, suggested tastefulness and love of home."[40] What the Trevornocks put out indicates not only their taste—that which Bourdieu describes as "social necessity made second nature"—but also their moral valuing of old over new, continuity and book learning over money, display, consumption.[41] Their interior design records not only that they abide by an emerging Queen Anne aesthetic but also that they hold true to what it sought to celebrate, the moral values felt to be under threat in a time of rapid capitalist and industrial growth.

THE DOCTOR'S WIFE

Braddon explores in other fictions what happens when women do *not* follow the Trevornocks' path, as if to lay out a kind of dire alternative to successful suburban-based labor. One of her most well-known texts, *The Doctor's Wife,* is an 1864 rewrite of Flaubert's *Madame Bovary,* and again it is set (at least initially) in mid-Victorian Camberwell.[42] At first blush, the text presents the suburb as enervating Dulham, a tedious place its heroine loathes. Isabel Sleaford, obsessed with popular reading, is careless and lazy, and her slipshod manner seems to match the environs in which she is pictured. But Braddon deploys familiar images of suburban dullness, tastelessness, and weediness only to point out that such ways of life need not happen, in much the way she draws on contemporary images of the passive woman reader only to point out the interpretive and deductive failures that lie behind them too. Indeed, the strategies Braddon develops to probe contemporary debates about women's reading shed light on the ways she simultaneously engages common imaginings of suburbia; in both cases, the text works to render available new associations to the reader who chooses to find them out.

Isabel is found among the weedy paths of her parents' rented Camberwellian house in the early chapters of the novel, reading beneath an old pear tree. Bored, she has turned to fiction and history for stimulation—or at least, "just so much of modern history as enabled her to pick out all the sugar-plums." Camberwell seems a place any young woman of spirit would want to escape—Isabel foreshadows, in this way, Nancy in Gissing's *In the Year of Jubilee.* The house Isabel inhabits is a "square brick building, with sickly ivy straggling here and there about it, and long narrow windows considerably obscured by dust and dirt. It was not a pleasant house to look at." The inside is yet worse—the parlor, for instance, is "large, but shabbily furnished and very untidy. The traces of half-a-dozen different occupations were scattered about, and the apartment was evidently inhabited by people who made a point of never putting anything away. There was a work-box upon the table, open, and running over with a confusion of tangled tapes, and bobbins, and a mass of different-coloured threads, that looked like variegated vermicelli. There was an old-fashioned desk, covered with dusty green baize, and decorated with loose brass-work, which caught at people's garments or wounded their flesh when the desk was carried about."[43]

The interior evokes chaos, idleness, lack of taste, and lack of commitment, the disorder of a middle-class family far from rich but not so poverty-stricken that it concerns itself appropriately with waste. The contents of the workboxes are not put away, the dust on the desk indicates that no one has put it to good use, while the brass work needs affixing, catching or wounding the inhabitants as if to recall them to their duty. The multiple occupations suggest the dilettante, rather than the worker driven by vocation. Isabel is not represented inside the home, signaling her disinterest in and distance from the domestic; she is invariably to be found idling away the days beneath her pear tree, and the cause of at least part of the home's disorder turns out to be the sensational books that are "beautiful sweetmeats, with opium inside the sugar."[44] Bored by Camberwell, uninterested in labor, Isabel is dangerously open to the blandishments of sensation texts.

Her reading practice is, as many critics have observed, escape and transgression, a means of avoiding duty and a signal of ungovernable desires—Isabel lives an "idle, useless life," and her subsequent marriage to a doctor runs into difficulties because her reading leaves her hungering for romance. Kate Flint's interpretation of reading in the text helps elucidate the narrative strategies in play: Flint argues that fictions like *The Doctor's Wife* "[invite] readers to join in a process which involves the active construction of meaning rather than its revelation."[45] She shows that Isabel was an instantly familiar portrait: contextualizing the novel with reference to the numerous periodical articles, paintings, advice and conduct manuals on women's reading in the nineteenth century, Flint argues that the image of a loose-limbed woman reading a novel sets off a chain of culturally produced signifiers a contemporary reader would indubitably recognize. An 1860s reader would thus bring to the experience of reading about Isabel an understanding of how to interpret her: hints of disarray in her attire, for instance, speak to what the author knows to be a reader's expectations—that a woman reader who cannot control her desire for plot may become unable to control her desire for other pleasures, and so "fall."

These expectations promptly meet, and are inflamed by, the words of Sigismund Smith, a professional sensation writer in the novel who from the start openly reveals the apparatus, and the market forces, behind the sensation novel. Smith makes abundantly clear the artificiality of the sugarplums Isabel devours—for instance, the trade phrase "combination novel" is translated by Smith to mean "frankly plagiarized": "Why, you see, when you're doing four great stories a week for a public that must have a continuous flow of incident, you can't be quite as original as a strict sense of honour might prompt you to be; and the next best thing you can do if you haven't got ideas of your own, is to steal other people's ideas in an impartial manner."[46] The Trevornocks' unwilling manipulation of words in the home advertisement is textually supported because it is driven by need, not ambition or avarice; what motivates Smith is his desire to advance his own career, which renders his manipulation of words far more dangerous. The reader who probes Smith's words and uses them to spot the risk in Isabel's reading is an active reader who proves her ability to resist the dangers of textual manipulation and puffery; risk lies not so much in the texts themselves, then, as in the business of reading them. The text's criticisms of sensation writing ultimately become criticisms of those who are unable to distinguish fantasy from fiction, those who cannot (like Captain Leland) decipher textual clues—criticisms of *other* readers, in other words, the ones who have not got the point.

The early chapters of *The Doctor's Wife* perform a similar linguistic and cultural gymnastic by raising, only to unsettle and complicate, stereotypes of the suburbs and the suburbanite. The image of the slapdash girl reading accompanies, as we have seen, another familiar image—the disheveled, disorderly, tasteless middle-class suburban interior. Camberwell is explicitly evoked as "suburban," a term fully freighted with associations of the tasteless and the ignorant—thus, for instance, when Isabel first sees the country, the narrator adopts the mantle of sympathy to remark: "[She] was a Cockney, poor child, and had spent the best part of her life amidst the suburban districts of Camberwell and Peckham."[47] Yet Braddon's narrator simultaneously works to test and overset such interpretations of the "suburban," for the novel shows us that the Camberwellian home *can* be different, if different residents, with different work ethics, inhabit it. Standing before the Sleafords' house, after journeying through the district, George Gilford, the young doctor, "compared it unfavourably with the trim white-walled villas he had seen on his way." Braddon builds very different adjectives into her narrative descriptions of those other "neat little mansions at five-and-thirty pounds a year; those cosy little cottages, with shining windows that winked and blinked in the sunshine by reason of their cleanliness."[48] Words like "trim," "neat," and "cosy" rescue the other villas for Dr. Gilford, suturing them into a middle-class ideal of the well-run home as sanctuary from chaos. (Presumably Mrs. Trevornock is one of the other residents and has been working hard to cleanse her villa of "smuts.")

Braddon also points out that the Sleaford home was itself once beautiful, pushing past its suburban meanings to pick up the threads of its rural past:

> It was an old-fashioned garden, and had doubtless once been beautifully kept; for bright garden-flowers grew up amongst the weeds summer after summer, as if even neglect or cruel usage could not disroot them from the familiar place they loved. Thus rare orchids sprouted up out of beds that were half full of chickweed, and lilies-of-the-valley flourished amongst the ground-sel in a shady corner under the water-butt. There were vines, upon which no grape had ever been suffered to ripen during Mr. Sleaford's tenancy, but which yet made a beautiful screen of verdant tracery all over the back of the house, twining their loving tendrils about the dilapidated Venetian shutters, that rotted slowly on their rusted hinges.[49]

This garden is a place where, interestingly, flowers of different countries and climates grow together; it is an Eden with a class and cultural dynamic, as the battle of the plants enacts in horticultural form the social battle of the suburb. "Rare orchids" and lilies-of-the-valley sprout and even "flourish" among common weeds and spreading plants—this is not merely a garden of native English flowers. The reader is prompted to see the plants as having human qualities through the verbs, an application of the pathetic fallacy in which the plants enact a remarkable coexistence of different species. While the house looks, at first, a product of deterioration and decline, the visitor who examines it more closely finds ample signals of lustiness and growth—indeed, the visitor who makes it around the back of the house finds that while the vines on the front are ill-looking and straggly, a "verdant tracery" to the rear grows so luxuriantly it is able to conceal the worst of even the Sleafords' mismanagement.

The reader is given access to familiar criticisms of the suburbs as a terrible place, then—dull and tasteless, chaotic and filthy—yet is shown through the narrator's tracking and focusing gaze a Camberwell that can be beautiful. Just as we come to see Isabel as the agent of her own downfall through her ungoverned reading, so we see that life in Camberwell does not have to be the life into which the Sleafords have slumped. The repetition of Emma Bovary's unhappiness does not have to happen; the suburb's very horticulture hints that what is needed is the endurance, patience, and willingness to beautify that the plants so ably exhibit.

BEYOND CAMBERWELL: REREADING LADY AUDLEY

Isabel is not the only iteration of a failed suburban woman in Braddon's oeuvre. Braddon was deeply concerned throughout her career with what agglomeration of character traits was produced in, and required by, the suburbs, given their peculiar problems. The text that made Braddon's name and career is an early investigation of the question: *Lady Audley's Secret* does not tread the streets of Camberwell, and it does not open with scenes of home advertisement or letting. But suburban areas play a pivotal role in the narrative nonetheless, and a plot spawned by an alien arrival, though it has taken place before the action begins, structures the narrative. Moreover, the bigamous lower-middle-class Lady Audley is strongly associated with the pushing new suburbs that hold so many of her secrets. She becomes a human embodiment of the suburban house whose appearance of grace and gentility is found to be faked, the smiling façade that conceals secrets the text works to uncover. Robert Audley, meanwhile, the man who penetrates her secrets, is a lawyer, and the text charts his progression from self-indulgence to self-discipline, from spendthrift to diligent worker.

Lady Audley—Helen Talboys—is destroyed at the end of the text, first through internment in an asylum (in a painful parallel to John Maxwell's first wife), then death. Audley Court, the courtly home of her titled *soi-disant* husband, is abandoned by her nephew and vanquisher. Aeron Haynie has argued that Lady Audley's sad end and Robert's move away from Audley Court at the close of the novel together "suggest an inability to imagine a peaceful merging of the classes."[50] This is a serious charge: Haynie presents the middle-class Braddon as unable to free herself imaginatively of her culture's constraints, unable to break down class barriers. This is, without doubt, a curious text; as generations of readers have noticed, Braddon inspires sympathy for the plight of her murderous heroine, while the putative victims and heroes are perplexingly hard to like. Yet if we attend to the place of the suburban, to the world that produced Lady Audley, reading the text in the light of other suburban popular fictions, some of the novel's contradictions begin to fall away. Lady Audley may number Bulwer-Lytton's Mrs. Copperas and Sala's Earl of Elbowsout among her kin; certainly other suburban characters and scenes offer more sympathetic visions of the world in which Braddon lived. But far from presenting two worlds that cannot come together, the author ultimately shows the upper class *embracing* the suburban environs and the life of the professional: the novel's final vision of a happy-ever-after ending is of a lawyer in Teddington, in a suburban villa, on the banks of the Thames. Braddon carefully unpicks the suburbs she loves, the suburban types she admires, from those she holds up to scorn, all the while holding out the possibility that life and work in the suburbs offers the greatest potential for happiness and human flourishing.

Lady Audley is evoked as a terrible fake, a woman whose airs and graces are revealed to be copies of gentility, as the suburban house aspires to copy the landed estate and the fake mantelpiece pretends to be marble. Her very face is a virtual duplication of her maid's, as a semidetached house's exterior is mirrored in the next-door façade. Helen Talboys—who, like so many suburbanites, assumes a genteel-sounding moniker in the pursuit of raised social class—is the product of a suburban discourse already a generation old. A younger, prettier Mrs. Copperas, in Lady Audley the spider-woman has broken out of the villa, to wreak havoc on the elite.

A woman with no intelligible history, like the suburban houses that conceal so many of her secrets, Lady Audley spins web after web to lure a wealthy man into her net, selling him, in the old phrase, a "bill of goods"—no mustard or green parrot here, but faked virginity—in order to secure title, social position, home. She is a precursor to Dracula in the way she employs the transportation and informational networks to serve her purposes, one step ahead of Robert Audley for most of the text. She works to exploit the possibilities of modernity for her own purposes, including the unreadability of the suburbs to those unfamiliar with their layouts, practices, and communities—her first attempt to evade exposure involves faking a telegram from an obscure suburbanite in Crescent Villas, West Brompton. When Robert journeys to West Brompton to uncover the history of his beautiful step-aunt, he finds, not the woman he seeks (indeed, she is as difficult to track down as Lady Audley no doubt guessed), but an architecture with façades that disturbingly remind him of Lady Audley. Driving through an unfamiliar wasteland, he feels "frowned" upon by chimney pots that sit atop "virgin plaster, undimmed by time or smoke." Too new, too clean, the strange whiteness of the plaster is soon echoed in Robert's musing on the curious whiteness of Lady Audley's skin: "He thought of . . . the soft, white hands tending on [Sir Michael's] waking moments. . . . What a pleasant picture it might have been, had he been able to look upon it ignorantly, seeing no more than others saw, looking no further than a stranger could look. But with the black cloud which he saw brooding over it, what an arch mockery, what a diabolical delusion it seemed."[51] The image of the white hand with a black cloud "brooding" over it, albeit undetectable by the ordinary or naked eye, echoes the plaster that has strangely not taken on the "frowning" effects of smoke.

A generation that knew to pour scorn on the "desirable suburban residences" advertised in the pages of the *Times* knew to expect dark truths from a woman who was both product and embodiment of the suburbs. *Lady Audley's Secret* stages and exploits an era's anxieties about suburbia, enacting through the young woman's relationships with Sir Michael and the Audley family the suburb's powerful deployment of the forces of modernity against the countryside, against the old ways of life, against the old ways of distributing cultural capital and securing social advancement. The only known history Helen Talboys/Lady Audley possesses is as a governess—a respectable enough position, if socially liminal: Robert Audley's attempts to uncover the truth about her and fit her back into the old class system from which she sprang soon take him into the darkest corners of the newest and most horrific suburbs. Scenes of entering West Brompton, then Peckham, take us behind Lady Audley's closed doors far more effectively than the moment of seeing her Pre-Raphaelite portrait (which is little more than exposure to another façade—Lady Audley as Gothic Revivalist projection).[52] When Robert arrives in West Brompton to interview the former schoolteacher who supposedly sent Lady Audley the telegram, he discovers a wasteland verging on a slum. Homes are hard to distinguish from construction: "The houses were large, but they lay half embedded amongst the chaos of brick and mortar rising around them. New terraces, new streets, new squares led away into hopeless masses of stone and plaster on every side." This is the suburban world of Tinsley Crescent, not Camberwell, and it forms an immediate contrast to the charms of long-established Audley Court, to which Robert was drawn in the early pages of the novel, "rich with fine old timber and luxuriant pastures." The adjective "old" is repeated dozens of times in the first description of Sir Michael's home, in stark contrast to the "new terraces, new streets, new squares" of West Brompton. Audley Court is a home "as was not elsewhere to be met with throughout the county of Essex": Essex was the home of Elbowsout, but Audley Court, surrounded by ancient trees, built over generations, is a home Elbowsout can never hope to build.[53] It seems established in the first pages of the novel as a paradigm of exactly what must be preserved in the war of modernity against tradition. West Brompton, by contrast, is a terrible, labyrinthine embodiment of Lady Audley, a canvas that reveals the "truth" of her character as painfully as Dorian Gray's picture later reveals his soul.

Yet while Audley Court is beautiful, filled with rich objects, glowing with the patina of old age, Braddon's text soon problematizes its apparent championing of past over present, "old" elites over the "new" middle class. Braddon's representation of time is quirky from the first: the "stupid, bewildering clock" in Audley Court does not work properly, for instance, while Time itself is figured as a quixotic architect. The great house, the narrator says, seems almost to have been built by "Time, who, adding a room one year, and knocking down a room another year, toppling over now a chimney coeval with the Plantagenets, and setting up one in the style of the Tudors; shaking down a bit of Saxon wall there, and allowing a Norman arch to stand here; throwing in a row of high narrow windows in the reign of Queen Anne, and joining on a dining-room after the fashion of the time of Hanoverian George I to a refectory that had been standing since the Conquest, had contrived, in some eleven centuries, to run up such a mansion."[54]

The novel is full of knowing references to the Pre-Raphaelite Brotherhood and the medievalist revival movement; Braddon surely knew Pugin's views. The architect argued in *The Present State of Ecclesiastical Architecture in England* that "architecture to be good must be consistent," and he disgustedly termed the blending of styles by his contemporaries "carnival architecture."[55] Yet here Braddon points out that stylistic purity is impossible in buildings that exist through time; no architect can control the aesthetic of a house that, standing in the world, must be shaped by age, fire, catastrophe, market, human caprice. For Pugin, stylistic consistency is at the heart of value: what, then, is the value of jumbled Audley Court? And if stylistic consistency is a practical impossibility in the real world, does it really matter if Time or a speculative builder brings styles together and makes them coexist? From its earliest pages the text allows for counterinterpretations of Audley Court, ones that disturb the hierarchy between the suburbs and great houses, between tradition and modernity, the old and the new. Again and again, parallels are slyly drawn between the Court and even the most terrible suburbs: both are places in which the stranger will get lost. The Court is a maze, "in which you incontinently lost yourself if ever you were so rash as to go about it alone"; Robert gets lost, for a full hour and a quarter, when he and a cabman hunt for number 9, Crescent Villas, in the "hopeless masses of stone and plaster" of West Brompton.[56]

Moreover, Mrs. Vincent, Robert's prey, is no Mrs. Copperas, even though the scene seems set for her to lure, spider-like, and lie. She is certainly trailed by a web of debt. But when Robert finds the middle-aged woman, in an even more run-down suburban home in Peckham, the narrative does not follow the Bulwer-Lytton model—the text detours dramatically, as Mrs. Vincent's existence at the very bottom of the social scale inspires not distaste but a terrible sympathy. "The drive from Brompton to the Peckham Road was a very long one," the narrator notes, and it is a journey down the social scale, a descent into lower and lower kinds of suburban hell: "The spare parlor into which Robert was ushered bore in every scrap of ornament, in every article of furniture, the unmistakeable stamp of that species of poverty which is most comfortless, because it is never stationary. . . . [T]he lady who loses the handsome furniture of the house she is compelled to abandon and encamps in some smaller habitation with the shabby remainder—bought in by some merciful friend at the sale of her effects—carries with her an aspect of genteel desolation and tawdry misery not easily to be paralleled in wretchedness by any other phase which poverty can assume."[57] It is the details we notice in this passage, the painful specificity; the friend who rescues some personal effects from the wreck, for instance, then passes them on, and the incongruous coexistence of fine and large objects with newer, meaner purchases. Braddon, who experienced calamitous social decline in her own life, turns a knowing eye to every detail of the Vincent sitting room; she was later to remember how, after her family broke apart, their first piano "dropped into the great gulf that [swallowed] our past years," how the whole home "collapsed suddenly in a house-quake that swallowed the nice new furniture and all Mamma's wedding-presents, silver, jewellery, china, everything except a set of Byron's poems."[58] The "quake" and "gulf" of economic loss is evoked as a catastrophe out of which a few remaining domestic objects are fragments shored against a ruin. The sitting room is read sympathetically, not as evidence of shallow pretensions to gentility, but rather for its "desolation" and "misery."

The ridiculousness of bourgeois taste is certainly sketched, most obviously in the "knitted curtains" that shade not only windows but also "wire baskets of horrible-looking plants of the cactus species, that grew downwards like some demented class of vegetation, whose prickly and spider-like members had a fancy for standing on their heads."[59] Like the green parrot of Bulwer-Lytton's novels, the out-of-place cacti are clear signals of suburbanism, in that they are exotics imported by means of a global trade network for the consumption of those swayed by advertising and dado-istic fads. Yet the cactus serves to underscore here not so much the spending power but the out-of-place character of the resident. Prickly, struggling to appear polite, Mrs. Vincent metaphorically stands on her head to appear charming and winning while pathetically navigating what she dimly sees is Robert Audley's covert agenda; he has all the power in the conversation. Her lies are very different from those of Mrs. Copperas, for her deceptions are not attempts to prise money out of Robert but rather efforts to maintain her own sense of self-worth and cling to an illusion of social place, so that she is kin to the sympathetic Trevornocks. Rather than deploying, say, Ruskinian criticisms of the mobile suburbanite who seeks to conceal the past, Braddon focuses on wringing every ounce of pathos from the situation. The schoolteacher appears but briefly in the novel, for Mrs. Vincent's colleague, Miss Tonks, is the one who eagerly gives Audley the information he seeks, and he soon departs. But the appearance of Mrs. Vincent serves an important purpose, for it is her life, after all, her lot, that Lady Audley has struggled so desperately to avoid. Deserted by her husband, the woman who was Helen Graham (later Talboys) became the bigamous spouse of Sir Michael Audley to avoid just this scene of poverty. Helen is left by her husband, she later tells Robert Audley, "with no protector . . . and with a child to support. I had," she says, "to work hard for my living, and in every hour of labour—and what labour is more wearisome than the dull slavery of a governess?"[60] Unwilling to end up like the schoolteacher Mrs. Vincent, Helen jumps at a chance of a union that rescues her from Peckham. Besides, what she has chosen is only what her culture values: who could ask a girl to choose life with an upside-down cactus when she could have green lawns and old timber?

Generations of readers have felt sympathy for Lady Audley, and generations of scholars have debated whether Braddon meant us to feel this sympathy or not. At times she is associated implicitly with the domestic tragedy of Mrs. Vincent. But at other times we see her as a woman who kills, rages, and exploits with little compunction. Still, few readers will fail to notice—especially the ones aware of Braddon's own history—that the decision by Lady Audley to leave her child and embark on a new life is preceded by her husband's cavalier abandonment of both. George Talboys leaves his wife and baby in the middle of the night, while they are sleeping, to board a ship bound for Australia to make a fortune; fidgety, moody, restless, a lover of card games and smoking, Talboys is seen first in the novel's second chapter "lazily" surveying his cigar case as a break from the hard business of apostrophizing the waves—"blue, and green, and opal; opal, and blue, and green; all very well in their way of course, but three months of them are rather too much."[61] The characterization of this extraordinarily inane man seems to borrow heavily from Henry Braddon, whom his daughter later remembered for his banal conversation, idleness, and devotion to activities like nail trimming. Moreover, we have only met George for a few paragraphs when we learn that another passenger on the same boat is a man who also made his fortune in the colonies but took his wife and children with him. Offering little explicit comment on George, his character, and his decisions, the text gives readers numerous opportunities to question its apparent narrative support of this particular absent father—at least, until he repents of his ways.

Helen Audley dies, alone and friendless. Yet while her practices are certainly wrong, what she wants fits her squarely into the grooves of an emerging middle-class culture that refused to regard birth networks as closed circuits. This is the world that reigns at the end of *Lady Audley's Secret*—not the downwardly mobile world of Mrs. Vincent, certainly, nor the horrifying squalor of Brigsome's Terrace, but the world of the suburbs, not the country house, all the same. The final chapter shows Robert Audley, now a successful barrister, "a rising man upon the home circuit," with his wife, Clara, living in what Braddon calls "a fairy cottage . . . between Teddington Locks and Hampton Bridge . . . a fantastical dwelling-place of rustic woodwork, whose latticed windows look out upon the river."[62] Aeron Haynie reads this as a "retreat" from the familiar world of the landed estate (Audley Court) into a "remote and unrealistic vision of rural, preindustrial England," focusing, perhaps, on the words "fairy," "fantastical." But this is to misunderstand the scene and its language, for Braddon evokes an entirely familiar suburban architecture at the top of the middle-class social scale. A few miles from Richmond, carefully sited—"between Teddington Locks and Hampton Bridge"—the home displays the kind of suburban whimsy that, certainly, many observers and architects despised. The rustic "cottage" is architecturally varied, equipped with "a little Swiss boat-house" that contains "a pretty rustic smoking room" (recall the designs in *The Builder's Practical Director*); this is the dream of *rus in urbe* in mid-Victorian form.[63] Pugin raged against his peers, in *An Apology for the Revival of Christian Architecture,* for what he considered a bizarre modern willingness to mix styles: "Does locality, destination, or character of building, form the basis of a design? no; surely not." His self-published treatise *Contrasts* laid down the gauntlet for the "cottages" and villas springing up across the country by critiquing buildings whose styles were uncoupled from location: "We have Swiss cottages in a flat country; Italian villas in the coldest situations; a Turkish kremlin for a royal residence; Green temples in crowded lanes; Egyptian auction rooms; and all kinds of absurdities and incongruities."[64] The Teddington cottage is the kind of suburbanite cottage Pugin loathed, a kind still decried in the press decades after his ideas were first published. Yet it is here that we find tumbling children and domestic bliss in Braddon's work, characters eating strawberries and cream in summer evenings on smooth lawns beside the Thames—*et in suburbia ego.* "A villa in Teddington, just above the lock," is also the second home of the newly married Flora and her doctor husband, Cuthbert, in *Lost for Love*, a "remote and sacred domicile" accessed by "a pleasant drive along suburban roads, where the roses and seringa [*sic*] were abloom in neat villa gardens"; the house itself has—again—"a landing-stage and a boathouse."[65] The "fantastical" Teddington house suits the curious mismatch of people who inhabit it and represents, in its very stylistic disconnectedness, the mobility of a new suburban population that, heterogeneous itself, chose a heterogeneous architectural form—as if to express itself visually. Meanwhile Audley Court is shut up and moldering, so that if the 1862 novel explores through Lady Audley a battle between old English house and new suburb, the suburb wins. The world of West Brompton and Peckham, edging into slums, is one that any suburbanite will leave if she can. Braddon left Camberwell for Richmond, and in similar fashion her worthy fictional characters find purposeful days and peaceful evenings on the Thames.

A PEAR TREE IN CAMBERWELL

If the suburban resident is hard-working, single-minded, devoted to the tasks of cleaning and home improvement, and morally conscious, her life will progress, her choices broaden. This is not to say that her journey will be easy, for no modern suburb is Paradise. Braddon incarnates the challenges of suburban life and labor in the image of a gnarled pear tree in many of her novels, an intriguing metaphor that suggests the drive to generate new associative connections for the suburbs, new images to replace green parrots, ring-tailed monkeys, and cacti as signals of suburbanism. Braddon's fiction of suburbia is full of references to Eden, Arcadia, and Paradise, and to the gaining of painful knowledge. When the now-married but still-oblivious Isabel comes to realize that Raymond Landsdell sees their future relationship as more than one of peaceful literary conversation, for instance, she is disturbed: "She had tasted, if ever so little, of the fruit of the famous tree, and she found the flavour thereof very bitter."[66] But while the image of a pear tree seems at first simply to ground the idea that suburbia is no Eden, it has other, more particular meanings also. The pear tree is a signal of the suburb's agricultural past, but it also stands in for what Camberwell offers new residents. Those who grasp at the meaning of the pear tree, those who pursue a vocation for social renewal, will thrive. Those who don't, fail. Appreciation of the pear tree is an invaluable index to character; the tree helps point out, through its very adaptiveness, its ability to thrive, what the best suburbanites embody.

Barbara does not talk about the tree in *The Story of Barbara,* but she chooses to walk beneath it as she thinks about her life (a practice that distinguishes her from the unthinking Isabel, who only reads under it). The pear tree bears little fruit—its "fruit was of small account"; it can only be appreciated, in other words, by one who does not highly value consumption. This is true of the long-suffering Trevornock women, who survive on little and have to bring in a boarder (as the Braddons did) to make ends meet. In a later scene, as Barbara sits on a wicker chair beneath the same pear tree, the narrator observes that the Trevornocks "had pinched and scraped, and been infinitely happy in doing without things." They are not "shabbily clad"—the girls live "hand to mouth," but they are sent cast-offs by a wealthier relative, which allows them to combine deprivation with a show of beauty, to produce the "general effect" of ease. The pear tree figures their life's struggle, in that it is a visual manifestation of making do. Showing signs of wear and hardship—"he" is "very much aslant in his trunk, as if he had outgrown his strength and gone crooked"—the tree nonetheless puts on a good show each year: he is "magnificent as to his foliage."[67] Like the vine clambering over the Sleaford home, the pear tree's leaves beautify the suburban hardship beneath it. Plants and the women who clean away the smuts of smoke work together to soften and conceal the harsher effects of modernity.

But the pear tree is more than a beautifier, it is a choice, and the elucidation of that choice in Braddon's fiction throws light on the meaning of Isabel's unconsciousness. In *Lost for Love,* two girls—who turn out to be first cousins—are raised in different circumstances but fall in love with the same painter. After pages of tragedy and confusion, when the poorer girl's father, Jarred Gurner, resolves to change his ways and give up a life of trickery and deceit (apart from blackmailing a man he believes, erroneously, he has killed, Jarred earns his living fixing and faking art and musical instruments), he decides on a move to Camberwell, an area he loved as a young man, to start life again. The pear tree decides the choice of house: his appreciation of the pear marks the seriousness of his change.

Jarred finds a "softer feeling full upon him" as he walks the streets of his old haunt. Happening on a "queer little lop-sided house, with a weedy neglected garden backing on to a canal," he discovers that "in the middle of the rank grass-plat there stood a fine old pear-tree—a tree that must have been planted a century ago, when Camberwell was among the most rustic of suburban villages—a tree with a thick rugged trunk and spreading branches, which in this autumnal season bore actual pears." The cottage seems to be the same house the Sleafords rented—with (of course) a larger garden than most available in Camberwell. Jarred is able to take it rent-free for the first quarter because of all the deferred maintenance and repair it requires. He likes the locale, barely notices the rooms, is tranquil about the weedy garden and smoky chimney. But he loves the pear tree—is positively "fascinated" by it and what it represents. As in the Trevornock garden, the fruit of the tree is unappealing (indeed, the narrator of *Lost for Love* notes frankly that the pears have "the flavor of turnips and the consistence of wood"). It is not the taste of the fruit that Jarred admires but what the tree represents, a meaning developed in relation to the pear's opposite—Dead Sea fruit, the ashy-tasting Apple of Sodom that Satan eats in *Paradise Lost* after tempting Adam and Eve to eat the fruit of the Tree of the Knowledge of Good and Evil. (Braddon's late-in-life account of her early years was called, significantly enough, *Before the Knowledge of Evil.*) Braddon indicates in *Lost for Love* that Dead Sea fruit means the drive for consumption, for worldly gain, which has tempted Jarred to outright trickery in the past but has not brought him happiness: "He had tasted too much of the dust and ashes that constitute the core of life's Dead-Sea fruit."[68] Here, Jarred's choice of the gnarled pear seems to represent the willingness to struggle over easy wins and duplicity, self-discipline over the drive for consumables and cash.

The novel *Dead-Sea Fruit,* serialized in *Belgravia* in 1867 and published in 1868, helps shake out a little more meaning, for in it worldly temptations derail and disrupt family relationships. The middle-aged Henry Jerningham is forced to see, years after the fact, the full implications, the profound wrong, of his early abandonment of a young wife and child. Even after Jerningham is reconciled with his son Eustace, the narrator remarks: "There is always the bitter taste of the ashes which remain for the man who has plucked the Dead-Sea apples that hang ripe and red above the path of life."[69] Both scenes, both references to Dead Sea fruit, concern erring fathers and suffering children; when Jarred chooses Camberwell and the pear tree, he is making the decision that Jerningham struggled to make, the decision to center his life on family relationships—in particular, to set a high value on his children. Braddon, abandoned by her own father, later remembered him as a thoughtless gentleman in "spotless linen, who took snuff out of a silver box, and who was associated with brown paper bags of winter fruit, which he would seem to have carried from Covent Garden."[70] Bitter memories of early years with a wastrel father who was "nobody's enemy but his own," carrying bags of expensive winter fruit that would set his wife and children on a path to impoverishment, and partial boarders, and making do, and hand-me-down clothes in Camberwell, may explain why the gnarled but indomitable pear tree gained such force in her later fiction as an incarnation of a very different set of well-rooted choices.

The pear tree rewards diligence and duty, love, self-discipline, and moral, ethical behavior by offering earned ease: "[Jarred] had pleasant ideas of long lazy Sabbath mornings, seated in a beehive chair under that tree, smoking the pipe of contentment, and listening to the church-bells as they called less independent-minded citizens to morning service. He liked the notion of Malvina Cottage, that domicile being in a peculiarly retired corner—a narrow little bit of lane between a church and a canal, which led nowhere. He felt that he could live his own life there."[71] Jarred is no ideal, and his unwillingness to enter a church is referenced wryly, but still his change of heart is delivered with pathos and narrative sympathy. The reason he can choose a life of Camberwellian quiet is not only because (unlike Isabel) he is a man but also because—unlike Henry Braddon—he begins, at last, to see the importance of living as a responsible, other-regarding worker. Turning from a life of exploitation of others, Jarred chooses a path of caring for others, a life in which Sunday indolence is earned by weekday work. Braddon recalled her own father, a solicitor, as a man who would not work, who tricked his wife into marriage with claims of a fortune he did not possess, and squandered what small income they drew in; Jarred, by contrast, assures his daughter: "I mean to reform . . . altogether in the future, Loo, and to live quietly in my retired little box, and restore pictures and manipulate violins, and earn my living like a man."[72] Jarred's speech in *Lost for Love* reads painfully like a daughter's fantasy of what an erring father might say, a storybook repenting of the ways. If Camberwell tests and reveals a woman's value, it also lingers as a potential Eden for a man ready to change, ready to become altruistic, to put his selfish needs aside.

WORKING SUBURBANS

Braddon's working characters are, for the most part, male. Jarred Gurner and Robert Audley are socially miles apart, of course, but both come to find satisfaction in a balance of daytime labor and evening/weekend leisure in the garden, a balance both feel the suburbs facilitate. The Trevornocks verge into professional action, advertising and renting out their home, but *The Story of Barbara* covers mostly the romance lives of its heroines. In the later years of her life, Braddon represents a few women taking actual professional positions in plots where, again, the suburbs play a critical part. As in Braddon's earlier texts, common suburban experiences generate plots in which characters find new lives, new connections, new roles, not as lawyers or doctors or architects, but as the kinds of professionals Braddon knew best.

After a career spent contrasting once-rural suburbs—Richmond, 1850s Camberwell—with the horrors of lower-class West Brompton and "Tilbury Crescent," Braddon gives the more urban Battersea positive treatment in *A Lost Eden.* The novel follows a familiar pattern—departure from Camberwell, precipitated by family tragedy, opens into new lives—but much of the middle of the novel detours to examine the life of the younger heroine, as an actress. Braddon originally intended to call the novel, according to her biographer, *The Suburbans;* if she had, it might more quickly have been viewed as a counter-narrative to another text of the same name published a year later, by T. W. H. Crosland. Certainly, *A Lost Eden* is every bit as deeply engaged in the suburbs and in suburban character traits as Crosland's sneering account. But in Braddon's work, suburbanites are not an undifferentiated mass of social failures, snobs and idiots but rather fall along a spectrum that encompasses struggling and admirable (if downwardly mobile) families to earthy, determined, diligent theatrical professionals.

A Lost Eden draws on familiar suburban plot threads but follows them to quite different ends, focusing less on suburban failures and more on successes.

In the early pages, a handsome titled artist sees a beautiful girl on an omnibus and follows her to Camberwell; so far, the novel recalls Collins's *Basil.* But the girl in question is no spider-woman. Marion Sandford is a member of a straitened family forced to move from Russell Square to Camberwell because of her father's unfortunate financial speculations. Threat is posed, not by the girl to the stranger, but by the stranger to the girl and her family; Edward Vernham (who, like Captain Leland, discerns the moral as well as the aesthetic value of the Sandfords' shabby furnishings, the meaning of a lack of "vulgar ornaments"), earns her trust, then asks her to become his mistress.[73] When Marion turns him down to accept an offer of marriage, Vernham abducts her, keeping her prisoner until she is able to make a daring escape.

Vernham knows the stereotypes of suburbia—the weakling clerk, for instance, pathetic and shabby. Crosland sneers: "It has been said by a more or less keen observer that suburban men are all clerks"; while this may not be exactly true, he concedes, the suburbs are dominated by low-ranking professionals, he assures readers, and "what a grubby, limited, old, unhappy, underbred crowd they are!"[74] Vernham is obviously of the same opinion: he pursues Marion partly because he thinks a suburban father will be too weak to withstand him. He is wrong. "The man Sandford had surprised him. He had expected to see a weakling, a shrunken threadbare atomy, like the shabbiest of the clerks in the Camberwell omnibus," the narrator observes, but Mr. Sandford was a man of old-world morals, "a magnificent wreck, a massive figure considerably above six feet," with "eyes that scrutinized him severely with a something of anger and distrust."[75] Though suburban stereotypes certainly flutter on the periphery of the Sandfords' social circle, fussing about nothing and boring their friends, Braddon's heroes and heroines are different, and the author endows them with moral stature and perception. The novel's plot leads the upper-class hero (at least, he appears a hero at first) to discover that he is ill-equipped to understand the depth and moral seriousness of the suburbs.

The best characters in *A Lost Eden* enjoy work, but they do it to help others, not just themselves. (Vernham, an artist, pursues his profession for all the wrong reasons, offering readers a cautionary alternative; his near obsession with discovering "abstract beauty, a light, a flame, to give life" to a new picture hints at a dangerous allegiance to Walter Pater's "Conclusion" to *The Renaissance* and nods at Basil Hallward in *Dorian Gray.*) Marion is working as a governess, and early in the novel she assures Vernham that she prefers this life to her former central London existence as a leisured lady: "If you knew how tired I was of that monotonous idleness, and the perpetual worry about trivial things. It has been my delight to work for my bread." Braddon hints that the claim of suburban monotony, made by the upper classes, is a case of the pot calling the kettle black, for what could be duller than a life with nothing to do? Later in the novel, when the family's fortunes sink even lower, Flora, the younger sister, takes a step further into professional life, announcing: "I am no longer going to eat the bread of idleness." Flora stoutly terms her sister "a lump of prejudice" for worrying about the dangers of the theatrical profession. After all, the choice, given their circumstances, is simple: "It lies between burying one's self alive or having a career." Flora's experiences as an actress, which draw heavily on Braddon's own, certainly involve knowing people who use slang, women who speak "with a mannish off-hand air," but in the theater, just as in the suburbs, there is variety, not to mention increased freedom. Flora loves the employment, passionately: "She was a working bee in the theatrical hive; and she had already begun to talk about *the* profession, as if there were no other, which is the distinguishing mark of an actress. She had attained the desire of her heart, and she was radiantly happy."[76] Besides, life off the stage proves more dangerous than life on it; Vernham is far more threatening to Marion than the actors are to her young sister.

Flora's engagement to Jim Rodney, a hopeful playwright, brings the young girl down the social scale, to Battersea, and to nightly rambles around the city and on omnibuses with her beloved. Marion's plot brings the heroine to Richmond, and, in this novel, the less affluent Battersea is the far safer place. Battersea, to the south of the Thames, grew rapidly at the end of the century, from a population of some 19,600 in 1861 to 107,000 by 1881, with multiple rail lines after 1838 spurring industrial growth while facilitating connections between suburb and center.[77] The Rodney family's ways, manners, and speech are never quite readable by Flora: their home is small and cramped, their streets noisy, their conversation filled with slang. Baffled in their world, she reminds us of Robert Audley, lost in the West Brompton streets. Still, while she never fully understands the Battersea family of her beloved, she comes to appreciate what its community offers and throws her lot in with it, energetically and joyfully, in the end.

Flora goes to Battersea with stereotyped expectations in place—not of a semidetached neighbor, as in Emily Eden's novel, but of a mother-in-law. Approaching the matriarch, she anticipates a character from a William Powell Frith canvas, or perhaps a grown-up Jane Eyre: "a domestic heroine, in a black silk gown and neatly braided hair; a person of supreme dignity." What she finds is quite different: "rosy and jovial," the woman's clothes are dirty and tumbled, with cap askew. Meanwhile the brothers and sisters of Flora's beloved Jim follow no system of manners or conversation that Flora can understand: "It could hardly be said that her lover's brothers and sisters were introduced to her. She gradually became aware of them, of their names and occupations." The lower-scale suburban interior is evoked with photographic detail, from the "trunks and wicker baskets all along one side of the room" and the "rickety pillar of band-boxes in a corner" to the "canes and parasols and swords in baize boxes," the "collection of cane-bottomed chairs of various patterns" set on thinning carpets. But the reader is led to conclude, with Flora, that the family's kindness is sincere, that its members love one another, that they make do; their unapologetic deviation from the ideal of gentility matters little, in the final accounting. Jim's younger sister, known as the Flower, is a particularly lusty and strong-minded character, who rattles her stick along the iron railings of all the nearby gardens as if hoping to raise Eden's Blanche Chester from the dead. The novel evinces startled admiration for such hardy creatures as the Flower, girls who have "thriven under suburban skies, and in the neighborhood of a candle factory." Those lower-class suburban skies and factories (most likely Price's Candles on Battersea's York Road) and the homes beneath them no more live up to bourgeois standards than their occupants—Flo sees, on the south side of Battersea Bridge, "a terrace of shabby houses, with skimped front gardens, mostly flowerless; then a house standing in a pleasance such as auctioneers call 'grounds;' then a pair of semi-detached hovels, yclept 'villas.' "[78] The old complaints about false promises linger. But life among such homes is redeemed, even rendered blissful, for those who see the problems of the world as a reason to work to alleviate them, whether as home managers, cleaners, or professional wage earners.[79] The idealism of the text sweeps up women who self-sacrifice in the service of their families and girls who work for a living: both, in their service to others, their self-discipline, are rendered worthy of joy. As Jim says, Flora's "happy in the present; and so am I. When we walk across Battersea Fields together, or sit side by side on the twopenny steamer in the sunshine, I don't believe there are two happier souls on earth."[80] Braddon's fiction suggests here and elsewhere that new professionals can thrive in suburban homes precisely because such houses offer daily checks on human selfishness. In this way, the novels help work out how professional labor is consistent with moral imperative.

The problems of the suburbs, a point so belabored in the press, reiterated by Braddon's fictional characters, require labor on the part of a heroine to fix them, just as they do in interior design and gardening texts. Sympathetic heroines rise to the task. To introduce a suburb into a romance novel is to introduce a heroine who, if she possesses authorial support, will be determined to improve it. Women who contribute to the suburb's problems, like Isabel Sleaford and Lady Audley, are critiqued; women who respond with diligence and determination, like the Trevornocks and Flo, move on and up—though still to marriage, in Braddon's literature at least. *A Lost Eden*'s Flora gives up her stage career finally, "to please Jim," so that the romance plot wins out at the end.[81] It is axiomatic in Braddon's novels that the real reward for suburban energy is, finally, a better home, not professional advance—at least not yet, not for most women. Jim becomes a successful playwright, building his career around the play that advises, in strikingly imperative form, *Go to Putney.*

SUBURBAN PLOTS AND LOOSE ENDINGS

Braddon's fiction engages the suburban plot arc, first discussed in chapter 3, where strangers meet in and around the suburban house, as boarders, housekeepers, landladies, tenants; such meetings connect characters with new possibilities, new adventures, new life courses. Yet while Braddon's fictions certainly show the suburban landscape as a place of journeying and adventure, the novels' conclusions continue to present the world of the suburbs as a space of domesticity, centered on marriage and wifely submission, rather as in *A Semi-Detached House* or *Great Grenfell Gardens.* In *A Lost Eden,* the meeting of strangers facilitated by suburban lettings and boardings generates a startlingly mobile life—we follow Flora on rambles around the streets of London, on buses, over bridges, to the provinces, and finally across the threshold of the professions. Still, marriage and professional life for a woman remain apparently inconsistent; in Braddon's fiction and elsewhere, suburban adventures facilitate romances that, in the end, bring about a heroine's socially advantageous union with a kindly, self-consciously superior man, who articulates his role as protector and wage earner. If the door of the villa opens at the start of such texts, it seems to close again at the end.

There are numerous examples of this pattern in Braddon's oeuvre, where the suburbs act as a portal into unexpected adventures that ultimately help the heroine fulfill a traditional wifely role. Braddon's horror story "Good Lady Ducayne" (1896) offers just one example. Bella Rolleston, a young impoverished middle-class girl living just off the Walworth Road, is introduced to the aristocratic but declining Lady Ducayne, who offers her the thrilling position of companion in Italy. Life abroad is exciting but dangerous; Lady

Ducayne drugs Bella and drains her blood in secret transfusions in a desperate effort to win herself "a few more years above ground." Bella was employed by Lady Ducayne because she seemed full of an energy and health that Lady Ducayne coveted: that health is built, the heroine comes to realize, on the rhythms of suburban existence, on "[trudging] to the West-end to buy half a pound of tea—just for a constitutional walk—or to Dulwich to look at the pictures."[82] The story's violence seems at first blush to suggest that access to strangers and adventures has led Bella astray—better to have stayed at home—but, by the end, Lady Ducayne is compelled to write the heroine a check for one thousand pounds to avoid exposure; with this nest egg Bella is able to marry a doctor and return to the Walworth Road, a subservient wife, but enriched.

Like so many other Braddon stories, "Good Lady Ducayne" suggests that the charm of suburbia is partly that it allows girls to find better husbands, that the lifestyle of train journeys and peripatetic ramblings allows middle-class girls to subvert the limitations of social class by giving them access to men outside their birth networks. Barbara's sister observes, in *The Story of Barbara,* that "a portionless girl with a pretty face is like a flower in a cottage-garden—she may bud and blossom, and fade and wither, and the world may know nothing of her existence."[83] A suburb is no cottage garden: Camberwell offers the portionless access to the world. The smoke and new houses and boarding advertisements and trains herald changes that alter the course of a girl's life, including meetings the women could never, in the cottage-garden way of life, encounter.[84]

And so the suburban adventure drives back toward marriage, in Braddon's fiction at least. Still, those marriages incarnate something of a challenge to an older social and class power structure nonetheless; Braddon only tentatively advocates women's professional life, but she exhibits clear support for the dismantling of traditional social hierarchies. Marriage is, in Braddon's work, a woman's first profession. But if women are to pursue it, Braddon tacitly suggests, they need more and better opportunities to pursue promotion and human flourishing. How are they to manage this, if they live confined in villages or country cottages? The suburbs offer girls expanded social networks, Braddon's fictions providing young women access to mobility (and more sympathetic men) through chance meetings with alien arrivals, much as professional life offers men, like Jim, a different, more structured means of social climbing. The suburbs' bringing together of disparate peoples in similar houses, with shared floorplans, further offers women access to a level playing field (so to speak) on which to display their worth in a way they could never hope for in the cottage-garden way of life: affluent girls and impoverished girls appear, to their swains, more or less the same. Suburban marriages are rewards for virtue, in the best tradition of the marriage plot, but they are also mechanisms for advance as well as offering satisfying relationships with emotional equals drawn from a more diverse pool. Companionate marriages fill the final pages of Braddon's texts. Those marriages are not only enjoyed by suburbanites, needless to say, but marriages into the elite and marriages of suburban residents are represented *side by side.* Braddon's following of suburban characters into successful marriages is clearly meant to dignify them, in novels like *A Lost Eden,* just as Crosland's *The Suburbans* works to set them at low price.

Braddon deploys the traditional arc of the marriage plot with considerable self-consciousness: this only makes her suburban narratives all the more interesting. There are other revisions too, to the romance paradigms on which she draws, which suggests that Braddon was working actively to address, in plot form, the shaping of women's life course and the norms that underpin its traditional arc. The dominant plot of *A Lost Eden* follows a young woman named Marion whose virtue is unassailable, and who is ultimately rewarded for her staunch adherence to moral precepts with a rich, virtuous, loving husband (in our final view of Marion, she is "wrapped in sumptuous furs"). Braddon draws, in other words, on a romance plot where love plus great feminine virtue equals class and economic advancement. As if to point out the very familiarity of the story, the narrator makes frequent references to *Jane Eyre,* describing it as another tale of "a man who tried to win his love by a fraud" and of a woman who, "alone and friendless . . . had yet been strong enough to resist her lover's pleading" and who is rewarded in the end. But Braddon revises the conclusion. The sin the text most reviles is not the sin of desiring a woman outside marriage but the fact that Vernham risks nothing for the woman he wants to make his mistress: "She had never been able to consider Rochester's sins with the severity which she knew they merited . . . Rochester would have risked assizes and the jail. Vernham would sacrifice nothing of his worldly welfare."[85]

Rochester is punished for attempting bigamy and extramarital sex with temporary blindness and injury. The aristocratic Vernham is destroyed, as Braddon makes clear in one brief, bleak final paragraph. He has already been punished by a failed artistic career—his wife looks on him, he reports in a letter to Marion, with pain, "only as an amateur." In the novel's last lines, we learn that, before a premature death, he suffered early dementia: "He was a good husband, and a model landlord, and always voted on the right side. He hunted a great deal, and shot a great deal, and kept racehorses, and wore himself out in rural sports and pleasures. He died in his fortieth year, after more than a year of living death, the death of a worn-out brain. For his wife, who fondly loved him, it was agonizing to see him playing with his dead brother's cup and ball, smiling, and apparently happy."[86] The heroines are happily married, rewarded, affluent; there is no need to linger on the now-peripheral Vernham (the paragraph was cut in an abridged version of the novel—whether by Braddon or an uncomprehending editor, we can't know). Yet in this late novel, as so often, Braddon lingers at the end on a scene of elite decline or collapse. Vernham, Audley Court, Lady Ducayne all die, sicken, or are abandoned, while the middle class is healthy, strong, married. The suburbs are far from utopian, but their networks facilitate change and opportunity, their challenges test and strengthen the middle classes who live in them. The suburban way of life makes people happier in Braddon's fiction, stronger, healthier, and more emotionally fulfilled.

CONCLUSIONS

The very existence of suburban problems gives women their vocation in Braddon's work, rather as in the design advice texts examined in chapters 4 and 5. Worthy heroines grasp that the world around them needs fixing, turn their sights toward the realm of business, and, in the process, begin tentatively to explore how and in what ways professional challenges can be managed. One does not reach Richmond overnight; the journey to the south bank of the Thames is a long one, fraught with difficulty and struggle. But it is an attainable dream for a woman with the appropriate self-discipline, the necessary moral character.

So why, then, did Braddon regularly excoriate the suburbs? Why would a writer who represented Camberwell, Richmond, Teddington, and Battersea as places of human flourishing so routinely pick up the old threads of dullness, tastelessness, and vulgarity? Throughout this book, we have seen that male and female writers employed stereotypes of the tedious, vulgar, or monstrous suburbs to position themselves and their protagonists as people of taste, incisive interpreters of the modern world at a time when categories of taste and value were in flux. Braddon fits this model. But Braddon also develops a counter discourse, I have suggested, that can be accessed by reference to specific suburban areas, forging new associative connections—for instance, between the suburbs and the gnarled pear tree. She grafts onto older fictional narrative forms, like the marriage plot, the newer suburban plot in ways that dignify suburban experience while rooting it in tradition and the past.

But the old stereotypes of suburban dullness and vulgarity remained. Indeed, on the threshold of the twentieth century, fiery conflicts over the dull suburbs erupted, becoming widely discussed, public spectacles in fiction and nonfiction alike. The complaints about the lower-class suburbs in the work of Gissing and Wells were not isolated, the well-known Charles Pooter and his hapless brother clerks were not, as we've seen, new figures to which the Victorians were just waking up; they evolved from types circulating widely for decades—performed, contested, repudiated, debated, overset. Speaking of suburbia as vulgar and dull was always performative, but by the turn of the century it was an act whose tremendous staginess revealed—like a vast, creaky piece of theatrical machinery—its own artificiality. Suburbanites were often described as good mimics; Bella Rolleston keeps her mother and their landlady in fits of laughter mimicking the people she meets: " 'Dear, dear, what a mimic she is!' said the landlady. 'You ought to have let her go on the stage, mum. She might have made her fortune as a hactress.' "[87] Mimicry and performance were, critics routinely snipped, enshrined suburban cultural practices, as the lower classes mimicked their betters. By the end of the century, speaking of suburbia, performing suburban identity, was rapidly becoming a way to make, if not a "fortune," then at least a thriving career.

In the final chapter, I concentrate on two professional woman writers who reached a wide audience in the same year: 1887. One published a novel about Maida Vale that became infamous; the other published a best-selling book of suburban home decoration. The names of both were, for the rest of their lives, intimately connected with the suburbs, although their performed positions on the suburbs changed and mutated. One critiqued different kinds of suburban practices and peoples under different identities, while the other oscillated between excoriating suburbia and accounting herself its staunchest advocate. Both experimented with genre and form in works that worked to shake loose the suburban from traditional plots. And both put on and took off subject positions with dizzying ease, performing multiple identities in fiction and nonfiction, book-length and periodical prose. Indeed, if suburbia encouraged performance—enacting "the correct thing," as the Trevornocks put it—the two writers taking center stage in my final chapter suggest that such role-playing may itself have helped prepare residents for the demands of late Victorian professional life.

CHAPTER 7

"The Quintessence of the Suburban"

JANE ELLEN PANTON AND JULIA FRANKAU SPEAK OF SUBURBIA

Jane Ellen Panton, introduced in chapter 4, is little known today. Yet she was famous in her lifetime as a spokeswoman for suburbia, an interior designer, novelist, poet, and journalist who not only lived in a variety of suburban locales but also successfully captured the interests of the rising middle-class masses. Her close association with suburbia did not help her reputation in the literary world, needless to say. Panton is the "quintessence of the suburban," the *Saturday Review*'s Frank Danby sneered in February 1897, "read with avidity by the lower middle classes" because she is cut from their cheap cloth. She speaks of trivial domestic life "in the best manner of Peckham Rye," reassuring "the aspiring wife of the City clerk" by sharing "acutely personal" memories to elicit a sense of community—"'Why to be sure, I had the earache myself' . . . rises to the suburban reader's lips." Danby's piece, a review of Panton's latest work on child rearing, *The Way They Should Go,* is a lesson in late Victorian takedowns. Starting with apparent respect, it moves into playful punches of sarcasm and finishes with roaring disdain: "Illiterate in form, incoherent in matter, appalling in its blatant ignorance, who are its readers?" The answer, of course, is suburbanites, from the lower end of the scale to the haut bourgeois: Danby sets "the intellectual stagnation of Clapham and Brixton, Hampstead and Highgate, Southgate and Winchmore Hill" at Panton's door, terming Panton's brand of literature "the Brixton Gospel," arguing that the opiates Panton delivers "[keep] her readers content with themselves" by allowing them to believe their lives worthy of text—the middle classes "are rejoiced to find," he sneers, that their domestic minutiae "can rise to the making of a Book."[1] Danby's critique of Panton is pointed and personal, but it draws on familiar fin de siècle arguments about the poor taste, poor grammar, yet terrifying new cultural, literary, and purchasing power of the masses.

Literature of the period is full of similar complaints. George Gissing's *In the Year of Jubilee* is, like T. W. H. Crosland's *Suburbans,* peopled with dreadful suburbanites. Fanny French, a frizzy-haired, chinless girl, "shallow-eyed," can't stop singing banal ditties; her showy dress "set the teeth on edge."[2] Samuel Barmby, in the same novel, is a supercilious and repellant "suburban deity"—these are the familiar embodiments of the late Victorian suburbs, together with the dreadfully, comically dull Charles Pooter of *Diary of a Nobody.* It is easy to read "The Brixton Gospel" as a similar critique of oppressively dull, petty bourgeois Victorianism, its embodiment in the sprawling landscape of the suburbs. "The supposed low quality of life encouraged by suburban conditions became a favourite theme for intellectual ridicule or censure," John Carey argues, and the speech, behavior, and tastes of suburb dwellers were frequently put down to their bad reading habits.[3]

But Danby's review is not what it seems. "The Brixton Gospel" is not, as it presents itself, an intellectual, metropolitan man's jab at an arriviste female suburbanite's work, for "Frank Danby" was the pen name of a woman, Julia Frankau, an Anglo-Jewish middle-class writer who lived in Bayswater, Maida Vale, and other suburban and urban locales in the course of a career as a sensational novelist, journalist, and historian of eighteenth-century engraving. Panton, meanwhile, was no Peckham Rye daughter; she was the daughter of Royal Academician William Powell Frith (1819–1909), a painter famous for capturing the spirit of the age in scenes of bustling everyday life, such as *Derby Day* (1858) and *The Railway Station* (1862). The two women moved in similar circles and knew each other: they shared literary and artistic friends and acquaintances, including *Punch* editor Shirley Brooks and his son Reginald, Oscar and William Wilde, and the great actor Henry Irving, who was the lover of Frankau's sister Eliza (Irving and Frith were great friends). Moreover, Frankau and Panton published, quite literally, alongside each other. Frankau contributed to the 1890s sixpenny weekly the *Gentlewoman,* discoursing, as her sister put it, "on Doctors and children" (while Eliza provided "Dress and drama with drivel sauce" to pay the bills when she separated from her husband). Panton was a fellow contributor to the same periodical, throwing, Eliza observed wryly, "some new light into the darkest domestic basements" in columns on home decoration.[4] Thus even as Frankau critiqued Panton for discoursing on domestic "commonplaces" in "enterprising weeklies," she was writing on similar topics in just such an "enterprising weekly" herself. "The Brixton Gospel" does not, in other words, express the distaste of a traditionally educated man confronted with a literature, language, and value system he despises, nor even the loathing of a middle-class modernist setting his face against the "feminization" of culture. Julia Frankau was a middle-class woman, writing about suburbia in the same magazine, at the same time, as Jane Ellen Panton (and so was her sister).

What inspired Frankau to speak of suburbia—and Panton—with such venom? Why publically savage a fellow traveler in the new and evolving business of claiming the cultural and literary value of fashion, interior décor, and design? An immediate answer to at least some of these questions must be: money. Tongue-lashings of the middle-class woman paid (as Eliza Lynn Linton surely realized when she trotted out infamous denunciations of "The Girl of the Period," "The Wild Woman," etcetera). Tongue-lashings of suburbia seem to have been especially attractive to editors in the later years of the century, as writers like Gissing realized, as Crosland's book-length *Suburbans* confirmed. Other possible reasons for the takedown include personal animus (Panton was anti-Semitic, which must have infuriated Frankau);[5] a wrangling over territory (*The Way They Should Go* walks into areas—medicine and family life—on which Frankau published herself); a sense of professional slight (Panton published as a celebrity in the *Gentlewoman,* while Frankau published, together with most of the other contributors, under a pseudonym—"MRS. PANTON is the best-known and admittedly the highest authority on matters of the Home," the editors trumpeted in a fawning introduction when Panton joined the staff); and/or a reviewer's reasonable irritation at what is, without question, a hastily written, unedited book.[6] Any one of these might be enough to explain Frankau's furious reaction to *The Way They Should Go* in "The Brixton Gospel," but, as we shall see, the implications of the spat encompass yet extend beyond career building and two writers' mutual dislike. Frankau stakes out the battle between herself and Panton as the conflict of elite versus nouveau riche, man versus woman, urban center versus margin—but suburban women occupy *both* sides of the ring. Indeed, "The Brixton Gospel" heralds, as we shall see, not the "intellectual stagnation" of the suburbs so much as their impressive cultural takeover—the ability of suburbanites, by the end of the century, to take center stage in debates about suburbia and confidently voice its positions.

Throughout this book, I have argued for suburbia's generative capacities. I have suggested that, for women in particular, the suburbs were not simply places of tedium, cultural aridity, and baffling anonymity—that their landscapes, ways of life, and problems produced new characters, new problems, and new possibilities, facilitating, even requiring, new plots. I have argued that the familiar image of the suburb as Dulham was a stereotype, a means of expressing anxieties about new social groups and practices rather than an expression of lived experience. A common suburban literary theme involves moving: in one strand of suburban fiction, a stranger arrives and must be assessed, while in another, a protagonist moves and must try to make sense of a new area. What guides characters in the face of constant mobility is a (supposedly) shared sense of what constitutes taste and gentility: performing "the correct thing," as one Braddon heroine put it, is not just a fussy adherence to the edicts of Mrs. Grundy but also an effort to find commonality and anchorage.

It is also central to the argument of this book that Victorian suburban experience was not one of terrible isolation, as so many of suburbia's critics have argued. The walls and privet hedges beloved by suburbanites marked out residents' modernity and newness every bit as much as they signaled a desire for quiet and privacy, while transportation networks brought suburbanites in and out of the city center to jobs, shops, parks, and amenities. I have suggested that the move to the suburbs involved the creation of new communities, rather than the erasure of *all* community: residents may or may not have "visited" next door, and many were undoubtedly separated from birth networks, but they shopped and took trains together, and formed new interest groups in print texts and professional organizations, rather as we form groups around shared interests online today.

In this final chapter, I examine not only the literary relationship between Frankau and Panton but also the communities of which both were a part. Suburban communities played important parts in both their careers, albeit in quite different ways. Frankau made her reputation with a novel about Jewish life in Maida Vale, while Panton rose to prominence writing about home decoration, especially in the suburbs to the south of London. Frankau finally sought to distance herself from her Anglo-Jewish suburban beginnings and enter the ranks of the English cosmopolitan elite; Panton, born Frith, detached herself from her great father and forged a new identity for herself as "Mrs. Panton," discovering in suburban Shortlands in Bromley a community of writers who helped her transition. The two authors viewed the suburban communities they encountered quite differently. Yet the two were united by a refusal to view their birth identities as defining their life course, pursuing lives and professional careers shaped by the suburb's thematic of mobility, new starts, and self-recreation.

JANE ELLEN PANTON

"I do not know anything more truly dreadful than these newer suburbs with their wildly-named houses," Jane Ellen Panton sniffed in 1914, sounding remarkably like Frank Danby—"their would-be artistic appearance, and their odious gentility." The thesis of her most well-known novel, *The Cannibal Crusader: An Allegory for Our Times* (1909), is that absolute cannibalism is preferable to life in London and its suburbs: when Ronaldino, child of two metropolis dwellers shipwrecked on an island of savages, returns decades later to his parents' home country, he is appalled by what he discovers: "The more he saw of civilization the less he liked it." Through his eyes, on a train journey, Panton shows us the horrors of industrial London, then the outskirts: "As London faded away through a mist of horrible slums, grimy gardens and gradually dying fields and commons, where the mark of the builder showed that they were doomed, Ronald closed his eyes. If London was bad, the suburbs were worse."[7]

But this, as we saw in chapter 4, is very far from the only view Panton articulated, in the course of a long career, of the suburbs. Panton's interior decoration texts offer endless ways for the resourceful suburban housewife to "circumvent" the houses that test her patience; her autobiographies, meanwhile, as we shall see in a moment, offer intimate and often affectionate articulations of life experiences in suburbs from the moderately urban and ethnically mixed Bayswater to the more distant, middle-class Shortlands. Her warm support of the suburbs in some works calls her familiar-sounding denunciations in others into question: criticisms of suburbia are, in other words, for Panton, just as for Danby, a mode of self-positioning, a means of associating with the tasteful, the astute, the other-regarding, the cultured. Panton's critiques, like Danby's in the *Saturday Review,* are so obviously performances that they remind us all over again that these refrains tell us little about the brick-and-mortar realities of the Victorian suburbs. But Panton does offer more positive accounts of the suburbs she knew, tending, like Braddon, to distinguish between generalized "suburbs" and geographically identified areas; while "the suburbs" are slum-like or places of "odious gentility," named suburbs like Bayswater and Shortlands are evoked as lively, full of good taste and encouraging, supportive communities.

Jane Ellen Frith was born in 1848 at 12 Park Village West (now Camden) in a house that "stood back from the main road of Albany Street, Regent's Park"; the house's gardens stretched to the Regent's Park Canal. The area, she later explained, was "a continual source of joy and delight to us" because, though it was "quiet and retired . . . in half a minute we could see the omnibuses go up and down the street."[8] Frith and his wife, Isabella, claimed that the canal's fogs and damp might be unhealthy, however, and in the early 1850s the family moved southwest, to 10 Pembridge Villas, Bayswater, a suburban area built on the Ladbroke Estate, flourishing since the construction of the Great Western Railway's new terminus at Paddington. This was emphatically a move up the suburban scale: Vivien Knight suggests that Frith may well have been "attracted by the advertisements for Pembridge Villas properties that appeared in *The Times* from 1850 onwards."[9] Certainly "Fashion, in its West End course," was "fading fast" from the Regent's Park district, so that Frith was signaling upward mobility by moving to the edge of fashionable Tyburnia, an area bounded to the south by the Bayswater Road.[10] Four months after the move, he was elected to the ranks of the Royal Academy.[11]

In 1887—the same year Frankau published *Dr. Phillips* and Panton issued her breakout *From Kitchen to Garret*—Frith published his well-received *My Autobiography and Reminiscences. My Autobiography* is a cheerful account of Frith's life as an increasingly successful painter and man about town. It begins with his leaving the provinces, hero-like, "to make [his] fortune" in London; it concentrates on the years after the move to Bayswater and Frith's election to the R.A.[12] The voice Frith adopts is one of a man in the know: friend to Dickens, Irving, Egg, and Turner, commissioned painter of Queen Victoria and her family (in *The Marriage of the Prince of Wales,* 1865), he appears to speak to us from within the narrowest of circles, the enclave of the elites. The *Whitehall Review* observed that Frith knew so many important people, was present at so many significant events, that his autobiography constitutes "a link in the historical chain of a country." His genius as a raconteur was to convey that he was at ease in his elevated position; the journal commended the artist for inviting readers into his world and making it interesting and accessible. Frith "smokes a pipe with us, as it were, in his studio," it remarked, "and the visions and ghosts of figures pass along the walls, but the visions are full of interest and harmony and the ghosts are merry fellows."[13] He is referred to on the title page as "W. P. Frith, R.A., Chevalier of the Legion of Honour and of the Order of

Leopold; Member of the Royal Academy of Belgium, and of the Academies of Stockholm, Vienna, and Antwerp." The Queen visited Frith's house in 1865 to see the painting of her family; Frith's text draws upon a familiar, long-standing tradition of post-Enlightenment autobiography, what Emily O. Wittman has called "the premise of a stable and triumphant sovereign self who narrates his autobiography" to show "the promise of personal growth and social advancement culminating in insight and self-assured reflection."[14]

In truth, Frith was far from a secure resident in the ranks of any elite, and the *Whitehall Review* was a sixpenny weekly with an aspirational title. Frith was emphatically a middle-class product, and not only because his father was an innkeeper from High Harrowgate. Frith's superstar status did not last his career: by the time he published his memoirs, his brand of detailed, hyperrealist painting had dropped out of fashion. He was on the wrong side of Impressionism, a style of painting he excoriated (even though Impressionism's urge to capture the everyday in many ways chimed with his own desire to render vivid a full social range). He termed it a "craze" that was certain to pass, "as everything foolish and false does sooner or later."[15] Excluded from the first rank of artists—John Everett Millais was, even in Frith's most successful years, more widely acclaimed—Frith was known as a painter who captured, in his very practice, the era's mania for reproduction, churning out new versions of successful canvases and rarely experimenting with either subject matter or technique. Famously, *Sherry, Sir?*, an 1853 picture of a winsome servant girl, was followed in 1854 by *Did You Ring, Sir?*, the engraving *Hot Water, Sir?*, and, in 1858, *A Maid with a Flagon*. The "vulgar" title of the first painting, assigned by Lloyd Brothers when they published the engraving, caused Frith embarrassment, he confided in his autobiography, but this did not stop him from cashing in on its success.[16] He was mocked for his willingness to produce art to order: the Shirley Brooks joke—"I ups and paints, hears no complaints, and sells before I'm dry"—evokes a very different man from the learned gentleman set forth on the title page of *My Autobiography*.[17]

Frith was a suburbanite, and he surely knew it. For all that he was favored by the Sovereign, he made his reputation in the 1850s capturing the world of the suburbs, using his own suburban home and family as inspiration, model, and backdrop. His painting renders the world of the suburbs the business of art, whether it is children's parties in his own Bayswater home (for instance, *Many Happy Returns of the Day*, 1856, fig. 19), servants, from the perspective of a paterfamilias (the *Sherry, Sir?* series mentioned above), or women with children (for instance, *When We Devote Our Youth to God, 'Tis Pleasing in His*

Eyes, 1852, a painting of a mother and child, for which his wife and daughter served as the models). The vast canvases for which Frith is most remembered, meanwhile, memorialize the masses about town and at play—*Life at the Seaside: Ramsgate Sands* (1854), one of his most famous paintings, was first turned down by six potential buyers, one of whom wondered, according to Frith, "how anybody in his senses could waste his time in painting such a tissue of vulgarity."[18] Yet as Mary Cowling observes, "Its purchase by Queen Victoria proved that Frith had caught the mood of the moment."[19] *Derby Day* and *Railway Station* soon followed, the latter offering, as Caroline Arscott remarks, "a compendium of observation, social commentary, comedy, pathos, adventure and moral reflection that perfectly fitted the appetites and expectations of the middle-class viewing public."[20] Frith was not a painter of the aristocracy so much as a painter who understood that art needed, now, to appeal to the middle class: his paintings of the elite, meanwhile, are not celebrations of their cultural authority, as in previous centuries, so much as opportunities for the bourgeois to see what the elites looked like. (It is worth noting that his representation of the wealthy did not always convince: the *Athenaeum* claimed that the rich women in the 1888 genre canvas *Poverty and Wealth* looked "vulgar," the babies "overdressed.")[21] At the same time, Frith lends dignity to the middle classes, giving their pursuits, pleasures, and places the grandeur of large canvases that had, for centuries, been devoted to important historical and mythological subjects.

Frith's daughter Jane learned, literally at her father's knee, that a career could be built catering to suburban tastes, interests, and practices. She also understood, all too well, that the triumphant upward trajectory Frith shaped in *My Autobiography* was substantially a fiction; she was to spend her own career evolving a literary form that allowed her both to retell his story and to narrate her own, more circular life journey. Frith makes little reference in *My Autobiography* to some unpalatable truths that might have called into question the text's narrative of "personal growth and social advancement culminating in insight and self-assured reflection": the scandalous twenty-six-year-long affair he had with a much younger woman named Mary Alford, who lived just up the road, the children they produced together, and the terrible pain this caused his first family, are squeezed into a few oblique references (for example, the gentlemen of the R.A. were all very understanding of his "position"). His mistress may have been his own ward; Whistler's counsel in the Whistler-Ruskin libel trial named her as such, in 1878, though Vivien Knight notes that there is no other evidence of this.[22] Certainly Mary was known as a teenager to the

19. *Many Happy Returns of the Day,* 1856, William Powell Frith (1819–1909). Mercer Art Gallery, Harrogate, North Yorkshire, U.K. © Harrogate Borough Council / Bridgeman Images. Frith used his own home as backdrop and painted himself and his family members into the group.

family, lived just a few streets away from the Friths, and Frith used to visit her, Knight observes, "under cover of the long walk he took daily before dinner."[23] (The story, possibly apocryphal, is that Panton's mother, Isabella, learned of the affair when Frith, who was supposed to be traveling, was spotted posting a letter down the road. If true, his downfall may be traced to the "letter-receiving pillar" that Anthony Trollope had advocated just a couple of years earlier.) Frith married Alford twelve months after Isabella's death, and he dedicated the second edition of *My Autobiography* to "My wife, in acknowledgement of her constant sympathy and ever-ready help."[24] His betrayal of his first wife caused his family, as we shall see, terrible pain. *My Autobiography* erases the scandal, the betrayal, and the suffering in the service of a story of professional success, marital harmony, and a journey from the provinces to secure embowerment in a community of elite Royal Academy men.

Panton's journey took a very different course, one in which the suburbs played a key part. Born in London, she spent much of her life in first the inner and then the more outlying suburbs, a progress that reflected broader contemporary patterns of migration: "London's center became increasingly depopulated between the 1860s and the 1890s and the wave of suburban growth moved outwards," Robert Woods summarizes.[25] Frith's provinces-to-center trajectory was, in a very real sense, the story of a different age, when (as we saw in the first chapters) the suburbs were substantially populated by provincial residents moving toward the city and urban opportunity.[26] Panton oriented herself around the metropolis, spending some periods in the countryside (Dorset) and the center (she died in Bloomsbury); hers was a common later Victorian story, and it is one her literature strains to narrate. At first, though, Frith's daughter hardly unsettled her father's narrative, repurposing Frith's text in her life-writing. The Panton works that most obviously present as autobiography include *Bypaths and Cross-Roads* (1889), *Leaves from a Life* (1908), *Fresh Leaves and Green Pastures* (1909), and *More Leaves from a Life* (1911). Other texts that seem to be first-person novels but draw heavily from life include *Leaves from a Garden* (1910), *The Year's Mind: Hamworth Happenings* (1913), *The River of Years* (1916), and *The Building of Whispers* (1915). Routinely, in the autobiographical volumes, but especially in the early works, Panton renarrates scenes and apes the upbeat narrative perspective of her father's *My Autobiography.*

"Now I am the last person to sneer at Bayswater," Panton observes brightly at the start of *More Leaves from a Life,* "for I too was born and brought up there, in the near neighbourhood of the squares and gardens and of the very 'Grove' itself, and in our day at least, Bayswater was a delight. Nowhere else were there such dear little gardens, nowhere else were the neighbours so neighbourly, nor the houses so well managed and the children so happy and numerous, so good and in some cases so clever."[27] Much of *Leaves from a Life* humorously describes the life the young Frith family lived in Bayswater in the 1850s and '60s, and it has been mined by Frith scholars extensively for the light it sheds on the domestic life of the painter in a time of professional flourishing. Certainly it offers fascinating insights into fashionable, socially mixed suburban Bayswater, rendered all the more piquant because of the veiled hints by Panton to her father's Great Secret. She references the affair with Mary Alford only obliquely, as Frith does in *My Autobiography;* she focuses more on the changing character of a suburb—the growing multiculturalism of Bayswater, for instance, or the way the community learned of news and current events at mid-century ("I have never forgotten the horror that seized me when the news-boys called through the foggy night: 'Glorious victory; appalling losses; fall of Sebastopol' ").[28] She also vividly describes the architectural features of their Bayswater rooms, the colors of fabrics and soft furnishings, the foods her mother made, the mixtures she poured down her children's throats, the Berlin Wools and laces Isabella worked.

Indeed, Panton is skilled at integrating finely drawn details into grand scenes of suburban middle-class life, producing in text something of what her father accomplished on canvas:

> The most tremendous "parties" were those given by Charles Lucas, the builder, and by the Cosenses, who both then lived at Clapham, and when we went to either house, we drove there in our warm winter frocks and coats, our "party" frocks packed up and carried on top of the fly, to be donned when we arrived there. . . .
>
> [T]he house was a blaze of light, and we were bundled upstairs to a room where a beautiful fire awaited us, and we were put into our very starched and stiff white frocks, silk stockings, and white shoes . . . our gloves . . . gave out a faint odour of benzine, that always recalls to me our earliest party days.[29]

The parties in Clapham—from the dresses of the other girls to the impressive scale of the Christmas trees, to Mr. Lucas's exasperating habit of picking up little girl visitors and spinning them around—are described in a way that fixes the importance of the domestic and the personal; the shift to the evocative scent of benzine in the gloves in this passage is typical of her prose. Panton's mid-century Bayswater is emphatically no Dulham but a place of riotous community and travel. Famous names mingle with the once famous, as in Frith's work; parties and social visits appear on almost every page, and Queen Victoria comes to visit. Panton also offers an exuberant account of her family's closeness, celebrating the painter as paterfamilias par excellence, a hardworking father who nonetheless managed to lavish time on his children: "Our dear young father! How we worshipped him, his talents, his never-failing, delightfully amusing talk, and his never-ending stories," Jane recalls, noting that he always made time for his children after a long day of work. And then, in a passage much quoted by Frith scholars, she observes: "The artistic temperament has its great and undoubted drawbacks, but such as they are they do not touch the children or young people of the household; and I can honestly say that, despite the trouble, the great trouble my father once gave my mother, I never remember the smallest 'row' or unpleasant wrangle in our household."[30]

Another reading of Bayswater, and of Frith himself, emerges in Panton's work slowly but steadily as Panton begins to diverge from the father-authorized life story and arc. *More Leaves from a Life* positions itself as a successor to *Leaves from a Life,* and it begins again in Panton's and Frith's Bayswater at mid-century. The near-identical red-and-gold tooled cover of the second book (published by Eveleigh and Nash) even copies, in a sense, its precursor. Yet *More Leaves* begins from, and centers on, the narrator's friendship with a man named Basil Hodges, who, born into a commercial family, becomes a celebrated painter and Royal Academician himself. The text references places familiar from both Frith's *My Autobiography* and Panton's 1908 *Leaves,* and it uses scenes such as Frith's studio to ground the narrative—which presents itself as memory—in fact: "Ah! they are painting the next house but one as I write, how the smell of the paint takes me back to those long dead days, and I see Basil still in the shepherd's plaid tunic leaning against my chair gazing at every stroke of the brush, while now and then my father steps back to look at his picture, gives us a humorous glance over his glasses, and then once more sets to work!"[31] The smell of paint is used, like the "odour of benzine," to signal the pull of authentic memory, the fall through a doorway into a world preserved across time, true and untouched. The narrative also integrates photographs: black-and-white images of Cornish towns, such as Tredickor and Morrab, French resorts like Bourget-les-Bains, and spots beloved by the narrator's friend (Hodges's Basil's Cove) face pages of text, so that the camera itself seems to provide supporting evidence of the narrative's veracity. Frith appears regularly in the book, for instance taking Basil with him on a trip to Bad Homburg with "another artist," to see the gaming tables as he prepared to paint *Salon d'Or.* Rosa Bonheur, Panton observes, "greeted them and made them at home" as they traveled back toward England; this was an important meeting, she observes, that set Basil firmly on course for the great artistic career that was about to unfold.[32]

Frith's own memoir is tugged into providing corroborating evidence. Frith certainly did go to Homburg with his friend Henry Nelson O'Neill, a fellow genre painter and member of the Clique, and the *Salon d'Or* trip is given its own chapter in the painter's autobiography. Frith met Rosa Bonheur. But he mentions no other travel companion. Hodges does not appear in *My Autobiography* on the Homburg journey, nor indeed anywhere else in the three volumes. Nor can any trace of the paintings Panton references as celebrated Hodges canvases be found, either in Frith's work or in Royal Academy catalogues.[33] No painter of that name became a Royal Academician; no Victorian

Academician matches Hodges's dates or career trajectory. Bourget-les-Bains does not exist, neither does Tredickor or Morrab, and none of the members of the aristocracy whose lives become entangled with that of Basil Hodges—the Arundels of Cornwall, whose marriage is destroyed when the heartless Lady Antoinette Arundel (Basil's "evil genius," a "soul-less butterfly") falls for him, and he for her—can be recovered.[34] While Miss Wright, the governess in charge of the Frith children when Basil first became friends with Jane, was certainly a real person, and is mentioned in other texts, including the 1908 *Leaves,* there is no reference to a child named Basil in the book, nor indeed to any child of a commercial family who rises to become a celebrated painter. Given Panton's patent desire to present herself, in the first *Leaves,* as a friend to celebrities (chapter titles such as "Some Literary People," "More Literary Folk," "Still More Literary Folk," "Theatres, Actors, Audiences" all hearken back to Frith's *Autobiography,* whose chapter titles reference celebrity "People I Have Known" or reflect on "The Great Actors of My Youth"), it is clear that Panton is not just fictionalizing or giving a pseudonym to a real person in *More Leaves,* in the character of Basil Hodges. She is, rather, creating a fictional character against a backdrop painted from real life.[35]

Departing from Frith's story, of "the boy who made good," Panton strains to tell a new story—or rather many new stories, in multiple voices. No longer merely authorizing the account Frith gave of his life, Panton comes to provide a new character for her father, as we shall see. But she also evolves a number of different narrative personae that circle around stories of betrayal, depression, unfulfilled promise, house moving, domestic discomfort, and unsatisfying marriages—dispensing with the arc of the traditional marriage plot deployed so often by (for instance) Mary Elizabeth Braddon. Some of Panton's narratives are arguably more honest than Firth's (Panton, by the end of her life, frames and fills in the story her father concealed), some more duplicitous (she uses photographs, fake "facts," and solemn assurances of veracity to claim the truth of highly fictionalized nonfiction, then uses fiction and fictional characters to tell what appears to be an approximation of the truth). Other narratives constitute bravura performances of what Danby termed the "quintessential" suburbanite, in slapdash, ungrammatical prose, for even as Panton comes to detach herself from her father she displays increasing affection for the suburbs that facilitate new lives, relationships, and identities. Her deployment of multiple personae in texts that refuse to follow traditional literary forms constitutes a gradual embrace, I suggest, of the suburbs as geographical spaces, cultural phenomena, professional portals, and finally literary mode.

The suburban resident, moved to a new area, was freed, at least in the popular imagination, to start again, to re-create himself or herself, to conceal the past (the fear of the alien stranger, concealing a mysterious history, surfaces in suburban literature dating at least as far back as Bulwer-Lytton; other suburban fraudsters include Collins's Mannion, Braddon's Lady Audley, Sala's Earl of Elbowsout, Eden's Baron Sampson, Buxton's Peregrine Latimer). Panton reinvents herself time and again, developing not just one but multiple narrating personae, even new areas of expertise, so that each text becomes a kind of restless literary "moving," a new house, new life, new character, new identity. Panton's interior design voice is authoritative and firm; when advising families, she is vague and breezy, sometimes querulous, sometimes sentimental, sometimes emphatic. As Jane in *Leaves from a Life* she is a loving daughter and in-the-thick-of-it observer (like her father) of artistic London. As the narrator of *The Cannibal Crusader* she aligns herself with the outsider who discerns social truth. In fictionalized nonfiction and in autobiographical novels, meanwhile, she develops a distinctive authorial voice that, uninterrupted by dialogue, discloses the workings and failings of communities from the perspective of a wise, hectored, struggling, but indomitable woman. (The *Times* commended, in its obituary of Panton, her "charming pictures of country life as a setting to narrative fiction without the aid of dialogue." This was, it added, "a mode employed by her with considerable success.")[36] Panton's first-person narrator is often severely tested, by the male tendency to sexual infidelity (in fiction) or the demon builder (in her works of interior design). She is no lover of children, marriage is a source of pain, and other women must be closely watched. Moving day is nightmarish ("The very sight of a furniture van, the smell of the horrid straw; the green baize aprons of the dreadful men reeking of shag tobacco and beer, the groans of the furniture as it is wrenched from the rooms and carted protestingly forth, are all so many separate horrors for me").[37] But the first-person voice heroically overcomes adversity and finds in the suburbs, especially of South London, ways of accessing long-hidden talents, and turning them, through access to professional communities, into a fresh start.

The River of Years, a work of fiction (supposedly) written from the perspective of a first-person heroine called Nancy, helps elucidate this point. The book presents as a novel but asks us from the start to draw a connection between it and Panton's autobiographies: just as *More Leaves* begs us to see it as a sibling to *Leaves, The River of Years* hints at a similar twinship. The text was published as "By the author of 'Leaves from a Life' etc," and it reproduces the chapter titles of the 1908 *Leaves,* which opens (hearkening to *David Copperfield*) with "I am Born," followed by "We Make a Move"; early chapters of *The River of Years* are entitled "I Wonder," "I Ask," "I am Rescued," "I am Educated," and so on. Nancy suffers from untreated earache as a child and loves *The Wide Wide World,* both of which Jane routinely mentions as features of her own childhood (the earache Frankau picked up in her review).[38] Like Jane too, Nancy is a member of a large family. But unlike the Jane of *Leaves from a Life,* who romps merrily with siblings and parents, Nancy strongly resents the large number and wonders why her siblings can't be drowned in buckets like puppies and kittens. If the Jane of *Leaves* follows her father in drawing polite veils over the unpalatable facts of life, Nancy in *The River of Years* tears them off, painting her early life as one that set her on the path to unhappiness.

The topics and events narrated in *Leaves* and *River* are similar, but the characters describe what happens quite differently. Nancy takes a far more critical view of the people round her than does Jane in *Leaves,* bluntly articulating anger with her family. The mother of a large family in *The River of Years* is suffering and overwhelmed, not (like the Isabella of *Leaves*) ever ready with friendship, good advice, and home-brewed medicine, and the narrator's frustration boils over on page after page: "My mother was always too much engrossed in the nursery to trouble much about me." The heroine adores her father, but he is distant; again the narrator recounts her frustration bitterly: "He so seldom, so very seldom, recollected that he had called us into a very overcrowded world." As Nancy grows up, she longs to become an artist but is told by her parents that it is not a career for a woman: she describes herself as tortured by the sights and happy sounds of more fortunate male artists working together. Married off by her parents to save them the trouble of caring for her, Nancy loves her husband but resents her limited choices: "I wonder always if every girl and woman rebels against her destiny, as I have always rebelled against mine? I hated living at all, much as I loved nature, some people, and all dogs." (Panton often remarked that she adored dogs.)[39]

Nancy finds a professional "vocation" when she realizes that she can make a career as an interior designer, saved by the discovery that she can turn her painterly eye to new purpose. In a passage that evokes Nancy's transition from uncertain, unhappy wife to confident designer, the bright, forthright Panton persona from the interior decoration advice texts surfaces:

> We were just then entering into the 'seventies, the 'sixties were dead, and there was a stir in the air. We knew that our houses were all wrong

> somehow; they were ugly and not even comfortable. Sir Jacob's house [a local who employs her] was gorgeous and glittering; the drawing-room all red silk damask and gold; a fearsome carpet blooming with gigantic roses, and lurid with arsenical green leaves, covered the floor from wall to wall; a most gorgeous but uncomfortable set of chairs and sofas stood stiffly about, and there were no flowers, no plants; the ornaments were ghastly, the engravings worse, and the books were laid out on vast centre tables placed in each division of the great double room, and were remarkable for their bindings, if for nothing else.[40]

Nancy's feelings of purposelessness and negation ("I hated living") disperse: Sir Jacob's catalog of failings are identified by his middle-class neighbor, who soon finds that possession of "taste" moves her from unhappy to happy, from margins to center. Nancy begins working as a successful designer and adds, she relates, "to my income by writing short articles and paragraphs. . . . I used my eyes. . . . Women journalists were rare indeed in the 'seventies. I knew just what country folk wanted to hear about"; "I was happy, happy."[41] As designer and as writer, she becomes no "mere" wife, then, but a local arbiter and soon even a national guide to taste. Landed gentry, country folk, and town dwellers depend on her.

Nancy's path from member of a large family, to unhappily married woman, to interior designer and finally professional journalist and author recalls the journey Panton recounts in her autobiographies. Frith's daughter moved to Pound Lane, Wareham, in Dorset when she married James Panton, a brewer. It was obviously an unhappy period. In *Fresh Leaves and Green Pastures* (which more nearly picks up the autobiographical thread from *Leaves from a Life* than *More Leaves*), Panton describes her life as a young married woman in rural Dorset, longing for London. Like Nancy in *The River of Years,* the Panton persona in *Fresh Leaves* admits to terrible low points in the countryside: "I have often and often gone down to what we called the 'lower garden,' and, watching the river from my pet seat under the privet-hedge; wondered if I should not be wise to slip in 'by accident,' and so put an end to an existence that began to bore me more frightfully than I can say. I used to think of our hilarious parties; of the roll of the traffic, like the sound of the sea on the distant shore away across the hills; of the theatres and parties I once despised; and I thought of how my life was slipping away."[42] Dreaming of life in Camden and Bayswater, Panton claims she was saved from despair only by finding vocations, first for acting in private theatricals, then interior design.

What really gave her a foothold, and a purpose, once her husband's brewing career was over, was the writing career she evolved when the couple moved to suburban Shortlands to start over.

Bromley's Shortlands is presented in *Fresh Leaves* as a sort of Bayswater Redux, a community of notables who dropped in on one another in much the way Egg and Landseer, Dickens and Turner once dropped in on the Friths. Bromley grew rapidly in the later nineteenth century, changing its character from Kentish market town after the arrival of the railway in 1858 and the opening of the Bromley Direct Railway Company branch line in 1878.[43] The Shortlands community Panton describes is less august than that of the Frith family in Bayswater, and it was less socially mixed (residents held out against a working man's train service, for instance, although Panton does not mention this in the book). But the people she meets—novelists Dinah Mulock Craik, Juliana Horatia Ewing, and Jean Ingelow and suffrage activist Clementia Taylor (Panton reports bitter disputes with Taylor over capital punishment and vaccines)—are nonetheless successful women who model artistic independence while offering the pleasures and the support of professional community. The great step is a meeting with Alfred Gibbons, the owner of the new weekly magazine *Lady's Pictorial,* who—Panton claims—offered her the editorship of the paper; although she turned down the offer, Gibbons helps her find her writing niche by drawing on her skill at interior decoration, much as Nancy managed to find happiness by writing on design in *The River of Years:* "'Well,' he said, 'have you any ideas that are new?' I had suffered a good deal when living in the country from not being able to get what I wanted from the London shops; I had, moreover, a very quick eye; and above all I had just been helping a dear young couple furnish their first house . . . so I replied, 'Yes I think I have'; and I explained that I thought a series of articles on the furnishing and managing of a house would take on; as most certainly the idea had never been used before by any lady's paper."[44] Gibbons immediately took to the idea and made a suggestion that initially bewildered her: write the article, and send it back to the office with "half a dozen 'replies.'" Panton observes that she was baffled, at first, as to how replies could possibly be written to an article that had not been published. Gibbons, entertained by her naïveté, offered to provide them himself, and, Panton remarks, "we very soon laughed together over the proposed "dozen replies."[45] What Gibbons reminds Panton, of course, is that characters can be created, the first-person voice of the letter made up. Panton took to the business of writing fake letters with abandon and soon found herself at the center of a thriving group of journalists and professionally employed women. "I loved the work," she enthuses; "the letters were so entertaining; I had such delightful presents sent me, and I made such charming friends."[46] She comes to find that her skill at acting parts and role-playing has direct application in the profession of late Victorian writer.

In the early years of her writing life, Panton positions her stories along the axis of a man's great achievements at the heart of literary London. In later years, the stories she strives to tell are more various and deploy different voices, different modes of speaking; if Frankau had multiple writerly identities, then so, most certainly, did Panton, even though (unlike Frankau) she published under her last, married name. Panton deploys different kinds of first-person narrative personae, though her works share common threads. Husbands, fathers, and even mothers thwart girls in their attempts to fulfill their dreams of professional advance; hope is offered by the ability of the protagonist to find outlets for her skills, not to mention a community and friendships oriented around professional work, in the suburbs. Still, family problems continue to get in the way; successes are short-lived. In *The River of Years,* Nancy's joy in interior design, the delight she finds in a vocation, are overtaken by unhappiness when her artist-husband has an affair with his model. The rest of the book narrates, not a journey from margins to center, but a long, awkward navigation of her husband's poor intentions and choices, followed by yet more uncomfortable house moving and travel with children in tow.

Autobiography as a genre is always preoccupied with, not just the facts of a life, but the business of interpreting them: if "*Darstellen* [the act of presentation] is a necessary part of the hermeneutic enterprise," Linda Peterson observes, "*Verstehen* [the art of understanding] is its focus."[47] Some of Panton's works are explicitly autobiographies, bristling with commentary designed to take charge of the author's life's meaning (although what that life means changes, discernibly, over the course of her career, as she begins to see herself as a product of parental misdeeds, not fair dealing). Other works insist on the interpretive rights of autobiography while exploiting the novel's arguably greater potential for reimagining, evolving in the process hybrid fictional/autobiographical forms that both interpret life events and imagine new events to interpret. Works of this kind, from the later part of Panton's life especially, choose not to mimic Frith's upward trajectory, or for that matter the rise to confidence articulated by so many gardening and interior design texts. We seek in vain for a story of assured ascent, for a triumphalist conclusion editing a newspaper (say) or nationwide success as a writer or artist. Instead, Panton's texts are full of detours, wrong turns, and new starts. Marriage is the beginning of a woman's problems, not their conclusion. Characters move, then move again, circling pain.

One particular story of marital disaster surfaces repeatedly. *River*'s disastrous break-up in the marriage of Nancy and Mark does not reproduce a real-life breakup in the marriage of Jane and James; the couple remained together until James's death, in 1921. But Panton releases her work from the constraints of what "really" happened in order to renarrativize a key scene of disloyalty—the betrayal by an artist of his wife—and then return to it, repeatedly. The relationship fictionalized in *River* is surely not Jane's but her mother's, as if Panton, years later, remains determined to disturb Frith's confident story of success. The great painters, Frith and Mark, are versions of each other, as they are of Basil Hodges in *More Leaves,* artists of great promise who are celebrated in the Royal Academy then fall for the charms of a designing woman; she, beautiful but heartless, takes what she wants without heed to the feelings of others, while the lawful wife and children are left suffering. Betrayal is followed, not to its biographical conclusion (wife dies, husband remarries happily a year later, writes cheerful autobiography), but to an alternative ending in which the erring husband sees the error of his ways, the suffering wife is vindicated and venerated, the temptress dies in misery. Panton counters Frith's gentlemanly story of lordly ascent with the moralistic narrative arc so popular in women's magazines like the *Gentlewoman, Belgravia,* and *Lady's Pictorial,* braiding the husband's moral downfall with another, less triumphant account of a heroine's muted professional achievement.

Book after book critiques the heartless temptresses and the weak men who, like Frith, fall prey to "evil influence," albeit in different ways.[48] Book after book shows the temptress suffering and tortured, her evil exposed. In a memorable scene in *The Building of Whispers,* a ghostly heroine who has returned to haunt the living sees her husband's lover, Yvonne, accompanied by evil imps that cling about her body and her skirts "as flies gather on carrion and the carrion neither knows nor cares what is happening to its dead flesh." In *The Year's Mind* the temptress ends up an abandoned alcoholic, while *Most of the Game* imagines the fallen man alone, abandoned, and, perhaps crucially, friendless: "I recollect another man, the world all before him, a sweet wife, pretty children, honors his for the asking. Then, the temptress arrived—he fell; it took years and years for him to creep back into his place; but he suffered until the end: all suffered, even his children never took the standing they ought to have in the world, for he had no real friends to help or advise them."[49]

What Panton seems to have found impossible to stomach was that she followed the course her family laid out for her (as a dutiful daughter she married and gave up her independent ambitions), while her father did not. In later years, after the First World War, under her own name, in a work more obviously autobiographical, Panton is explicit that her mother, burdened by child rearing, paid her little attention; that her father ignored her for his career; that she was forced to marry, to get her out of her parents' way; that her ambitions as a writer and artist were scotched; that her family's façade was a lie; that behind her father's great story of success many other stories unfolded, unheard; that her life's narrative was plotted out for her, and that she strongly resented it. "I had endless wants in my girlhood, but they were one and all ruthlessly crushed," she recalls in 1919. "I wanted—oh! how I wanted!—to paint and draw . . . and, above all, I meant to write, and this I did, though I should have done far better than I have ever succeeded in doing had I had a fair chance, been taught properly, and, moreover, been sent abroad in some way or the other."[50] The Jane of the 1908 *Leaves,* who affectionately laid out her parents' good humor and kindness, is replaced by a voice that demands, cajoles, and storms: "Do not parents owe something more to their children than this? Do they not owe them unending patience, unfailing guidance? Surely yes. But there was nothing of the kind for me. Well! fortunately I have never really required much; and now that the grave has closed over the last of the elder generation, I will forget, I cannot forgive—that, at any rate, is an impossibility as far as I am concerned!"[51]

To write an autobiography is always to choose among narrative paths, to select events or meetings so as to tell a certain story of a life. Held at a point of betrayal and rage, Panton refuses to move past it—to give readers the climax of happy success that shapes Frith's *Autobiography.* Instead she evolves narrative forms that are consistent with her own life experience of circling, emotionally and geographically, forms that defy the conventions of the literary autobiography deployed by her father but also refuse the arc of the marriage plot. Pushing at the boundaries of genre, she flouts the conventions of Victorian fiction and autobiography alike—as if "to disclose aspects of [her life] and experience that could not be revealed in any other format," as Maria DiBattista and Emily O. Wittman put it in *Modernist Autobiography.* The editors continue: "In place of the traditional life-narrative that traces the progress of the self as it moves toward, and ultimately claims, what is truly its own, modernist autobiography might concentrate on short periods of a person's life . . . or else it might restrict its focus to a particular, life-defining, and often life-altering problem."[52] The life-defining problem Panton faced was her father, his treatment of her and the rest of his family, and his duplicity—the dark side, one might say, to his superb ability to perform. Frith positioned himself as a member of the secure elite in the very form of his autobiography, using it as part of an effort to control the story of his life; Panton tells a different story, circumventing the marriage plot laid out for her by her family and deploying the suburbs as practical aid as well as biographical, thematic, and formal inspiration.

Frankau accused Panton in "The Brixton Gospel" of talking too much about her own personal experience, and it is no accident that Frankau equated the "acutely personal" with the suburban. In the suburbs, the most obvious points of contact between people were the houses that formed a common experience, and Panton built her career speaking to that common experience, from kitchen to garret. Silenced as a young woman, she seems to have found in the suburbs the community and friendships she sought, not to mention ways of transforming both skills and painful past experiences into professional opportunities. Advance was not, as Panton well knew, easy, or even straightforwardly upward: indeed, some would call her downwardly mobile. She who began her life entertaining the Queen at home ended it entertaining, in print, "the aspiring wife of the City clerk." But Panton surely grasped that the future lay in the suburbs. Urgently seeking a new mode of writing, a new literary form, she eschewed her father's province-to-center trajectory, as well as the marriage plot, and founded a career on the perambulations of the suburbs.

JULIA FRANKAU

Panton was not alone in writing on the "acutely personal" or the suburban domestic in the 1890s, needless to say. Indeed, Julia Frankau's writing for the *Gentlewoman* in the 1890s makes her thunderous disdain for suburbanism in "The Brixton Gospel" appear, on first reading, frankly hypocritical. The *Gentlewoman* was a thoroughly middle-class publication whose bread and butter was women's family life and domestic experiences; to scan its advertisements is to confront all over again the extraordinary range of late Victorian middle-class commerce and its penetration of the domestic. Vendors offered everything from wedding cakes to silver plate to hat pins to cures for baldness and corpulence, traveling bags to nursery lamp food warmers to corsets, Hovis biscuits, "Antirougine" ("hides redness, pimples, scars, blushing"), and sanitary towels. The "Exchange and Mart" section of the *Gentlewoman* proposed tamed goldfinches, budgerigars, and parrots ("free from all vice"); Bolingbroke House on Wandsworth Common advertised hopefully "for Middle-Class Invalids." Letters addressed such topics as life as a lady shopkeeper and sibling disputes, while the rest of the magazine combined thrilling fiction (for instance, in 1894, by "The Hon. Sybil Hardyman, Detective"; sample line: "Aileen had not fainted. Aileen was dead") with regular columns on relationships, cooking, fashion, and celebrities, such as "Weddings of the Week," "Daily Dinner Menu" (by "Epicurious"), and "Famous People I Have Met" (by Mrs. George Augustus Sala, that is, Ada Rehan, an American actress).[53] There were also notices of births, marriages, and deaths: Croydon, Cricklewood, South Hampstead, Putney, and other suburban London locales, high and low, appeared regularly. The *Gentlewoman* was the quintessence of the suburban.

Frankau was in the thick of the mix, positioning herself as not only a friend to but also an ally of suburban readers, one who grasped their hopes and fears. Born in 1859 into an Anglo-Jewish family, Frankau lived in a variety of suburban streets, including Warrington Crescent, Maida Vale. (Her father, Hyman Davis, wanted to be a painter, but, with a family to support, he practiced dentistry in Dublin before becoming a portrait photographer in London.) Julia and her sister Eliza were educated at an Orthodox Jewish school, after which Julia was for a time tutored by Laura Lafargue, daughter of Karl Marx. Julia's brother James introduced his sisters to a more bohemian life that included the Wilde brothers, with whom the young women played tennis; Julia married Arthur Frankau, an agnostic and cigar manufacturer, at a Reform synagogue in 1883.[54] The couple later broke with their faith and raised their children in the Church of England. Arthur resigned his membership from the synagogue in 1885 after refusing to circumcise their eldest son, Gilbert, who was to become a well-known writer himself.[55]

As "Ariel," Frankau was a fond mother in the *Gentlewoman,* exploring in the winter/spring 1891 column "Children: As Their Mothers See Them" the everyday moments parents cherish (or, to their cost, fail to cherish) as their children grow. (The pieces were published posthumously in 1918 as *Mothers and Children,* when financial need forced Gilbert to rifle her pages for "treasure.")[56] As "Medicos," Frankau put "medicoes under the microscope," offering a guide to London's best doctors, a sort of Angie's List of the 1890s: "a Guide to the leading medical men of the Metropolis; a guide which will steer the neophyte through the shoals of incompetent or semi-competent men into the safe harbourage of the consulting room of the doctor who combines the more essential qualities of ability, experience, and high character."[57] The

Gentlewoman reported that the column inspired fury in the medical establishment: "The strongest pressure was brought to bear upon us to induce us to forego the publication of the intended series. Lawyers were set to work, the power of the Colleges of Physicians and Surgeons was invoked, and it was even asked if Parliament could not interfere. Having at heart the interest of our readers, however, we determined to go on."[58] Here the woman suburbanite takes on the male establishment, the Frank Danbys of the world, and the woman suburbanite is, the column exuberantly assures readers, emphatically in the ascendant. The *Gentlewoman* presents itself as friend to and supporter of the suburban woman, its very issues an embodiment of a community oriented around shared interests. All that was needed was an enemy, and this the College of Physicians ably provided.

Frankau wrote quite differently as Frank Danby, as we have already seen. As Danby, she aspired to sound urbane, gentile, and male, the sort of person who would sooner smoke a pipe with the gentlemen of the College of Physicians than denounce them from the flimsy pages of a woman's weekly. Yet her male persona was complicated, for by the time Frankau's critique of Panton was published Frank Danby was already synonymous with Frankau's infamous and sexually frank novel, *Dr. Phillips: A Maida Vale Idyll.* Danby's identity seems to have been an open secret in literary circles from the time of the novel's publication: George Bernard Shaw certainly knew of it when he wrote a reference to the furor in the *Pall Mall Gazette* on 25 March 1887, having met Frankau in person at the Gaiety Theatre.[59] "Frank Danby" was put in quotation marks in *Hearth and Home* in 1891, signaling the writer's recognition of the pseudonym and perhaps expectation of the reader's similar understanding.[60]

A fierce fight that unfolded in the pages of the *Saturday Review* in 1895 reveals just how far Frankau's cover was blown—or, to put it another way, gives us access to the complexity of the persona Frankau brought to the Panton review a few years later, in the same publication. Frankau published, as Danby, a denunciation of the work of George Moore, her former mentor, for a "lack of [sexual] reticence" in the pages of the *Saturday Review.* The ensuing back-and-forth turned into a fight over Frankau's supposed ingratitude and whether Danby had the standing, given the content of her own work, to criticize her fellow. Moore explicitly brought up *Dr. Phillips* as evidence against his adversary, referring to the novel's author as "she," thereby reminding readers not only that Danby had written an infamously "coarse" text but also that Danby was a female Maida Vale resident.[61] "Frank Danby has forgotten everything; she is a great disappointment to me," Moore storms, at the end of the first of several replies to Danby's review of his book *Celibates:* "Very few years are required for the desert to go back to the desert, and the return of Maida Vale to Maida Vale is even more rapid."[62]

Moore positions Danby as not so much a critic of London's Anglo-Jewish community but an embodiment of the vices Frankau associated with the suburb.[63] *Dr. Phillips* follows the career of its titular hero, a married Jewish doctor with a gentile mistress who detests her lover's caresses. Mary Cameron pretends to accept the touch of her stooping, black-haired lover in order to maintain her comfortable circumstances and social position, all the time despising him, their daughter, and his community. The Jewish suburbanites to whom Benjamin Phillips introduces the soi-disant Mrs. Cameron are represented as obsessive card players, closed-minded, overweight, diamond-loving, money-grubbing; three-quarters of the way through the text, Dr. Phillips cold-bloodedly murders his unconscious wife while she is recovering from an operation to remove an ovarian tumor, in order to help right his financial fortunes and, in the process, win the freedom to wed Mary. Mrs. Cameron (who barely notices when her little daughter dies of a fever that could, with care, have been treated) promptly abandons him and marries a younger, richer man. Few characters possess authorial sympathy, and the open representation of extramarital intimacy startled reviewers almost as much as the supposed peek into a world of Jewish suburban greed and malfeasance. *Punch,* it was said, stormed: "It should never have been written. Having been written, it should never have been published. Having been published, it should not be read."[64] Sexual relations between unmarried lovers are clearly laid out, the murderer is not punished for killing his ailing wife, and the novel ends with the hero reaping the rewards of a successful medical career while enjoying a casual sexual relationship with Bessie, his housemaid.

Frankau's first novel treats Maida Vale as a suburb where Jewish community fosters, not mutual support, but crime and degradation, even murder. Indeed, its vitriolic representation of Victorian Jewish life may test, as Michael Galchinsky remarks, our era's urge to reclaim fiction "from the silences of the archives." Galchinsky interprets Frankau's efforts to distance herself from her Jewishness as indicative of a "Jewish self-hatred" animated by later Victorian biological and evolutionary discourse, in which Jews—who, not coincidentally, were immigrating to England in increasingly large numbers in the 1880s and '90s—were articulated more and more in Britain as members of an inferior race. Galchinsky points out that Frankau's vision of Jews is atypical of contemporary Jewish writers like Israel Zangwill and Amy Levy who, though forced to confront the era's growing eugenicist discourse, did not follow Frankau's line and embrace it. Nita, the suffering product of the union of Phillips and Mary Cameron is weakly even before fever strikes, as if to hint at the dangers of interracial union, while throughout Frankau's book Jewishness is associated with a suspicious physical blackness that contrasts with the starry white beauty of gentiles.[65]

The novel is certainly a difficult read. But its challenges may be illuminated if we read it as a suburban-engaged text, one whose disdain for the suburbs is at least partly produced by the literary and cultural tradition I have explored in this book. Frankau is critical not only of Jewish suburbanites but of *all* suburbanites in *Dr. Phillips,* in her later fiction, and in her writings for the *Gentlewoman,* not to mention in her critique of Jane Ellen Panton. The gentile Mrs. Cameron in Frankau's first novel is beautiful but amoral, as we have already seen; in Frankau's second book-length fiction, *A Babe in Bohemia* (1889), a heroine living with a married man in Twickenham commits suicide, crushed by realizing the consequences of her actions. Frankau's pseudonymous personae in the *Gentlewoman,* meanwhile, are far from straightforwardly enthusiastic champions of the magazine's middle-class readership. "Medicoes Under the Microscope," the column that aspires to critique the medical establishment, ultimately tilts more at female readers than at doctors, holding up to weekly shame not so much instances of medical malpractice as the female hypochondriacs and hysterics with whom medics are apparently forced to contend.[66] In the first column, the reader is addressed as "you," a member of "the great guinea'd army of *malades imaginaires*"; the doctor, Sir Andrew Clark, will, the column assures us, quickly diagnose our weakness and dispense moral advice ("avoid self-notice"), and we shall depart wiser, healthier women.[67] The column constitutes in the end less a guide to doctors than a guide to the kind of behavior a woman must embrace if she is to gain access to the ranks of those culturally admired: the values the column commends, week in and week out, are modesty (none of the admired doctors seeks fame), diligence, and accomplishment (all of the doctors work hard and publish in leading professional magazines), coolness in the face of pain or suffering (few of the doctors display emotion, and the only patients Frankau represents sympathetically are those who seek advice with an actual terminal illness), good English (she applauds her doctors' accents and grammar), and good taste (the best medics cleave to a Queen Anne aesthetic, with a touch of Arts and Crafts about their textiles). "Ariel," meanwhile, presents the children in her column as a barometer to the comportment of parents. The suffering of a child is invariably connected to a failure on the part of either father or mother to live up to the virtues Frankau espouses—"sobriety, energy, and self-restraint."[68] (Gilbert was at pains to stress, in his preface to the 1918 edition, that his mother did not make the same mistake herself, and that if she struggled as an artist it was only because she gave so magnificently of herself to all her children.)[69]

Frankau, like Panton, adopted multiple writing personae and narrated multiple different stories of life in the suburbs. But one common premise runs as a substratum, and that is the need for suburbanites to self-critique—to hold themselves to certain standards of taste and behavior if they are to align themselves with the worthy and advance. Like so many other writers of the period, Frankau treats the suburban domestic as, fundamentally, a crucible for behavior modification and taste making. Worthiness depends, in the work of Frankau just as in that of Mary Elizabeth Braddon or Bertha Buxton, or for that matter interior design and gardening texts, on viewing suburban problems as a reason to think, to act, to change. Notably, the competing values in Maida Vale are not laid out along Jewish/gentile lines—Mrs. Cameron is utterly corrupt, a terrible mother—but pit the Philistines against the cultured as so many other suburban-engaged narratives did. The very term "Philistine"—which Frankau deploys explicitly in "The Brixton Gospel" to describe Panton and her ilk—is one that takes on Arnoldian meaning in a late Victorian context, as discussed in my Introduction: Arnold remarked, in "Sweetness and Light":

> The people who believe most that our greatness and welfare are proved by our being very rich, and who most give their lives and thoughts to becoming rich, are just the very people whom we call the Philistines. Culture says: "Consider these people, then, their way of life, their habits, their manners, the very tones of their voice; look at them attentively; observe the literature they read, the things which give them pleasure, the words which come forth out of their mouths, the thoughts which make the furniture of their minds; would any amount of wealth be worth having with the condition that one was to become just like these people by having it?"[70]

Arnold is quite clear that such a perspective must be articulated if culture is to police itself in a time of plenty and production: "And thus culture begets a dissatisfaction which is of the highest possible value in stemming the common tide of men's thoughts in a wealthy and industrial community."[71] This, I suggest, helps us understand the narrative perspective of *Dr. Phillips,* as it does other writings critical of the suburbs. No reasonable person today could read Frankau's text and think her representation of the money-grubbing, beetle-browed Anglo-Jewish community in Maida Vale in any sense "accurate"; her articulation of Maida Vale as a place of Philistinism is similarly no mirror held up to reality. Frankau, like many of her peers, *feared* that Maida Vale was verging toward the side of the Philistines, not the cultured, and thematized that anxiety, exhorting suburbanites, Jewish or not, to value culture over money, to practice self-denial over self-pleasure. The novel is a speech *to* suburbia, not *about* suburbia.

The price of being a "good" suburbanite was, to Frankau, as to so many other Victorians, self-criticism and rigorous self-policing. To that end, *Dr. Phillips* is full of pointers toward the ways in which the gap between Maida Vale and Mayfair may be lessened by any Jewish suburbanite who chooses. Benjamin Phillips's complexion must remain dark—but it is quite clear Frankau thinks he could cut his facial hair, manage his finances better, choose his companions more carefully. The Jewish community in Maida Vale, meanwhile, has not (Frankau suggests) grasped elite standards of taste, and here again she offers pointers to improvement. On the first page we enter a Jewish home of "gilt chairs and satin draperies . . . exquisite china lay on inlaid tables," but the room is "filled with floating suggestions of a Bond Street show-room; the furniture looked as if it were on view." Some pages later, we enter Mary Cameron's home and see that she, by contrast, has dispensed with high Victorianism and educated herself in the aesthetic of the emerging Arts and Crafts movement: "Bluish-grey druggeting blended into the green of the ferns that filled the conservatory. . . . Here Liberty had been allowed to use his own discretion."[72] Mary may be sexually immoral, but at least she understands good taste; Julia hung the drawing room of her own Eastbourne holiday cottage at the turn of the century, her son recalled, "with a peacock wallpaper."[73]

Frankau's critique of her community for its "failures" in *Dr. Phillips* constitutes not only Anglo-Jewish self-hatred, then, but also a suburbanite's sense that social advance required repeated, emphatic self-criticism and a careful self-positioning in relation to contemporary categories of taste. Advance, what it took to advance, and how to signal advance in fin de siècle London are topics that surface routinely in Frankau's work: in the fight with George Moore, for instance, Frankau and her erstwhile mentor battle as much about access to the elite as about sex and its place in realist fiction.[74] In her answer to Moore's claim that she had returned to Maida Vale, for instance, she is at pains to intimate that, au contraire, she long ago left Maida Vale behind: "My intermittent acquaintance" with Moore "died a natural death," she informs readers. "That he is unaware of my present address is, therefore, neither remarkable or interesting; whether it be Belgravia or Maida Vale, St. James' or St. Giles', does not affect the value of my criticism."[75] Moore, she concludes, "has missed the ear of the *elite* and escaped the eye of the public"; she hints that he is "un-English." The Irish-born Moore was enraged by Frankau's claim that she knew more about the elite than he, citing this line first in his answer; he proceeds to conjure "the elite" as his own ally throughout his letter of complaint about her review of him: "It is well known to the *elite,*" Moore observes, "that I spent long days toning down and suppressing sentences in 'Dr. Phillips.' . . . What will the *elite* think when they read this passage?"[76] Moore's reply positions him as one who emphatically has the ear of, and speaks with, the cultured, the intellectual favored few. Frankau promptly replies that Moore has misunderstood certain Latin roots and takes aim at his "ungrammatical indignation," as if Moore, like Panton, is an ill-educated Putney product, spawn of the semiliterate masses.[77]

Todd Endelman observes that Frankau ended her career in "the largely gentile worlds of journalism, publishing, literature, theater, and the arts," while her later work on engraving "put her in an elite group of cultivated persons." Julia herself remarked, in the preface to a book on John Raphael Smith, that the topic of engraving appealed only to a "cultured, perceptive public," and she presented herself as the means by which a small, elite readership could gain access to an even smaller, even more cultured circle—the "private custodians of our national art-treasures," "collectors and connoisseurs" who have shared their objets with her ("Sir Charles Tennant has positively dismantled the walls of his staircase at 40 Grosvenor Square" for her, she tells us).[78] Her effort to leave her Jewishness behind her is a biographical fact; her desire to slough off suburbia and enter the august portals of Belgravia and Mayfair seems similarly clear. The family moved to 11 Clarges Street in 1903, thus apparently completing the upward journey; Frankau celebrated her arrival in Mayfair by purchasing a Victoria and a brougham.[79] (After her husband's death, she removed to the Ritz.) Aline Bernstein, daughter of the American actor Joseph Frankau, who was a cousin of Arthur's, later recalled that Julia lived in what seemed a perfect "Georgian house," full of the signals of established wealth, not the nouveau riche—"the silver and old woods looked as though they not only had just been polished, but had been polished for hundreds of years." Julia herself was "superbly tailored until tea-time, and then every afternoon she received in lovely tea-gowns," so that, to the star-struck Aline, Julia and her drawing room seemed the embodiment of elite Englishness.

Frankau policed herself rigorously and made considerable advances into the literary and geographical centers of turn-of-the-century London. This may help us understand why she turned, in 1897, to skewer Panton with such passion in "The Brixton Gospel." Her critique of her *Gentlewoman* colleague at last makes sense, for Frankau points to Panton's cavalier, casual attitudes with particular exasperation: "There is a cocksureness in Mrs. Panton's way of dealing with great State questions," she contends. By authorizing "sweeping statements," Panton "keeps her readers content themselves"—that is, she does not push her suburbanite readers to the appropriate self-examination, self-fashioning, self-cultivation. Panton's readers are left, from Frankau's perspective, languishing in a state of unselfconsciousness, not excoriated or exhorted, as she exhorted her own readers, to change.[80] Panton's run-on, excitable, unedited prose in *The Way They Should Go* must have seemed, to Frankau, not only exasperating to read, but also a terrible betrayal of their shared readers' interests. To Frankau, self-aware self-critique was not just a practice, it was an imperative for any suburban resident who hoped to move, in late Victorian society, from Maida Vale to Mayfair, Bayswater to Belgravia.

Panton embraced the suburbs. But Frankau's life and work reminds us that it was easier for some to articulate celebrations of the suburban than for others, that the margins remained equivocal spaces for those positioned farther, for whatever reason, from the heart of the elite. In the background to the fight that played out between Moore and Frankau in 1895 was surely a joint understanding that access to the elite remained difficult to secure. Oscar Wilde, a good friend to both, not to mention a fellow Irishman to Moore, had just been imprisoned, a tragedy Frankau references in the third letter of the 1895 exchange: "Recent events have proved that, whatever a man's ideas or code of morals may be, no amount of talent will save him from the necessity of living and writing with due regard to the conventions and decencies of English life."[81] Here we see her grasp of the value of a deft performance that verges into outright disguise: "conventions and decencies" must be adopted no matter what one's "ideas or code of morals may be," Frankau remarks—she does not indicate that Wilde's ideas or codes are, of themselves, wrong, but rather that he needed to conceal them, to perform a different (safer) identity. Wilde's historic downfall, from the epicenter of literary London to prison, must have offered a lesson to many of those who felt themselves, in one way or another, more firmly set on the margins. Frankau's adoption of the pseudonym "Frank Danby" in the 1880s and '90s may well bespeak, then, as Galchinsky argues, a tortured self-hatred, a longing to efface her own Jewishness. But we can also read Frankau's self-positioning not only psychologically, as indicative of inner pain, but also as a skillful, self-policing performance of what her community termed the "correct thing."

CONCLUSIONS

Eliza Davis Aria, née Frankau, was surely only speaking the truth when she remarked that, as an old woman, Jane Ellen Panton remained obsessed with the past. "She sits at ease now gowned in black silk, diatribing against the ways of to-day, airing her old grievance against her father, Derby Day Frith, R.A., whose double matrimonial life remains eternally amongst her disgruntles," Aria observed.[82] The fury Panton felt—that she was pushed aside, that her ambitions were thwarted, that her father's son by Mary was to become the painter she longed to be, that her father lied to them, to the world—finds explicit expression in the end, but not before she has done battle with the conventions of the autobiographical form her father deployed, not to mention the marriage plot she felt she had been forced to live out.[83] Writers of Victorian autobiographies typically selected episodes to convey a journey on which worth produces understanding, recognition, success, and her father's narrative certainly fits this model, as Frith charts his journey from the provinces and the lower-middle classes to the Royal Academy, and so to the cultural and urban heart of 1880s Britain. His narrating persona is an extension of his painterly eye: he positions himself as a member of the elite who nonetheless understands and has sympathy with the masses. Panton's work at first cautiously adopts a similar model. But Panton later abandons it, creating multiple textual voices who are at war with the past, insecure in their advance, grappling with the fiction of who and what they are, fighting to establish a new place for themselves. She had direct, personal experience of being fictionalized, as a daughter; Frankau was fictionalized, far more profoundly, as an Anglo-Jew. Both writers, over the course of their careers, experimented with new voices, new identities, telling new stories, finding new plots, adopting new roles—speaking of suburbia in multiple voices, as reviewers, seers, critics, professionals.

Frith's daughter embraced the identity of suburbanite, performing traits, practices, preoccupations, and speech patterns that writers like Frankau associated with the suburban-dwelling masses, the uncultured, the Philistines.[84]

Panton's remarkable self-positioning as "the quintessence of the suburban" indicates that, to Frankau at least, the masses appeared in the ascendency; "secure in her public," as Frankau expressed it, with perhaps a trace of wistfulness, Panton built a career speaking to suburbanite interests. Her work suggests that Panton saw the suburbs as the future: her own life was one where the suburban landscape facilitated entrance into what was rapidly becoming the nation's cultural heart—the professions. The suburbs, places of moving and work, of exposure to new people, connected residents like Panton to professional life through networks that did not just run by rail or road. Suburbs brought disparate groups together, transplants and aliens who forged communities based on shared interests and occupations. The suburbs had their problems, but their promise of new beginnings was tantalizing. Besides, not everyone viewed the journey away from birth networks with fear and trepidation. To those with uncomfortable or painful pasts, breaking with family could be freeing.

To the very ends of their lives, Frankau and Panton deftly deployed their skills in performance. Both, interestingly enough, were commended somewhat humorously by those around them for their ability to play roles. Eliza Davis Aria—lover of Irving, friend to Ivor Novello, and a thespian who not only wanted but actually managed to die in a theater—surely knew a good performance when she saw it: she called the Panton of the 1920s "[a] very wise creature with a delicate air of a Cosway miniature and slim white fingers encircled with many coloured jewels . . . although only about a dozen years older than I am, she persists with a flattering smile to talk to me as if I were in my first youth."[85] Gilbert Frankau, meanwhile, remembered that his mother's axiom was "When considering the words of people who write, always allow for a little insincerity." A young American relative watched in fascination, as we saw earlier, as Julia received in elegant tea gowns, the quintessence of Englishness, and observed, in tellingly theatrical language: "It was like a story, an elegant and beautiful interpretation of ordinary life. It was the sort of thing I always hoped to see when I went to the theatre."[86] Suburban women both, Frankau and Panton ended their lives as they had lived them, setting scenes, making up stories, playing roles, and adroitly turning their suburban skill set to personal and professional use.

Conclusions
STEPPING OFF THE THRESHOLD

The later decades of the nineteenth century saw a number of reformers turn their attention to the suburban landscape; the city took a back seat. Ebenezer Howard famously developed the idea of the "garden city," a self-sustaining space with different zones that could provide leisure, government, and industry harmoniously, integrating green spaces and agricultural land together with an active civic heart. A rather less ambitious model was the "garden suburb," which was not intended to fulfill all a community's needs, as Howard envisaged, but which nonetheless combined housing with green spaces and aimed to foster community by integrating social meeting places. Hampstead Garden Suburb was one of the first places successfully developed along this model, driven by the redoubtable activism of Henrietta Barnett and her husband.

The garden suburbs and garden cities designed and developed over the course of the next century sprang from the idea that the first suburbs were not fulfilling their residents' needs: Ebenezer Howard's first book was full of the problems of the suburbs as they had evolved, not to mention the draining countryside that had produced them. Yet while Howard thought more, if better, suburbs were the answer, many disagreed: male cosmopolitan writers especially expressed themselves appalled by what they termed suburbia's cultural as well as architectural and spatial takeover of the nation. The suburbs, they argued, were not worthy of their prominence. Walter Besant presented life in the suburbs as one "without any society . . . as dull a life as any mankind imagined." T. W. H. Crosland, with particular animus, skewered suburb after suburb in his book-length study *The Suburbans,* raining down criticism on its men, women, children, and servants, its religious practices, churches, and theaters, its art and architecture, gardens, music, and literature. Sounding very like Frank Danby, Crosland sneers at suburbanites for consuming cheap books: "Show me a house with its rows of skimpily-bound, undersized shilling or eighteen-penny volumes, and I will show you a house in which the spirit of Dalston and Clapham and Surbiton and Crouch End rules supreme."[1] Indeed, suburbia seems to inspire Crosland, like Danby, to list suburbia's characteristics, as if to signal that they share no internally logical connection. He offers a catalog of supposedly shared horrors—"red-brick villas, seven-guinea saddle-bag suites, ceraceous fruit in glass shades, pampas grass, hire-system gramophones, anecdotal oleographs, tinned soups, music in the parks" yet nonetheless terms suburbia a landscape of absences, "a place wherein nothing is, save villas; where no bird sings excepting in front-windows; where the principal objects of cultivation are the stunted cabbage and the bedraggled geranium."[2] George Gissing's suburbs, meanwhile, are peopled with the unhappy striving to get ahead and failing, or languishing in their own self-satisfaction, and consequently falling prey to the rapacious, like the hapless husband sucked into marriage by his landlady in "The Prize Lodger." Sherlock Holmes moves through opaque South London suburbs that need a mastermind to interpret them, while Grossmith's suburban "Nobody" is both smug and lost. In Arnold Bennett's work, in the fiction of Jerome K. Jerome and Keble Howard, we find trivial and mundane existences on every page. The title of a chapter in Howard's *The Smiths of Surbiton* (1906) is "Concerning a Toothbrush."

Ged Pope observes, in a recent book on the suburbs in literature, that "much late nineteenth-century London suburban-set fiction . . . concentrates precisely on the almost imperceptible trivia of . . . everyday domestic life" and "on semi-visible suburban 'Nobodies.'" The story of the suburb, as he sees it, is a "problem of knowledge in the suburb. Again and again, in fiction, we meet isolated individuals agonizing over what can be seen and what can be known, in this new-built, peripheral and inscrutable domestic habitat, inhabited by displaced strangers and new arrivals. Information is crucial and scarce: in the suburb no one knows anything for sure, no one can see anything . . . . this inability to fully read the suburb means that any full or rewarding sense of place or belonging is unavailable and is replaced by a feeling of alienation from place and local historicity and by a profound sense of the unreality of the world."[3] Pope goes on to present the suburb as a place that forces us to consider the question of how we make the places in which we live meaningful, if those places lack easily accessible cues, familiar lineages, a connection to family and the past; this is an important point, and he is surely right to point out the unrelenting focus on the horrors of domestic trivia in the texts he focuses upon. "Suburban place is always in the process of coming into focus, of being imaginatively rendered (or not) as a meaningful place," he argues, and the Victorian suburbs posed great problems to those working to make legible "the new mass metropolitan suburbs," given that they were "both banal and unremarkable, and deeply strange."[4]

It seems clear that the Victorian suburbs were very far from utopian. The texts discussed in this book are full of reference to unseasoned floorboards, drafty chimneys, yelling potboys, rattling railings, screeching macaws, upside-down cacti, not to mention alien strangers, anxious mothers, avaricious speculators. But that is not all the Victorian suburb was; it cannot be so easily dismissed as a real-world incarnation of Crosland's hideously dull and tasteless wasteland nightmare. There was another way of speaking of suburbia, another story that does not take "unbelonging" and alienation, dullness and mechanical following as its predominant theme. This story has remarkably escaped attention, an oversight that is, I have suggested, caused substantially by selection bias. Literary critical readings of the suburbs focus almost always on texts written by male cosmopolitan writers, like Gissing, Doyle, Wells, Bennett, and Crosland; their interpretations of the suburb consequently shape discussion of the Victorian margins. In an era that famously argued for the separation of the spheres of men and women, those whose sphere was ideologically domestic were associated with suburban homes from the first: the apparent femaleness of the suburbs strongly reinforced its association with the trivial, the small-minded, the petty, and the boring—a life "as dull a life as any *man* imagined," as Crane put it (my italics). Suburbia was imagined as a trap with a spider-woman at its heart, from Bulwer-Lytton's pre-Victorian fiction, to Collins's mid-Victorian *Basil,* to Gissing's "Prize Lodger" and beyond. To be in suburbia, it seemed to many, was to be in women's world, subsumed and out of place, struggling to read the signals and navigate an unfamiliar feminized territory; struggling to survive. Crosland claimed, in a putative letter to "The Female Suburban," that "the male suburban is a henpecked, shrew-driven, neglected, heart-sick man," and laid the blame for this lamentable state of affairs squarely on the "monstrous regiments" of suburban women.[5] Crosland is not only quoting John Knox, for the suburbs were often likened to monstrous women. The sweeping of homes across the landscape was compared to the releasing of a raging female monster with brick teeth, tentacular arms, and dangerously closing doors, so that heroes who enter suburban houses regularly live out a kind of castration fantasy. A commonly narrated Victorian scene, as we have seen, shows a man looking up at a suburban house that watches, then slyly "embraces" him. He enters the house, only to find himself powerless and devalued inside, frightened and foundering. Eventually he leaves, but he is forever weakened. Famous accounts of the Victorian suburbs as monstrous beasts squeezing out the creative juices of residents must be read against this backdrop.

But the suburbs were spoken of in other ways, as we have seen—in women's magazines, fiction, and nonfiction especially. Lara Baker Whelan, examining Gissing's suburban literature in the light of Matthew Arnold's work, suggests that, "judging by its numerous starring roles in turn-of-the-century literature, the 'new class' inhabiting these suburbs was problematic for those who watched it develop precisely because it lacked any emphasis on 'the best' either in thought or in action."[6] Frank Danby would have said an emphatic "yes, quite," to this, of course, but "Frank Danby" was a ghostly projection, a phantasmagoria. Time and again, we find women writers deeply committed to the topic of what constituted "the best" and emphatic that the suburban home is in fact the space in which "the best" can be most actively pursued. Frances Wolseley argued, in a 1920 chapter entitled "Suburban Gardens," that "a garden is . . . the clear mirror of soul and character" because here "no deceit gains admission"; a large house, she contends, is undoubtedly revealing, but "in small gardens even more can be learnt about the character of those to whom they belong" because the very challenges show off taste and skill more starkly.[7] Wolseley does not contend that all suburban gardens are models of good taste, needless to say, but she presents them as especially fertile ground for its growth and display. Even those women who critiqued their suburb—and many did—pursued their criticisms in ways that remind us that discussions about what constitutes "the best" were deeply suburban conversations.

Those conversations were surely raging in the suburbs encircling other Victorian cities also. *The Promise of the Suburbs* has concentrated on London, for reasons of space and focus, but the nation's many other suburban communities beg for sustained attention in the future. Other cities in England were growing with a rapidity that equaled London's: the census recorded a population growth in Birmingham from 73,670 in 1801 to 522,182 by 1901, the city "increasing at nearly twice the national average rate." These census figures do not even include surrounding areas like Yardley, Handsworth, King's Norton, Aston, and Northfield, "even though they were rapidly expanding as suburbs of Birmingham." The earliest Birmingham suburban railway station, in Perry Barr, opened in 1838, with tramlines also facilitating movement in and out of the city center, so that the networked lives explored here in London surely evolved in Birmingham—and Leeds, Liverpool, Manchester, Bristol, and so on—as well.[8] Further lines of suburban inquiry might turn on how residents of these and other suburbs regarded and represented their environs, suburban problems and possibilities, how and in what ways magazines and periodicals aimed at residents of other cities' margins flesh out the story of the generative and beguiling suburb uncovered in this book.[9] Women and "self-made men" in these areas seem, from a very preliminary survey, to have been just as likely to view their suburban locales as generative, enabling friendships, amateur creativity and, ultimately, professional opportunity. Railway clerk Atkinson Grimshaw made the suburban streets of Leeds by moonlight the subject of many of his most famous paintings—and he left the railway behind in the process, becoming an acclaimed late Victorian professional artist.[10] Photography, meanwhile, was an important means, from the middle of the century onward, by which the leisured suburbanite could express and develop his or her creative and scientific interests and, in the century's later decades, transition to professional life. Full examination of the topic lies, again, outside the scope of this book, but *Practical Photographer,* begun in 1890, contained a regular column entitled "Photography as a Business," even as it also answered the questions of amateurs. The pages of the *Amateur Photographer* in the 1880s and '90s are full of reports from suburban photographers' organizations, advice on finding talks and darkrooms, "Sale and Exchange" columns and "Queries" pages through which enthusiasts could connect and share tips. Women were welcomed, at least initially, into the fold: the *Amateur Photographer* "cordially [invited] the co-operation of either sex" in its first, 1884 issue, stressing "that ladies make excellent manipulators" (it also presented photography as an art "in which the amateur soon equals, and frequently excels, the professional in proficiency").[11] L. T. Meade, author of girls' stories, contributed to the publication, and advertisements for photographers' apparatus targeted women through approving quotes on the healthfulness of the art from magazines like *Lady's Pictorial.* Some of this welcoming tone faded, over the course of the magazine's next fifteen years, but women undoubtedly persisted in the business: *Practical Photographer* presented Mrs. Jeanie A. Welford in

1891 as one of the "leaders in the field" of photography. Welford (née Jeanie Agnes Morgan) lived in the Birmingham suburb of Edgbaston in the 1880s and was to have studios in London, Birmingham, and Rottingdean, on the edge of Brighton, in the course of her professional career. She exhibited images in the Royal Photographic Society Exhibition and earned hundreds of awards.[12]

Older markers of class difference were gradually losing their force. As "culture" emerged as a newer signal of superiority, women, immigrants, provincials, and the lower classes surely grasped that they were positioned (once again) on the margins of a category that, for all Arnold's optimism, required an education, training, and social position they did not possess.[13] But women were beginning to work out new ways to train themselves, to work on what one might call *self*-culture. This is an important part of the hidden story of the suburbs, the narrative climax of a plot that has so far escaped attention. Middle-class women could work on *themselves;* they could practice self-discipline and service to others, they could test their moral character, in the suburbs. They could garden and design the homes they lived in and participate in print communities oriented around matters of taste. They could write letters, enter competitions. They could learn about, and participate in, new schools and courses in design, gardening, cooking. They could buy furniture, textiles, paints—and then move, and deploy what they had learned, all over again. Commerce, and the transportation systems that facilitated travel out of and around the suburbs, allowed women to experience the challenges, problems, and opportunities of the marketplace. Shopping for paints or annuals did not just afford pleasure, it gave women a means of entering into a relationship with the modern world, experiencing its challenges, learning how to navigate its problems. In time, women could parlay the skills they had acquired, not to mention their experience in managing money and commercial exchanges, into paid labor that they represented as, in the emerging language of the professions, "vocational." In this way, professional work could be rhetorically presented as altruistic rather than selfish, a means of responding actively to the world's challenges, rather than merely benefiting from its opportunities or being duped by fraudsters' tricks.

Importantly, a language of professionalism and even explicit discussion on how to manage client relationships, legal obligations, and company finances increasingly appear in advice texts aimed at women about the suburban home. In 1920, Frances Wolseley includes, at the back of *Gardens: Their Form and Their Design,* a text whose chapters advise on "Suburban Gardens," a five-page bibliography for readers who intend to take on "advisory work for private gardens, jobbing gardening, or the larger scope of laying out public parks and gardens." There is even a specimen legal "Agreement" that can be clipped out when contracting to garden for clients, a kind of LegalZoom precursor. Extra notes warn on the kinds of practical problems that can develop in relationships with clients, sketching out the minutiae of drawing up contracts: "The agreement should be prepared in duplicate. Each party—that is, both gardener and client—should sign both copies, and each should hold one part."[14] In this way, the reader could not only imagine herself becoming but also actually become a professional by reading Wolseley's book.

Novels set in the suburbs, meanwhile, provide literary spaces for the working out of the stakes of women's professional identity. For it is in such texts that writers engaging an audience of women show how the new landscapes women inhabit are conducive to the development of an identity that was, as critics from Harold Perkin onward have argued (with varying degrees of approbation), increasingly at the cultural—if not the geographical—center of the English national identity: the professional. Novels like Panton's *River of Years* offer an obvious example, a text that shows how a woman gains purpose, and finds community, in a suburb of professionals who guide her into the life of a professional writer, where she finds happiness and purpose. But even novels that do not explicitly represent the suburbs as a community of professionals, or the professional life of the architect, interior designer, writer, or actress, lay the foundations all the same, by representing women networked from margins to centers; commercially engaged, not locked into remote "cottage-gardens"; oriented around interest groups, not birth communities; active in the world of capital relations, as landladies. Suburban popular novels turn on the need for residents to respond to new kinds of people and rise to the challenges of new kinds of relationships, and new commercial interactions, with people to whom they are not connected by birth, faith, or ethnicity. It is axiomatic in such fiction that women are not only able to manage such relationships, they are unusually good at it because of their skills in reading human emotions, their ability to find points of human connection, their selflessness. They are also tremendously skilled at performing a role: women, as stage setters, know the "correct thing" when they see it and how to produce it. The role-playing that suburban living required and regularized helped acculturate women in the kinds of rituals that Albert Pionke identifies as key to the constitution and perpetuation of the professions.[15] In this way, fictions present women's entrance into the worlds of capital relations and professional labor as harmonious with the past, with women's traditional roles, rather than a dangerous schism.

The broader reimagining of women's professional work as continuous with the past is everywhere evident in the catalog for the first-ever exhibition of women's professional achievements, held in the spring of 1885. Located in the affluent Bristol suburb of Clifton, the Loan Exhibition of Women's Industries sought to reveal the scope of women's professional work, the scale of women's creative achievement and innovation. With a reported eighteen thousand visitors, the exhibition was dubbed by local and national papers alike a great success. Visitors were reminded in the catalog "that all the modern work they will see in this Exhibition is done by women who make a profession of their pursuit, either for the arts' sake, or for the sake of earning a livelihood. No work is shewn done for recreation or amusement only." (Agnes Garrett designed an entire room; special admiration was directed at the all-woman-manufactured carpet.) But while the members of the exhibition's organizing committee were keen to paint the producers of the displayed objects as professionals, not amateurs, they worked simultaneously to connect the modern woman professional to the skilled amateur of the past. A woman seated at a spinning wheel was a central theme of the exhibition (she is visible, for instance, at the top left of the catalog); quilts of yesteryear hung near displays of ebonized door handles, and portraits of artistic women of the past sought to remind viewers that those "who have left their mark on the world remind us of many efforts for the progress of Society, which can neither be engraven nor embroidered, in stone or tissue, but in the fabrics of Society and the memories of history."[16] Insofar as modern professional work may be a break with the past, moreover, the organizers were at pains to stress that this was only because the industrial revolution had brought it about. Women's traditional means of artistic production and remuneration—like the spinning wheel—had been taken over by machines: "We have, in these days, to face the fact that factories are destroying home industries; that women are being deprived of home work of marketable value. The greater number of industries once wrought by women at home, by the mother, assisted by her daughters and her maid-servants, are now to be bought, factory-made, for hard cash in the shops. In other words, the possession of cash has increased in importance, while the woman's range of domestic industries has decreased."[17] At once celebrating the industry of the past and weaving it carefully into the industry of the present, the exhibition's ultimate goal was explicit, and explicitly

20. Catalog for "The Loan Exhibition of Women's Industries." The Mistress and Fellows, Girton College, Cambridge.

political: professional training (that is, training in turning skills into marketable labor) is imperative for women in a new age of intense competition. "Only those who are trained to understand principles as well as to exercise manual skill can hold their own in the race," the catalog explained.[18]

The first exhibition of women's professional work in England chose, not a quaint cottage, or (for that matter) a purpose-built exhibition hall, but a suburban villa for its location. The spacious Queen Villa, in the rapidly expanding Clifton suburb, was fortuitously empty and considered "suitable in every respect" (the committee members trooped in a number of times to investigate it, en masse).[19] The exhibition's display of women's achievements was organized to reflect the house's more conventional arrangement: thus cooking lessons were placed in the basement, portraits of Great Women hung in the hall, and "an improved system" of baby's clothing was exhibited on the second floor, in a room that echoed a nursery (complete with wax baby). The villa location surely signaled to attendees that women's labor was consistent with Victorian domestic values, that what professional women did could be placed on a continuum with the practices of generations of skilled housewives.

Yet the choice also signaled a more intimate relationship between the suburban home and women's professional labor. The villa was not only *consistent* with women's professional work, it *produced* it. Many of the exhibition's industries were intimately related to women's work in the home, from clothes, furniture, carpets, and landscape gardening designs to door hinges and door handles. And, even as it overflowed with throngs of fascinated visitors, the Loan Exhibition memorably staged for its eighteen thousand visitors that women were outgrowing the villa. "Every nook and corner of the moderate-sized house in which the exhibition is held is full," the *Pall Mall Gazette* remarked, in a long, admiring review of the event, while the *Queen* observed, of one of the evening lectures: "The only drawback to the evening's enjoyment was the crowded state of the rooms, which were so blocked that it was almost impossible for the guests to move about."[20] And even as the exhibition focused on domestic productions, there were clear signs of interest in new industries and new professions, such as telegraphy and shipbuilding. Not for much longer could women's work be contained within the doors of a villa; not for much longer could women's interests be limited to the four rooms of ground floor and first floor. A generation of women stood on what Virginia Woolf termed "the threshold of the private house."[21] They were ready to step off.

Notes

INTRODUCTION

1. Forster, *Room* 118; Crosland 17; Wells qtd. by Cunningham, "Houses" 422. As Cunningham notes, Wells's title is strikingly incorrect, since the Martians largely follow the commuter railway as they blast and kill: "The furthest point of the Martian advance is the Thames estuary." Cunningham, "Houses" 430.
2. The 1851 census showed an aggregate urban population exceeding the rural, "albeit by less than one percentage point." "During the third quarter of the century . . . the census classified more than half the population as urban," so that "by the year of Victoria's death, three-quarters of the population of Great Britain was classified by the census as urban" (Lampard 4, 6). At the same time, as Raymond Williams points out, "at the end of the nineteenth century more people were living in the rural districts than in the whole nation only a century earlier" (Williams 188). See too Dyos and Reeder 362.
3. Williams 289, 297.
4. Williams 9–12.
5. Chaucer 8.657–61.
6. Clubbe and qtd. by Clubbe 15.
7. "On the Mischievous Effects of Fairs" 3; *Times* (20 July 1826) 1.
8. Dyos and Reeder 362.
9. Other major impetuses in the growth of suburban areas include the abolition of turnpikes in 1863, through the Metropolis Amendment Act, and the building of bridges over the Thames (Barratt 207–12). Other transport options seem less to capture the spirit of the age but were no less important in moving people around the city and its environs, such as the hansom cab, a two-wheeled vehicle pulled by a one-horse

tram (at the end of the century), and the boat: "At the start of the 1850s, far more people travelled along the Thames in boats than sat in railway carriages." Barratt 185.

For more discussion on the factors precipitating and driving suburban growth see Thompson, "The Rise of Suburbia"; Olsen, "House upon House"; Kuchta 3–56; Long, "The Origins of the Edwardian House." An especially accessible account of London's growth is Jenkins, *Landlords to London.* Most agree that "the first English suburb was St. John's Wood, developed from 1815 by John Shaw on the Eyre Estate; the detached and semi-detached houses became the blueprint for later suburban houses. Suburban development round other major cities began in the 1820s and 1830s." Long 49. John Shaw was the architect-surveyor for the Eyre estate in St. John's Wood; a superbly detailed survey of this particular suburb's growth may be found in Galinou, *Cottages and Villas.* Williamson's *Coping with City Growth* offers a detailed survey of the demographics behind urbanization; discussion on the designs of terrace streets and houses of all classes, including floor plans, may be found in Muthesius, esp. chaps. 11–13.

10. Thompson, "The Rise of Suburbia" 10. For more on the class arrangement of the early suburb of Edgbaston see Flanders xxiii.
11. The first London rail line, to Greenwich, was opened in 1836, with further routes connecting north and south opening in 1840. Expansion (and extensions to existing lines) proceeded apace through the 1850s and 1860s. The first underground line opened in 1863, with the Hammersmith and City Railway opening in 1864. Extensions opened into Middlesex, Hertfordshire, and Buckinghamshire, with further extensions in the 1880s and '90s into Rickmansworth and Pinner. The Metropolitan District Railways opened between South Kensington and Westminster in 1868, extending east to Aldgate and Whitechapel, south and west to Earl's Court, Richmond, and Ealing in the 1870s and '80s. Electrified lines came as early as 1890; the integration of what is now the Underground took place in 1908. (I am indebted to Barratt for this brief overview; see esp. 186–91.)
12. Dyos 70. For more on the transportation system in early and pre-Victorian Camberwell see Dyos, 66–80. For more on the impact of the railways generally see Simmons, "The Power of the Railway" and Kellett's classic *Impact of Railways,* esp. 408–9.
13. As Richard Rodger argues, straight terraces help with "labor-intensive building work" by reducing "the costs of foundations, roofs, and piped supplies of water and gas." Rodger 238.
14. For a detailed analysis of how these factors played out in the development of Camberwell, see Dyos passim. Dyos focuses particularly on the conditions and circumstances of pre- and early Victorian development in chapters 2, 3, and 4.
15. *Builder's Practical Director,* "Design for an Italian Villa" 232, "Design for a Suburban Villa" 247. Plates 95 and 115. For more discussion on changing designs over the period, see Barson 61–102, esp. 75–93. I discuss Queen Anne Revival in more detail in chapter 4.
16. Dickens, *Barnaby Rudge* 253.
17. Barthes 38–39.

18. Qtd. by Rappaport 25, 42. For more on Bayswater's growth in particular, as well as the heterogeneity of the suburbs, see Rappaport's excellent first chapter. The suburbs were, Rappaport points out, "at the crossroads of the public and private, both domestic havens and thriving marketplaces. During the second half of the nineteenth century, several suburban streets evolved into flourishing retail centers with elegant small shops and monumental department stores." Rappaport 22.
19. Thompson, "The Rise of Suburbia" 20.
20. Rappaport 24.
21. Carey 5, 58.
22. Qtd. by Whelan, *Class, Culture* 151. Lara Baker Whelan is, to the best of my knowledge, the first to argue that Arnoldian terminology "had a significant influence on the way late-century commentators framed the discussion surrounding Culture and the suburbs" (151). I am indebted to her argument here. Arnold was optimistic that an entire society could become cultured; he did not suggest that only the educated middle classes could ever acquire taste.
23. Carey 47.
24. Carey 80.
25. "What can I do in Rome? I never learned how / To lie" (Juvenal, Satire III); qtd. by Williams 46.
26. Jameson 225; Daly, *Literature, Technology, and Modernity* 3.
27. "Our Views" (1895), 298. The passage continues: "When, as seems only too likely, our towns and villages are alike 'abominations,' it will be pleasant or painful to be able to look back at what they once were in the 'dark ages,' before our new lights had dawned" (298).
28. Suburban photographs do exist, of course; Bedford Lemere and Co. staged particularly wonderful images of suburban interiors and exteriors at the end of the century. Photos of the Warner Estate include gardens, kitchens, dining, and drawing rooms from Walthamstow flats and "Villas": http://www.exwarnerproject.co.uk/lens_portfolio/bedford-lemere-co/.
29. Thompson, "The Rise of Suburbia" 3.
30. The most important book-length studies of Victorian literature about the suburbs include Hapgood's *Margins of Desire,* Kuchta's *Semi-Detached Empire,* and Whelan's *Class, Culture and Suburban Anxieties.* Pope's *Reading London's Suburbs* contains several chapters on the nineteenth and early twentieth centuries. Other key literary critical studies of the suburbs include Cunningham, "Houses in Between" and "The Riddle of Suburbia," and Flint, "Fictional Suburbia."
31. Cunningham, "Riddle" 51.
32. Hapgood 1.
33. Cunningham, "Riddle" 52. "For many writers . . . the prime response to the new suburbia was one of anxiety and disorientation," Cunningham argues. "How were they to conceptualize the sudden appearance of the new spatial environment?" Cunningham, "Houses" 42.
34. Kuchta 15.
35. Kuchta 15; Whelan, "Clash of Space" 152.

36. Dickens, *Dombey and Son* 52–53.
37. Carey 69.

CHAPTER 1. JOHN CLAUDIUS LOUDON AND THE NEW SUBURBAN LANDSCAPE

1. Loudon, *Suburban Gardener* 10.
2. Flanders xxiii.
3. Hapgood 8. For more on the separation of housing from commerce and retail spaces, and how this reinforced emerging ideologies, see Thompson, "The Rise of Suburbia" 13–14. I suggest, here and throughout, that the separation of public and private in the suburbs was more theoretical than actual from the first; as Rappaport's study makes clear, suburbs like Bayswater, where Loudon lived, were thriving marketplaces.
4. Rappaport 25.
5. The most sustained work on Loudon's contributions to architecture and landscaping styles is Simo, *Loudon and the Landscape;* for a more general examination of Loudon's relationship to other contemporary theories of the landscape, see Taylor, *The Vital Landscape.*
6. Loudon, *Suburban Gardener* 10.
7. Flanders xliii; Whelan, *Class, Culture* 9.
8. See also Burnett: "The new town inhabitants were partly the result of natural increase but, more importantly, they were immigrants from the countryside." Burnett 7. This is obviously not to argue that there was *no* movement out from the center, but rather to argue that the movement *in* from the countryside is too easily forgotten.
9. Feldman 189.
10. Woods, *Demography* 311. For more on the age of migrants from the countryside, see Williamson 30–47. For more discussion on the factors behind the move away from agricultural living, and statistical analyses of patterns of rural depopulation, see Armstrong's "Flight from the Land" 118–35.
11. Simmons 298. Barratt also points out that, later in the century, "as the population of the outer suburbs continued to rise, so that of some of the inner suburbs started to decline. Between 1851 and 1901 the population of the City of London fell from 128,000 to 27,000. Between 1871 and 1901 the population of Westminster slipped from 524,000 residents to 460,000." Barratt 213.
12. Dyos 58.
13. "In the last ten years of the century the increase of about 24,000 persons was wholly accounted for by natural increase, and would have been higher had not more people—over a thousand—left the suburb than came into it." Dyos 58.
14. Thompson, "The Rise of Suburbia" 16. Thompson draws on Kellett's classic *Impact of Railways.* The pattern continued: "It is significant that in London in 1881 a greater proportion of provincials were to be found in the rapidly expanding suburbs than in the central districts such as Bethnal Green," observes Armstrong (128). Dyos and D. A. Reeder make the same point: while "the slums of Victorian London were mostly occupied by second or later generation Londoners . . . the suburbs were the ultimate destinations of the incoming provincials" (359–86, 373).

15. Lampard 6. Hapgood observes, writing of the suburbs at the fin de siècle, that "rural England belonged in the past" (7).
16. Loudon, *Suburban Gardener* iii. Loudon restates the point in his introduction; *Suburban Gardener* 2.
17. G.S.B. [Boulger], "John Claudius Loudon," *Dictionary,* vol. 34, 149–50.
18. Loudon, *Suburban Gardener* 325.
19. Loudon, *Treatise* 425.
20. Loudon, *Suburban Gardener* 2.
21. For more on middle-class attitudes to manual labor see Davidoff and Hall 22.
22. See, for example, Loudon's *Suburban Gardener* 236–38, a section tellingly subtitled "To lay out and plant a Fourth-Rate Suburban Garden, where the Occupier intends to cultivate some Culinary Vegetables and Fruits, with a few Flowers."
23. Loudon, *Suburban Gardener* 235.
24. Loudon, *Suburban Gardener* 6.
25. Loudon, *Suburban Gardener* 3.
26. Note that the judicious use of science was something contemporary reviewers admired particularly in Loudon's work; the *Gentleman's Magazine* observed of Loudon's *Suburban Horticulturalist* that "all the latest discoveries in agricultural chemistry have been applied in this work to the subject of gardening" (172).
27. Loudon, *Suburban Gardener* 9.
28. Loudon, *Suburban Gardener* 217.
29. Loudon, *Suburban Gardener* 8–11.
30. Loudon, *Suburban Gardener* 9.
31. Loudon, *Suburban Gardener* 9.
32. Davidoff and Hall 190.
33. Garson 198, 184.
34. Davidoff and Hall 191–92.
35. Olsen 213–18; qtd. in Olsen, *The Growth of Victorian London* 217.
36. Loudon, *Suburban Gardener* 30, 29.
37. Loudon, *Suburban Gardener* 30.
38. "The exterior appearance of manufacturing buildings is now undergoing great changes in almost every part of the country; and, instead of huge masses, presenting a mean appearance, from the absence of architectural design, or deforming the landscape by their unsightly chimneys, they are becoming magnificent masses." Loudon, *Suburban Gardener* 30.
39. Dickens, *Curiosity Shop* 44.
40. Loudon makes this point in the service of an argument about careful attention to location when choosing a home. Loudon is emphatically *not* advocating friendship with those out of one's social class, but he is arguing that because neighborliness is important, potential suburbanites must consider first whether they are willing to be neighborly with those living next door.
41. Loudon, *Suburban Gardener* 32. Loudon's vision of the suburban home with garden as ideal precisely because it lends itself to improvement by the tenant is common in early Victorian gardening texts. For example, Whiting, in the *Manual of Flower*

Gardening for Ladies, remarks (in an entirely positive vision of suburban living) that such a home "owes half its beauty and comfort to characteristic planting" (84).

42. Loudon, *Suburban Gardener* 10.
43. Loudon, *Suburban Gardener* 30.
44. Dickens, *Dombey* 651; Loudon, *Suburban Gardener* 30–31.
45. For further discussion on middle-class criticisms of aristocratic practices and vices in particular, see Davidoff and Hall 22. On the subject of defining middle-class daily practices, Davidoff and Hall argue that "professional men dealt more with abstractions, symbols and ideas; they sold services not goods. They could more easily keep their hands and clothes clean" (270).
46. Daly, *Literature, Technology, and Modernity* 2.
47. Loudon, *Suburban Gardener* iii.
48. Loudon, *Suburban Gardener* iii.
49. Garson observes that "though the book is, according to its subtitle, written 'for the instruction of the female part of our readers,' it is clear that the implied reader of its more practical sections is the man of the family" (195).
50. Jane Loudon, *Practical Instructions* 26–45.
51. Whiting 84–85.
52. Loudon, *Suburban Gardener* 8.
53. Loudon, *Suburban Gardener* 9.
54. Loudon, *Suburban Gardener* 9.
55. Loudon, *Suburban Gardener* 7.
56. Loudon, *Suburban Gardener* 6–7.
57. Loudon, *Suburban Gardener* 7.
58. Loudon, *Suburban Gardener* 609.
59. Loudon, *Villa* v.
60. *The Villa Gardener* looks far more like the book described by critics such as Davidoff and Hall and Garson—a text oriented around family seclusion and privacy.
61. Emphasis added, *Villa* 4.
62. Loudon, *Villa* 73, 121.
63. Hapgood 12. Hapgood is talking in particular about novels by Arthur Conan Doyle and Keble Howard.
64. "By 1860, [Westbourne] Grove [in Bayswater] was lined with milliners, tailors, grocers, tobacconists, ironmongers, bakers, linen drapers, watchmakers, photographic artists, auctioneers, house agents, fishmongers, confectioners, butchers, and stationers," Rappaport concludes, drawing on the *London Post Office Directory* for that year (26). Sala described the Grove "as a sensual Eastern marketplace in which men delighted in looking at women who, in turn, enjoyed looking at goods." Qtd. in Rappaport 21.

CHAPTER 2. SETTING SUBURBAN STEREOTYPES

1. Hammerton 169.
2. Cunningham, "Riddle" 54.

3. "Dulham" is the name of the suburb Emily Eden's characters inhabit in *The Semi-Detached House.* The text will be discussed presently.
4. For a useful overview of the development of lower-middle-class housing in the last third of the century, and the ways in which fin de siècle writers associated the suburbs with the tasteless clerk, see Whelan 147–50. The phenomenon is also thoughtfully discussed, in detail, by Hapgood in *Margins of Desire,* esp. 170–93.
5. Thompson, "The Rise of Suburbia" 2.
6. "Stereotyping" meant, originally, "the practice of typesetting with 'a printing plate made by making a cast, usually in TYPE METAL, from a mould of a printing surface.'" Morris 9. Surrounding the mechanical practice of stereotyping were, from the beginning, concerns characteristic of the process of industrialization generally: traditional printers were at pains to point out the "unquestionably infinitely superior" qualities of the old presses. Johnson's *Typographia,* for instance, runs through a series of objections to the stereotyping process, ranging from the incurring of new start-up expenses (because of the cost of the metal) to the standardization of texts: "The plates once cast must ever remain so, as no alteration in the size of the page, or cut of the type can ever take place, without incurring all the original expense" (Johnson observes that this cost makes it far more likely for texts to be produced with errors). The author is especially concerned about the potential proliferation of unauthorized texts (because of the "'facility with which Stereotype plates are cast from Stereotype plates'") and, perhaps above all, the loss of jobs in the profession. In answer to one advocate of stereotyping, who argued it would benefit "both pressmen and compositors," Johnson acidly observes: "It could only be of service to them, if Mr. T[illoch] could prove that men are better off without employment than with it." In stereotyping, as in so many other advances of the industrial age, discourse surrounding potential (cheaper production in the long run, new kinds of jobs in new industries, the growth of a mass reading public powered by an expanded industry) was contested and balanced by discussion of threat (job loss, higher short-term costs, gross standardization practices, the annihilation of traditional skills). See Morris 9 and Johnson, *Typographia* 658–59; for a more detailed discussion of stereotyping (and electrotyping), its costs and benefits, as well as its use until late in the nineteenth century, see Weedon esp. 73–76.
7. "The Art of Puffing" 159.
8. For example, in a tale of searching for work in a depressed printing industry, the narrator uses the language of the presses to describe the wearying sameness of the reply he receives from every door: "'We are doing nothing, and have not work for our own hands,' was the stereotyped form of the reply I received." A Working Man 224. Stereotyping in its contemporary sense (as applied to people and their characteristics) is usually dated to 1922 and the work of social scientist Walter Lippmann, although the *OED* dates the use of "stereotyped" as referencing phrases "fixed or perpetuated in an unchanging form" to the 1840s. Mrs. Gaskell uses "stereotyped" in this way in *North and South,* first serialized in 1854: "She made all these reflections as she was talking in her stately way to Mrs. Hale, and uttering all the stereotyped commonplaces that most people can find to say with their senses blindfolded." Gaskell 92; chap. 12.

9. For a detailed examination of Bulwer-Lytton's misanthropic criticisms of his peers and of social injustices generally see Lane passim.
10. *N&M* xiv.
11. *Disowned* I.65, 66. The text imagines (in a passage clearly designed to amuse the reader) what suburban methods for advancement may be: "'Marriage with a fortune,'—here [Linden] paused, and looked at the glass,—'the speculation of a political pamphlet, or an ode to the minister; attendance on some dying miser of my own name, without a relation in the world.'" *Disowned* I.66. At least one of these appealing options turns out, ironically enough, to come true; this novel does not seek to mount a serious analysis of middle-class social mobility.
12. Gray 223.
13. *Disowned* I.71.
14. Hammerton 171. Cunningham makes the same point; see "Riddle" 66. For further discussion on the predatory suburban woman plot see Cunningham, "Riddle" 60–62.
15. Cunningham, "Riddle" 60–61. See, for example, Richard's uneasy passage into Mr. Aked's Fulham home in Bennett's *Man from the North,* where a strange girl ushers Richard into a tastelessly decorated domestic interior—small, heavily curtained, horribly wallpapered, with excessively large furniture (84–85), or Catterson and West's passing into Nellie Hooper's Teddington villa ("Rose Cottage") in Ella D'Arcy's "A Marriage."
16. Cunningham, "Riddle" 60. Cunningham also discusses this moment—as a *rite de passage*—in "Houses" 427–29.
17. *Disowned* I.71.
18. Flint, "Suburbia" 114
19. *Disowned* I.72.
20. *Disowned,* I.44.
21. *Disowned* I.72, 73.
22. *N&M* 1.92.
23. *Disowned* I.4.
24. *Disowned* I.158. Raymond Williams's vision of the modern city begins "with a man walking," Deborah Nord observes. Women's walking in Victorian city streets is inevitably complex. Nord's book is an examination of when, how, and in what circumstances women can occupy the streets; see Nord 11.
25. In *Night and Morning,* the weariness of a priest at his retired existence leads directly to his death in the novel's first volume. Set apart from the rest of the villagers by training and birth but lacking the means for regular contact with the well-born, Caleb Price has long lived for the brief visits of better-positioned men who come to fish the local rivers. After the excitement of a secret wedding to his friend, Price finds himself unable to settle again into rural "monotony" and yearns desperately for the "animal life of passionate civilization" (*N&M* 1.30)—the town.
26. Building owners in London were typically craftsmen and builders. Sometimes gentry invested in homes in the expectation of a six or seven percent return on their investment; see Chalklin 36–7.

27. On the supposed separation of home life from work life in suburbia around this time, in areas around England, see Davidoff and Hall esp. 57–58 and 251–52. The authors describe the separation of home life and work life as one of the key features of suburbia: "The gradual move of manufacturers to suburban areas seems to have been both cause and effect of the gradual separation of the family home from the works," they observe (251). The authors also discuss the fact that this separation was far from uniformly experienced (232): lower down the social scale separation from the place of work was obviously an impossibility.
28. Tosh 25.
29. Sala 218.
30. Sala 219.
31. Sala 220.
32. Dickens, *Barnaby Rudge* 253; Sala 227.
33. Sala 221–22.
34. Riddell, *City and Suburb* I.159.
35. Sala 228.
36. Whitehead 119.
37. Whitehead 121.
38. Whitehead 121–22.
39. Dickens too tends to represent the suburbs as places where criminals prey. Sometimes those criminals are the speculators and developers building terrible houses and deafening railways, but Dickens also makes the point that urban problems spill easily into the suburbs. The boys in Fagin's gang do not confine their activities to the city, for instance; Mr. Brownlow in *Oliver Twist* has his pocket picked in Pentonville. Dickens's suburban interiors receive more positive treatment; homes and hearths tend to be—especially if governed by an angelic woman—refuges from chaos.
40. Whitehead 124.
41. Whitehead 124.
42. Wiener 12.
43. Taylor 185. The other two facets are "self-responsible independence" and "the individualism of personal commitment."
44. Marcus 7.

CHAPTER 3. PLOTTING THE SUBURBS

1. The *OED* dates the first use of the word "suburbia" to 1870; the term is, from the first, as other critics have argued, strongly culturally associated with the tasteless, the lower-middle class, the dully bourgeois (see esp. Whelan 147–50).
2. Long 8.
3. Jovchelovitch 67.
4. Jovchelovitch 71.
5. Shared knowledge may be confined to just a few. In philosophical terms, the idea of common knowledge is of something everyone knows, and *knows that everyone else knows;* knowledge is open among all. For more on the distinction see Horsten and Pettigrew 512.

6. This is not to deny that the new suburbs were typically constructed in areas shaped by class markers; for detailed discussion on the designs of terrace streets and semidetached houses, including the floor plans that indicated class affiliations of residents, see the classic work of Muthesius, *English Terraced House* passim, esp. chaps. 11–13.
7. "The Art of Puffing" 159.
8. Jovchelovitch 68.
9. For further discussion see Hammerton 171; Cunningham 60–61.
10. Wagner 207.
11. Collins 113.
12. Collins 113.
13. Collins 134.
14. Schwarzbach 239.
15. As Kate Flint has argued, suburban occupancy was, theoretically, a sign of "one's ability to purchase leisure," and thus a way to buy, "at least in the imagination, into the tradition and culture of the aristocracy." Flint, "Suburbia" 114.
16. Collins 34.
17. Collins 62–63.
18. As R. R. Thomas puts it, "What is vulgar is quite literally defined as that which belongs to the mass, to the crowd, to that which is widely and commonly disseminated among the populous." Thomas 187. Bernstein and Michie's extremely useful collection of essays on Victorian vulgarity explores in detail the ways in which notions of the vulgar were used, in an era of increased social mobility, to assert distance from those in the group just below. (See, for example, Newman 19.) Kucich's thought-provoking afterword to the book, meanwhile, suggests other potential reasons (including changing notions of Englishness) for why vulgarity was, in the period, "an unprecedented cultural flashpoint." Kucich 242.

    Disgust, meanwhile, a response Bernstein and Michie suggest is "inherent in the term vulgarity" is, as Miller shows, "not just raw, unattached feeling," but an emotion "linked to ways of talking about" feelings; we learn rules for what is disgusting in our social and cultural context, and thus disgust "implicates . . . social and moral judgments." Bernstein and Michie 7; Miller, *Anatomy* 8, 113.
19. Jann 85.
20. Collins 32.
21. Disgust is produced by our training, but it is, McGinn argues, a "sense-based emotion." McGinn 44. That is to say, it is triggered by sensory appearance, so that it appears to the experiencer to possess the force of something like instinct. A fuller discussion of disgusted looking lies beyond the scope of this chapter, though I note here that gazing disgustedly and painfully at the suburbs was an act that placed one in good company, as we shall see later.
22. Collins 63.
23. Miller, *Anatomy* 120. For fuller exploration of the idea see 109–42.
24. Collins 181. Another clear signal of impending disaster: "Had I seen [Margaret's father] under ordinary circumstances, I should have set him down as a little-minded

man; a small tyrant. . . . But he was Margaret's father; and I was determined to be pleased with him." Collins 64.

25. When Basil first sees the house, the full passage reads: "I arrived at the house. The blinds were all drawn down over the front windows, to keep out the sun. The little slip of garden was left solitary—baking and cracking in the heat. The square was silent desolately silent, as only a suburban square can be. I walked up and down the glaring pavement." Collins 34.
26. Collins 63.
27. Knight, *English Cyclopaedia* 363.
28. Cole is memorably caricatured in Dickens's *Hard Times* in the figure who tells Sissy Jupe: "You don't walk upon flowers in fact; you cannot be allowed to walk upon flowers in carpets. You don't find that foreign birds and butterflies come and perch upon your crockery; you cannot be permitted to paint foreign birds and butterflies upon your crockery. . . . This is fact. This is taste." Dickens, *Hard Times* 10.
29. Sala's *Gaslight and Daylight* is similarly addressed to those who seek to differentiate themselves from characters like the much-mocked "Earl of Elbowsout" and his kin.
30. Crosland 21.
31. Gissing, *Whirlpool* 327. For more discussion on both Crosland's and Gissing's attitudes to women and suburbia see Cunningham, "Houses" 426.
32. Besant 17. The passage is much discussed, for example by Flanders (xliii) and Olsen (213).
33. Federico 66–67.
34. Eden 13. Blanche's stereotypes are outlined esp. at 13–15. Mrs. Hopkinson, Blanche observes in the full passage, will "be immensely fat, wear mittens—thick, heavy mittens—and contrive to know what I have for dinner every day." Eden 15.
35. Eden 19.
36. Eden 25–26. The screech of the imported macaw, displaced from its natural habitat and lost among the anonymous doors of Victorian suburbia, prefigures the secret in suburbia that was to become an organizing principle in sensation fiction in the next decade; a disruptive force, it unites the community only in the ways in which it forces inhabitants to become stealthy detectives of each other.
37. Eden 21.
38. Eden 48.
39. Eden 54–55.
40. There are other benefits too, as the redoubtable Aunt Sarah observes: "You may add, my dear, that a semi-detached house has its merits; if one half catches fire, you can take refuge in the other." Eden 58.
41. Eden 61.
42. Eden 194.
43. Eden 195. With wonderful Victorian pragmatism, Eden remarks that birth is "the only moment of a fine boy's existence in which his presence is more agreeable than his absence, so let him make the most of it." Eden 196.
44. Eden 223.

45. In that the novel represents the middle classes schooling the upper in the area of domestic skills, the plot reminds us of Theda Skocpol's analysis of nineteenth-century American clubs and lodges where skilled lower-middle-class and even blue-collar individuals could rise to leadership roles. See Scocpol 106.
46. M. Cohen 38.
47. Eden 223.
48. The pioneering historical and literary survey of stereotypes of Jewish people is Rosenberg's *From Shylock to Svengali.*
49. Field 295.
50. The bill was repeatedly rejected by the House of Lords in the late 1840s and early 1850s, but in 1858 the Lords finally agreed to allow each house to decide on its own oath, clearing the way for Lionel de Rothschild to take up a seat (to which he had been repeatedly elected by his constituency) in 1858. For more discussion on the background to and fallout after these developments, see Alderman esp. 282–84. Eden makes disdainful fun of members of Parliament "who had manfully voted for the removal of Jewish disabilities. Whether they knew what the disabilities were, or what would be the effect of their removal, is doubtful; but they somehow had an idea that they were voting against gentlemen and bishops, and church and state, and they felt proud of themselves." Eden 142–43.
51. For more on stereotypes of a virtuous daughter's conversion—a stereotype that reaches back to Shylock's relationship with Jessica, of course, via Scott's Isaac and Rebecca—see Galchinsky, *Origin* esp. 51–53. Ragussis argues that narratives of Jewish conversion played a critical role in redefinitions of Englishness and English nationhood from the 1790s to the 1870s (passim).
52. Bertha Buxton (1844–81), born in Tufnell Park, had published a number of novels by 1879, particularly about theatrical life, including *Nell—On and Off the Stage.*
53. See Bernstein and Michie 1–2.
54. Buxton I.1. While not a common feature of the Victorian suburban landscape, gardens in squares can be seen in the Ladbroke estate of the 1840s, while later versions, where shared gardens are set between the backs of houses, may be seen fairly often in (for instance) Maida Vale and South Hampstead.
55. Jovchelovitch 73.
56. Buxton I.81.
57. Buxton II.221.
58. Buxton I.3.
59. Buxton I.3.
60. Buxton I.18.
61. Forster, *Room* 27.
62. Buxton I.72.
63. Buxton I.62.
64. Buxton I.16.
65. Buxton III.179.
66. Buxton III.193–94.
67. Buxton I.101.
68. S. D. Bernstein 104.

CHAPTER 4. "ART AT HOME"

1. Barker 55.
2. Deborah Cohen notes that "measured in real terms, average income per head doubled between 1851 and 1901. At the same time, the cost of necessaries, especially food, plunged, with the consequence that more people had more money to spend on luxuries previously unimaginable" (D. Cohen 13).
3. For more on women's handicraft culture, see Talia Schaffer's absorbing *Novel Craft* (2011). Handicrafts functioned as ways of both participating in and contesting a newly industrial commodity culture, Schaffer argues, but the rise of the culture of the connoisseur saw the devaluation of such pastimes—the vanishing of fish-scale sequins, painting-by-numbers embroidery, paraffin-forged wax coral, and the like. Writers like Charles Eastlake and John Ruskin sought to dismiss handicrafts as early as the mid-1860s, and "young ladies" from the scene of Art; writers decamped into interior decoration manuals, I suggest in this chapter, presenting the work of designing a room and a house as no "mere" decoration but rather an architectural subspecialty, a reconception that dignifies women's labor, or at least renders it more consonant with the values of the era.
4. Panton, *From Kitchen to Garret* 4, 3.
5. Ruskin, *Modern Painters* 4.
6. Ruskin, *Seven Lamps* 164.
7. Ruskin, *Seven Lamps* 165–66.
8. Ruskin, *Seven Lamps* 166.
9. "Philosophers and Negroes" 326; "M. Vitet's Essays" 539.
10. Crosby 103.
11. Crosby 103.
12. *Suggestions for the Formation of a New Style of Architecture,* which argued for a splicing together of different architectural styles, was memorably dismissed by the *Athenaeum* as a defense of "Frankenstein Art." Review of *Suggestions* 633.
13. Forster, *Howards End* 96.
14. Forster, *Howards End* 242.
15. Forster, *Howards End* 59.
16. Collini, *Public Moralists* 64.
17. Aestheticism as a term and as a movement has long been associated with the male dandy, with the male-edited journal the *Yellow Book,* with male artists and writers like Oscar Wilde and Aubrey Beardsley. Yet as Talia Schaffer's *Forgotten Female Aesthetes* makes clear, aestheticism was always a more complicated movement (passim; for a summary see 2). Part of Wilde's achievement, Schaffer makes clear, lies in the ways Wilde embraced, rather than distanced himself from, a "supposedly debased women's culture" of decoration and design, in the process transforming aestheticism "to carry the narratives of male-male desire." Schaffer, *Forgotten* 30.
18. See esp. chapter 1, "Material Good" (1–31). This is not to say the idea was invented by the Victorians: "The argument that art elevated character was . . . an ancient one. A tenet of Romanticism, it had been given extensive play during the 1835 hearings of the Select Committee on Arts and Manufactures, by the London Art Union, and in the writings of Pugin, Ruskin, and Morris" (D. Cohen 78–79).

19. D. Cohen 13.
20. Panton, *Kitchen to Garret* 68.
21. Boyd 337. The Art at Home series, in which Barker and Orrinsmith published, was proposed to Macmillan by an Anglican curate, the Reverend W. J. Loftie, who subsequently published his own *A Plea for Art in the House.* J. J. Stevenson also published in the series.
22. Boyd 338, 317.
23. Boyd 321–22.
24. Ruskin, "Queens'" 122.
25. For more on Ruskin's despairing vision of the city, see Mallett 38–57. On Ruskin's hatred of the suburbs especially, see 45. Ruskin's beloved Herne Hill became progressively suburban over the course of his life. For more on Ruskin's indebtedness to medievalism, see Bell and Offen 384–85.
26. Barker 19–20.
27. Beecher and Stowe 98. I am grateful to Talia Schaffer for pointing this out to me.
28. Barker 57; Panton, *Kitchen to Garret* 25. As Deborah Cohen makes clear, a central tenet of interior design literature was that objects were ugly and tasteless if they pretended to be what they were not; see esp. 14–31.
29. Panton, *Kitchen to Garret* 10.
30. Panton, *Kitchen to Garret* 22–23.
31. Panton is unabashedly partisan: "I always consider that the southern suburbs are at least twenty-five years in advance of those in the north," she asserts, "the houses are more modern; they are much more tastefully arranged." Panton, *Kitchen to Garret* 5. I explore her own experiences in South London in more detail in chapter 7.
32. "A bedroom paper ought never to have a distinct, spotted pattern on it, lest, if you are ill, it should incite you to count the designs or should 'make faces at you,'" Lady Barker observes. Barker 9. Panton makes a similar point, years before Gilman's "Yellow Wallpaper" shows a protagonist driven out of her mind: "The first thing to recollect in choosing one's paper is that there should be nothing aggravating in it; no turns and twists that shall bother us as we lie in bed; no squares or triangles that flatly refuse to join." *Kitchen to Garret* 133.
33. Long 171. Long argues that the moveable Cosy Corner was especially attractive to suburbanites, a population at once mobile, penny conscious, and keen to stay up to date. Long 169–75.
34. Panton, *Kitchen to Garret* 3, 4.
35. Panton, *Kitchen to Garret* 110; *Nooks and Corners* 71–2.
36. Panton makes this explicit: "Remember, please, I am not writing for votaries of fashion or for rich people, who could tell me doubtless a great many things I do not know; but for the ordinary educated middle-class girl who may never leave her country home until she is married, or may have had few opportunities of seeing the world, even in London." Panton, *Kitchen to Garret* 109–10.
37. Panton, *Kitchen to Garret* 111; *A Gentlewoman's Home* 175–76; *Kitchen to Garret* 112.
38. Braddon, *OTN* I.18. See Steinbach 1–11, esp. 7–8.
39. "A piece of brocade should be put carelessly on the end of the piano, and kept in place by a few books, and a tall palm should be placed on the table in the bend," Panton

opines in *Suburban Residences* (157), but by 1896 her advice is even more detailed: the material should be "a square of Japanese embroidery," the fabric should be kept in place with "a few music books and a flowering plant in a brass pot," the nearby table should contain multiple books and flowers, while several "tall" palm trees should repose on stands. The piano should further be surrounded by "a Chippendale escritoire, flat against the wall, and an appropriate chair should be in front thereof." Panton, *A Gentlewoman's Home* 176.

40. Barker 53, 79.
41. Panton, *Kitchen to Garret* 86.
42. Panton, *Suburban Residences* 150.
43. Schaffer, *Novel Craft* 46.
44. Panton, *Suburban Residences* 133. Notably, Panton thinks it obvious that one should ignore one's actual neighbors if one wants to avoid "endless friction." *Suburban Residences* 17. Her vision of community is of a group brought together by interests, not location.
45. See Schaffer, *Forgotten* 250.
46. Schaffer, *Forgotten* 250.
47. Barker 92–93.
48. Swift 529, lines 116–18.
49. Neiswander 118; Loftie 91; qtd. Neiswander 122. For more discussion on conflicts in interior decoration styles in the 1870s see Neiswander 115–45.
50. Weiner 70–71. For further discussion on the uneasy relation between Gothic Revival and Queen Anne Revival in the 1870s and '80s see Weiner esp. 76–80.
51. For further discussion see, for instance, Girouard esp. 77–78.
52. Mary Eliza Haweis is an interesting exception to the trend identified in this chapter. As Judith Neiswander observes, Haweis's books on interior decoration, *The Art of Decoration* (1881) and *Beautiful Houses* (1882), were inspired by the Renaissance, not Queen Anne—Haweis's prose even uses the long *S* to indicate a debt to the age of Shakespeare. She critiques what she takes to be Queen Anne features as "noisome" and puts "Queen Anne '*taste*'" in italics, with speech marks, to indicate her scorn. See *Beautiful Houses* 80, 81; for discussion see Neiswander 102–3.
53. Qtd. by Weiner 76.
54. Qtd. by Weiner 72. For more on the battle between architects in the 1970s see Brooks esp. 274–75; see also Muthesius, *The High Victorian Movement* 205–6.
55. Rhoda and Agnes Garrett 3; my emphasis.
56. Rhoda and Agnes Garrett vii, 7; my emphasis.
57. Adams 158. For further discussion on the role of women activists in Queen Anne Revival architecture, see Adams 158–61.
58. Panton, *Kitchen to Garret* 199, 198, 202.
59. Panton, *Kitchen to Garret* 8–9.
60. *Suburban Residences and How to Circumvent Them* also calls for women to enter the profession of interior decoration because (Panton argues) only women grasp domestic detail, thus only women can bring a house to the state of "perfection" residents require if they are not always to "move on" in search of better. Panton, *Suburban Residences* 250.

61. Reader 2.
62. Peterson, *Becoming* 2.
63. Smyth et al. 5.
64. Smyth et al. 5.
65. Hadjiafxendi and Zakreski, *Crafting* 11.
66. Woolf 155–56.
67. Woolf 102.
68. For more discussion see Peterson, *Becoming* 13–49; M. Cohen, *Professional Domesticity* passim.
69. Peterson described the woman's insecure but evolving status as professional in the period as one of "becoming." For examinations of women's entry into other kinds of professions, from the nineteenth into the twentieth centuries, see Smyth et al; Hurtado. These tremendously useful studies of the difficulties women faced invariably present the home and domestic responsibilities as challenges to be managed (the women, as Hurtado puts it, had to organize their careers "while maintaining a diminished but socially acceptable level of domestic involvement," 69). While I do not deny that there is truth to this claim, I suggest that the home and the domestic realm were not only stumbling blocks.
70. Hadjiafxendi and Zakreski, *Crafting* 11–12.
71. M. Cohen 40.
72. Rhoda died in 1882, aged forty-one, but Agnes continued the business under the name "the Misses Garrett."
73. Smyth et al. 260. The Garretts' journey into the professions was not easy—it took years before they were able to find an architect who would apprentice them.
74. Rhoda and Agnes Garrett 54, 55, 13, 68.
75. For more on women's entry into the design profession see Neiswander 83–113.
76. This is, as Anne Witz argues, a patriarchally defined notion of professional work.
77. For further discussion on professional labor in the nineteenth century and, specifically, on why women's professional work was so troubling to some, see Marcus, "The Profession of the Author" 155–56.
78. D. Cohen 105.
79. For more discussion see D. Cohen 108–13.
80. The exclusion of female aesthetes from modernism, in spite of their movement toward professionalism, and in spite of the fact that modernism celebrated "a new image of the author as an elite, high-art professional," is explored by Schaffer in *The Forgotten Female Aesthetes;* see esp. "Postscript," 251–52. Schaffer discusses the ways in which modernist writers worked to "denounce her, praise her, publicize her, conceal her, resent her, and imitate her" (251).

CHAPTER 5. WOMEN AND THE SUBURBAN GARDEN

1. Wolseley, *Gardening for Women* 15.
2. "The upper middle class might have been the 'pioneers' in selecting new areas for living . . . but the suburbs quickly assumed an even wider heterogeneity as other income groups moved in." Cherry and Sheail 1570.

3. See Elliott esp. 17–18, 28–32, and 107–10 and Carter 67–102. Sheet glass, first developed in 1847, was free of bubbles, which could cause burn marks on plant leaves.
4. The bedding system was the bugbear of later Victorian and Edwardian gardeners. For early twentieth-century criticism of bedding-out see Jekyll, "Some Decorative Aspects" esp. 39–42.
5. Elliott 16–20. Elliott stresses that the most significant innovation was probably the advent of the railway, which meant that nurseries and gardeners could stock nonnative plants and import materials such as stone quickly and easily (16–17).
6. For an investigation of the very earliest gardening books in England, from the seventeenth century, see Tabaroff 1–5 and Bushnell passim. Bushnell points out that, interestingly, the early books "[imagined] a female reader," whether a country housewife or a Queen (122).
7. Ruskin, "Queens'" 134, 110.
8. Ruskin, "Queens'" 121.
9. Waters 241, 242, 242–45. The reference is from Ruskin, "Queens'" 122.
10. Weltman 119.
11. I have written elsewhere about the "garden of Eden" plot in popular women's texts, which serves to structure a heroine's disappointment with the limited options available to her as she grows up and seeks to move beyond her family. See Bilston, *The Awkward Age* esp. 60, 143–44.
12. Bardswell 5. Bardswell references the last line of "Come Down, O Maid" when she mentions the "innumerable bees." I am grateful to Stefanie Markovits for pointing this out.
13. Bardswell 6.
14. G.S.B. [Boulger], "Jane Loudon," *Dictionary of National Biography,* vol. 34.
15. Jane Loudon, *Companion* vii.
16. Jane Loudon, *Instructions* v–vi.
17. Jane Loudon, *Instructions* v.
18. Jane Loudon, *Instructions* 7; Whiting 14.
19. Jane Loudon, *Instructions* 7.
20. L. Johnson 4.
21. Many "mainstream" gardening publications seem to have anticipated female readers: Shirley Hibberd's *The Floral World and Garden Guide* juxtaposed advertisements for lawn mowers with ones for face cream and included articles on "Ladies' Flowers," while the *Florist and Garden Miscellany* included a monthly "Ladies' Page" by Henry Burgess. The latter assumed a level of considerable expertise.
22. See, for example, Jane Loudon, *Practical Instructions* 255. I discuss the late Victorian instantiation of the conflict in more detail later in the chapter.
23. Jane Loudon, "On Flower Gardens: II" 200–206; R. G., "On The Natural Love of Flowers," 69–70. For discussion on Chevreul's theories see Elliott 125–26.
24. To give just one example, Loudon's magazine provides an account of *Daubentonia tripetiana,* a plant from Buenos Aires introduced into Europe by a French nurseryman in 1840. See the *Ladies' Magazine of Gardening* 1 (1842) 65–66.
25. For discussion on representations of gardens in British, French, and German literature of this period see Finney, *The Counterfeit Idyll.*

26. Helmreich 2.
27. Jane Loudon, *Instructions* 125–26. Note, of course, that Loudon's conception of unconstructed nature is not of brutal nature, nature untamed, but nature ordered—by God. For discussion on Victorian preferences for the ordered garden above uncivilized nature see Waters 159–61.
28. L. Johnson 4.
29. This is not, of course, to accept the depoliticization of women's activities (which is hardly possible) but rather to remark on the strategies operating in the texts. Helmreich helpfully summarizes, "We should take heed of Barthes's warning that 'the most natural object contains a political trace.' Thus it is useful to conceive of the garden as embodying a collection of ideologies, sometimes contradictory, bundled together and put to numerous uses." Helmreich 2–3.
30. Jane Loudon, *Instructions* 344.
31. For discussion on gardening as analogous to Britain's "civilizing" imperial project see Waters 159. Waters stresses that Victorians viewed their civilizing agenda as a carrying out of God's own plan.
32. Scott, "Landscape Gardening" 307. I owe this reference to Waters 9. As Shirley Hibberd put it, in a book celebrating the "progress in domestic aesthetics": "It should be borne in mind by every cultivator of taste in gardening, that a garden is an *artificial* contrivance, it is not a piece scooped out of a wood, but in some sense a continuation of the house." Hibberd, iii, 330.
33. Jane Loudon, *Instructions* 246.
34. Jane Loudon, *Instructions* 258
35. Rappaport 222, 221, 5. Rappaport outlines the transportation options available from the Loudons' suburb of Bayswater into the West End on 24–25.
36. Ruskin, "Queens'" 122.
37. Ruskin, "Queens'" 142.
38. Gardening had a fuddy-duddy image in the Victorian period, just as today. Theresa Earle remarked, in her highly successful *Pot-Pourri from a Surrey Garden,* "Gardening is, I think, essentially the amusement of the middle-aged and old. The lives of the young, as a rule, are too full to give the time and attention required" (19).
39. Batson 974.
40. Boyle, *Days and Hours* 3.
41. Boyle, *Seven Gardens* 27, 29.
42. Boyle, *Days and Hours* 9. The essays and articles from the book were first published in *Gardener's Chronicle. Days and Hours* was an enormous success and was reprinted seven times; the author went on to write three other gardening books.
43. Boyle, *Days and Hours* 10. For discussion on the later Victorian love of "old-fashioned" plants, and the growth of this aesthetic throughout the century, see Waters 48–71.
44. Schaffer, *Forgotten* 50.
45. Barbara T. Gates, in her discussion of the garden as a site "in which an aestheticized nature is already literally in place," goes on to point out that "garden writing sets out to further reenvision this nature-as-garden linguistically, a daunting task for several reasons . . . although the garden itself is a locus, the garden transformed into

writing must become portable, representing a place but never literally tied to it." Gates 189.

46. Boyle, *Seven Gardens* 25–7.
47. Maryon 26, 27.
48. For discussion see, for example, Elliott 226–27. Note too that members of the "same" side often disagreed strongly with one another: for instance, two of the participants in Robinson's *English Flower Garden* (1883), J. D. and Gertrude Jeykll, expressed very different views on ideal color combinations in the garden. See Elliott 205–7.
49. For discussion on the development of this myth through the 1880s see Elliott 160. Note that Robinson was not against the use of exotic plants but rather argued they should be planted in masses. In fact J. D. Sedding and Reginald Blomfield, associated with the formal approach to gardening, were "among the promoters of native plants" (Elliott 195) in the later years of the century. It is perhaps unnecessary to point out that Robinson's account of the annihilation of native plants by bedders was almost certainly false, as was his claim that cottage gardens provided a safe haven for the embattled herbaceous border. Some contemporary commentators remarked that cottage gardens were in fact starting to go over to bedding just as the upper classes "discovered" the so-called cottage aesthetic. See Elliott 161–62.
50. Jekyll's aesthetic will be discussed in more detail presently.
51. Waters stresses that "the canonization of 'cottage' garden plants was motivated by a perceived need to shore up, revitalize and purify the imaginatively bankrupt floral culture of the philistine bourgeoisie. It was thought in some quarters that the middle classes, though economically dominant, were culturally impoverished—as their monomania for the imaginatively sterile and crassly ostentatious bedding system clearly showed" (129).
52. Schaffer's *Forgotten Female Aesthetes* discusses the professionalization of the domestic arts at some length; see in particular 70–77.
53. For further discussion on the later Victorian distaste for bedding plants see Waters 124–25, 128–29.
54. Maryon 183–84. Von Arnim's text is, as Schaffer points out, in many ways a dissection of the author's unhappy marriage to Count von Arnim, who appears as the "Man of Wrath," sneering at his wife's gardening efforts and memorably advocating wife beating. "[Yo]ur garden is not your Duty, because it is your Pleasure," he remarks at one point, high-handedly, and Elizabeth's response is pointedly sarcastic: "What a comfort it is to have such wells of wisdom constantly at my disposal! Anybody can have a husband, but to few is it given to have a sage, and the combination of both is as rare as it is useful." Arnim 80–81.
55. Maryon 184.
56. Jekyll, *Home and Garden* 149; Maryon 106–7.
57. See also, for example, Chamberlain and Douglas's *Gentlewoman's Book of Gardening:* "Flowers are like children, beautiful, irresponsible, helpless things; and we may say that the good gardener will make a good mother, and the good mother—after her children are grown up—the best gardener" (210).
58. Maryon 65.

59. Arnim 20.
60. Arnim 59.
61. Jekyll, "Idea" 38.
62. Chamberlain and Douglas 207.
63. See Schaffer, *Forgotten* 119.
64. Earle 246.
65. Earle 40.
66. Maryon 167.
67. Arnim 21, 83.
68. Arnim 22.
69. Jekyll was uncomfortable describing herself as a "professional" because the term connoted, to her, a man of limited education and possibly limited gifts. She preferred to refer to herself as an amateur and/or an artist gardener. See *Home and Garden* 151–52. We would clearly describe her today as a "professional," however.
70. Qtd. by Earle 258.
71. For a detailed overview of women's horticultural colleges, and of the young women who quickly excelled in them, see Horwood.
72. For a thorough investigation of the designs of Lutyens and Jekyll, see Ottewill 67–95.
73. Chamberlain 5–6. She champions the woman gardener at length in *The Gentlewoman's Book of Gardening,* 207–18, and managed the Women's London Gardening Association.
74. Earle 40.
75. Wolseley, *Gardening for Women* 108, 35.
76. Wolseley, *Gardening for Women* 22, 79.
77. Wolseley, *Gardening for Women* 78.
78. Earle 309; Wolseley, *Gardening for Women* 83.
79. Wolseley, *Gardening for Women* 85–86.
80. Wolseley, *Gardening for Women* 22, 23, 88.
81. Earle 40.
82. Long 42.
83. Scott 190.
84. Ravetz and Turkington 180.
85. Jeykll, "Idea" 35.
86. Jekyll, *W&G* 2.
87. Jekyll, *Wall and Water* 41.
88. Jekyll rarely referred to her gender, taking her position as paid gardener for granted and touching only occasionally on the frustrations she experienced. Still, there are hints of the problems that other writers articulated more openly. In a book for children, for instance, Jekyll remarked that as a child she was "always strong and active in my limbs, and in many ways more like a boy than a girl," "delighting to go up trees, and to play cricket, and take wasps' nests after dark, and do dreadful deeds with gunpowder and all the boy sort of things." Jekyll, *Children and Gardens* 9.
89. Weltman 105. For a fascinating series of essays on the ways in which Queen Victoria, and queenship generally, were and continue to be read, see Homans and Munich, *Remaking Queen Victoria.*

90. *Queen of the Air* was the title of Ruskin's 1869 study of Athena. In the 1890s, Alice Corkran used the idea of the pole star to explain Ruskin's purpose to readers discouraged by the loftiness of the ideal : "We sail by the pole star, we do not expect to reach it." Corkran, "A Chat with the Girl of the Period" 965.

CHAPTER 6. SUBURBAN OPPORTUNITY IN MARY ELIZABETH BRADDON'S FICTION

1. Forster, *Howards End* 102.
2. Carey 6, 23–24.
3. Carey 6, Jekyll, "Idea" 35.
4. Qtd. by Wolff 11.
5. Dyos and Reeder remark, with terrible condescension, that Braddon's "tedious novels were set in the suburbs because they were designed to be read there"; at most, they argue, Braddon records "some of the chatter" of mid-Victorian life. The only suburban-engaged authors they admire are male. Dyos and Reeder 374.
6. Qtd. by Wolff 179.
7. Braddon, *One Thing Needful* 259, 261, 271. Mrs. Mulciber views interior decoration in Arnoldian terms, as facilitating "sweetness and light" (260).
8. Dickens, *Dombey* 53; Braddon, *DSF* I.18.
9. Braddon, *DSF* I.18.
10. Braddon, *LAS* 187.
11. Dickens too bemoaned the careless attitude speculators took to the human occupants of the new suburbs, noting that early residents could find themselves living in a wasteland. Of the chaotic part-built streets, bridges, and houses of 1840s Camden, Dickens observes: "One or two bold speculators had projected streets; and one had built a little, but had stopped among the mud and ashes to consider farther of it." *Dombey* 53.
12. See Wolff esp. 28.
13. The smell of the muddy riverbed in summer was terrible, and development of the area was on hold until the problem (a drawn-out bureaucratic nightmare) could be resolved. See Maxwell 6. The testy, drawn-out issue to restore the river's levels at low tide—making it both navigable and usable as an amenity, particularly in the summer months—is discussed in Chancellor 279–81; for a modern analysis see Savinson 12–13. In 1894 a lock and a footbridge were opened.
14. Maxwell named Marchmond Road and Audley Road after characters in Braddon's novels. Chancellor evoked the area, in his 1894 history of Richmond, as still rural, yet rapidly covered by "a colony of small houses" (278). The process of suburbanization was effectively under way in the area as early as the seventeenth century—mineral wells were discovered in 1696, after which, Chris Miele argues, "speculators, following the example of West End builders, erected terraces and single houses (and even one very early pair of semi-detached houses)" (39). A second boom happened in the middle of the eighteenth century, followed by the development of more middle-class housing from the 1820s. Lichfield House was demolished in the twentieth century. For a useful overview of the borough, see Saint 222–24.

15. Booth xxvii.
16. Coyne 30–31, 49–50.
17. Braddon, *Eden* 249.
18. For discussion of Dyos's work, see Thompson, "The Rise of Suburbia" 4.
19. Branca 154–56.
20. "Dr. Lettsom" was Dr. John Coakley Lettsom, botanist and horticulturalist, who bought land in Camberwell in 1779. See Hunting 221–35. Lettsom's admiration for Camberwell, its good situation and healthful climate, is much quoted by Allport in the 1841 book.
21. Allport 101, 98, 99.
22. "Memorabilia of Two Literary Men" 413–14. The piece focuses on Allport's biographical notes pertaining to the Peckham experiences of Oliver Goldsmith.
23. Dyos and Reeder 371.
24. Thompson, "The Rise of Suburbia" 6, 11.
25. "The horse may rightly be credited with much influence over the form which the suburban environment took," Thompson remarks. "It would be going too far, however, to suggest that the availability of horse-drawn public passenger transport was decisive in triggering the birth of the suburb. The sequence of events was that the suburb came first and the short-stage coach or omnibus followed once the potential passengers were established. It is true that this came to be such an automatic development that people came to live in districts with very poor, or no transport services in the confident expectation that a new bus route would be opened." Thompson, "The Rise of Suburbia" 11–12.
26. Dyos and Reeder 373, 374. Dyos and Reeder point out that Sultan Street, like many another slum, was not (as was popularly supposed) the home of immigrants but of second- and third-generation Londoners. Ninety-two percent of children living in Sultan Street in 1871 were London born; the figure rose to 98 percent by 1901. For discussion on Irish experience in the horrors of Camberwell and Sultan Street specifically see Lees 69–70.
27. Braddon, *Barbara* III.2.
28. Dyos and Reeder 376.
29. Braddon, *Eden* 59.
30. Braddon, *Eden* 74.
31. Braddon, *Eden* 74.
32. Braddon, *Barbara* I.13.
33. Braddon, *Barbara* I.13, I.257.
34. Braddon, *Barbara* I.12.
35. Miller, *Anatomy* 136. William Ian Miller's earlier work examines in detail the ways in which humiliation punishes "moral and social failure" (Miller, *Humiliation* x–xi). Love, meanwhile, offers "the suspension of disgust rules" (Miller, *Anatomy* 132), which may partly capture why the Trevornocks are not, at least within the family, disgusted by what they are doing.
36. Bourdieu 95. On the concept of the habitus, and the traditions on which Bourdieu draws in formulating his conception of the term, the introduction to the 2013 edition

of *Distinction* summarizes: "The habitus, for Bourdieu, consists in the set of unifying principles which underlie . . . tastes and give them a particular social logic which derives from, while also organizing and articulating, the position which a particular group occupies in social space" (Bourdieu xix). Dyos 58. As Dyos has shown, suburbs closest to the city—like the Trevornocks' own Camberwell—were swollen by a "stream of migrants" from the very earliest decades of growth: 28 percent came "from the neighbouring south-eastern counties of Sussex, Hampshire, Berkshire, Essex, Suffolk, and Norfolk," 40 percent from "adjacent areas of metropolitan Middlesex and extra-metropolitan Surrey and Kent," while most of the rest came from farther north. Dyos concludes that "the cumulative effect of these prodigious transfers of population was to create urban communities in which not more than half their members had been born within South London at all" (58).

37. Collini 65. For further discussion see Collini passim, esp. chaps. 2 and 3, "The Culture of Altruism" and "The Idea of Character," 60–117.
38. Colón 9.
39. Colón 12.
40. Braddon, *Barbara* I.22, I.31, I.21.
41. Bourdieu 476.
42. For discussion on the relationship between the two texts see Carnell 214–18.
43. Braddon, *Doctor's Wife* 27, 17, 21.
44. Braddon, *Doctor's Wife* 24.
45. Flint, *The Woman Reader* 292.
46. Braddon, *Doctor's Wife* 45.
47. Braddon, *Doctor's Wife* 81.
48. Braddon, *Doctor's Wife* 17.
49. Braddon, *Doctor's Wife* 23.
50. Haynie 72.
51. Braddon, *LAS* 247, 250.
52. Katherine Montwieler reads Lady Audley as especially skilled at creating versions of herself to appeal to men: "She is a craftswoman constructing an elaborate identity—a living, breathing, display-window doll." Montwieler 50.
53. Braddon, *LAS* 246, 43, 44–45.
54. Braddon, *LAS* 43, 44–45.
55. Pugin 2.
56. Braddon, *LAS* 44.
57. Braddon, *LAS* 251–52.
58. Qtd. by Wolff 22, 24.
59. Braddon, *LAS* 252,
60. Braddon, *LAS* 361.
61. Braddon, *LAS* 54.
62. Braddon, *LAS* 445, 444.
63. Braddon, *LAS* 445.
64. Pugin 301.
65. Braddon, *Lost for Love* II.121, II.155, II.150, II.156.

66. Braddon, *Doctor's Wife* 255.
67. Braddon, *Barbara* I.48, 110.
68. Braddon, *Love* II.272, 273, 272, 274.
69. Braddon, *DSF* II.319.
70. Qtd. by Wolff 22.
71. Braddon, *Love* II.273.
72. Braddon, *Love* II.297.
73. Braddon, *Eden* 17.
74. Crosland 44–45.
75. Braddon, *Eden* 78.
76. Braddon, *Eden* 12, 86, 135, 136, 139, 167.
77. For more on Battersea's suburban growth after the arrival of the railways in 1838, and the problems of rapid population growth, see Barratt 215–21.
78. Braddon, *Eden* 252, 255, 254, 261, 251.
79. Flo no sooner sees Jim's cramped parlor-cum-bedroom in Battersea, with a sleeper sofa, than she starts "wondering what she could do to make it prettier"—specifically "whether pink-glazed calico with muslin over it" would help. Braddon, *Eden* 265.
80. Braddon, *Eden* 259.
81. Braddon, *Eden* 469.
82. Braddon, "Ducayne" 86, 95.
83. Braddon, *Barbara* I.66. Other characters who suffer in Braddon's work are those who do *not* find their way to the suburbs—those who are "stuck" in inner city or countryside. In *Lost for Love,* for instance, a heroine named Loo suffers when she sees the "world of beauty" that is Richmond for the first time, "down by the Thames, and onward towards Thames Ditton and Moulsey. Loo was gazing around with wide admiring eyes. The solemn avenue yonder skirting the Palace grounds, the clear rippling water, the pretty villas, all bright with tulip-beds and hyacinth-boxes, and early roses on southern walls; the cottage-gardens full of wall-flowers breathing sweetest odours." *Lost for Love* 1.172. The pain of the scene is that Loo fears this scene is closed off to her: in spite of his kiss and his expressions of admiration, Walter feels he cannot offer marriage to a girl of the lower class, a girl raised in the narrow, dirty environs of Voysey Street, central London. Loo retains reader sympathy because she does not do what Lady Audley does in the face of her affliction, murder and lie, and she is ultimately rescued, breaking out of her birth networks, finding new opportunities.
84. Barbara is ultimately separated from Captain Leland because Flossie and the mother, in a fateful decision, prioritize money over Barbara's happiness.
85. Braddon, *Eden* 469, 221.
86. Braddon, *Eden* 469–70.
87. Braddon, "Ducayne" 74.

CHAPTER 7. "THE QUINTESSENCE OF THE SUBURBAN"

1. Danby, "Gospel" 226.
2. Gissing, *Jubilee* 2.

3. Carey, 51.
4. Aria, *My Sentimental Self,* 33.
5. In *Leaves from a Life,* Panton is emphatically prejudiced against the Jewish families she knew in Bayswater. "[In] our time," she says, they "were never allowed to reside there; they could never keep respectable servants, and the landlords refused to let the houses to them." Things have deteriorated in the suburb, apparently, "for the Jews are an hilarious set, and appear to visit each other continuously, and keep up large card-parties to a late hour of the night. The place is, indeed, very much altered for the worse" (128). The stereotype of raucous Jewish card parties gained traction with the publication of *Dr. Phillips,* so that Panton may have been digging here at Frankau herself.
6. Editor, "Other Folk's Houses. By Mrs. Panton," *Gentlewoman* 504. Frankau is right about the prose of *The Way They Should Go:* at the very least, Panton needed a good editor. A sample sentence: "While sensible indeed is that grandmother who has not her own opinion and expresses it on the unsuitability of all her daughter's surroundings at the time the babies begin and continue to come, from the choosing of the doctor to the dress and manners of the nurse who has to look after mother and child" (*The Way* 243).
7. Panton, *Leaves from a Housekeeper's Book* 14; *Cannibal Crusader* 142, 255.
8. Panton, *Leaves* 1. The woman sculptor Mary Grant took a lease on a studio at 12a Park Village West in the 1870s, putting a door in the back garden wall to allow access to her family living in Gloucester Gate. See Hurtado 101.
9. Knight 9.
10. Panton later remembered that the change of houses was enabled partly by Frith's financial successes as an artist and partly by financial bequests from two relatives (Frankau later moved, for a similar combination of reasons, to 11 Clarges Street). Close to Belgravia, across Hyde Park, Tyburnia was an area of increasing wealth and importance inhabited (a contemporary noted) "by those who are undergoing the transitional state between commerce and fashion"; Cunningham xiii, xii. For Panton's account of the move, see *Leaves from a Life* 25–26. See also G. Frankau 76–77.
11. Knight 14.
12. For Frith's account of the day he left for London see Frith, *Autobiography* I.20.
13. "Mr. W. P. Frith Speaks" 17–18. The *Whitehall Review* serialized thoroughly middle-class fiction by, for instance, Mary Elizabeth Braddon.
14. Wittman 194.
15. Frith, "Crazes in Art" 191.
16. Frith, *Autobiography* I.262. See also Knight 17, note 20.
17. Qtd. by Woodcock 145. Frith gestures at the public's estimation of him in his own memoir: "I know very well that I never was, nor under any circumstances could have become, a great artist; but I am a very successful one." Frith, *Autobiography* I.7.
18. Frith, *Autobiography* I.252.
19. Cowling 57.
20. Arscott 79.
21. Cowling 69.

22. Knight 16.
23. Knight 17.
24. See Knight 16–17.
25. Woods, *Demography* 378.
26. The stories of individual suburban areas inevitably complicated this broad-brushstroke account: for a more fine-grained analysis of census returns, one that takes into account the class of residents, see Dyos and Reeder 372–73.
27. Panton, *More Leaves* 2.
28. Panton, *Leaves from a Life* 41.
29. Panton, *Leaves from a Life* 209–10.
30. Panton, *Leaves from a Life* 23. See, for instance, Knight 17.
31. Panton, *More Leaves* 8.
32. Panton, *More Leaves* 25. Frith discusses his trip in *Autobiography* II.1–26.
33. *Sunlight in Holland—Winter* is an "exquisite painting," Panton remarks, noting that she, breaking the Academy's rules, let Basil know it was to be included in the exhibition. It subsequently became, she tells us, like Frith's own earlier *Ramsgate Sands,* the "picture of the year." *More Leaves* 26.
34. *More Leaves* 248, 291. Panton certainly did spend a great deal of her life in Dorset, and visited Boulogne.
35. For the most part the volume's fictionalizing of its author's life has escaped attention. A rare counterexample may be found online: "The third volume, *More Leaves from a Life* (1911), is very odd—it purports to tell the story of a childhood friend of Jane's who became an artist, ran off with another man's wife, and came to a sad end, but a perfunctory Googling has not found any of the protagonists, nor a period in Jane's life where the story would fit." https://cambridgelibrarycollection.wordpress.com/2012/10/09/how-to-be-a-gentlewoman/ (accessed 3 August 2016).
36. "Obituary: Mrs. J. E. Panton" 11.
37. Panton, *Leaves from the Countryside* 12–13.
38. She calls Susan Warner's text "a book which used to delight me, and which I can never forget," *Leaves from the Countryside (*121). *Leaves from the Countryside* paints an autobiographical backdrop, but the story that unfolds (full of titled people and dreadful tragedies with parentless children and misalliances and infidelities) is the stuff of Panton's fiction. Thus I suspect that, like many of her other apparent autobiographies, it is substantially fictionalized. I discuss Panton's genre splicing in more detail presently.
39. Panton, *River of Years* 43, 61, 127. See, for instance, Panton, *Fresh Leaves and Green Pastures* 354.
40. Panton, *River of Years* 131.
41. Panton, *River of Years* 141, 142.
42. Panton, *Fresh Leaves and Green Pastures* 229–30.
43. See Rawcliffe 28–91, esp. 34–40.
44. Panton, *Fresh Leaves and Green Pastures* 357.
45. Panton, *Fresh Leaves and Green Pastures* 358, 357.
46. Panton, *Fresh Leaves and Green Pastures* 359.

47. Peterson, *Victorian Autobiography* 4.
48. Panton, *Leaves from a Life* 128.
49. Panton, *Whispers* 221, *Year's Mind* 46, *Most of the Game* 171. In *The Building of Whispers,* the narrator loses her husband, Humphrey—not a painter, but easily tempted for all that—to a woman who possesses "a light nature, all the sparkle on the surface"; " 'tis for such as she that men are mad—forget their duty, their parents and themselves; and 'tis such as she who light the fires of hell and beckon on men until they fall into her deep-laid traps" (*Whispers* 104).
50. Panton, *Garret and Kitchen* 229.
51. Panton, *Leaves from a Garden* 289.
52. Di Battista and Wittman, xiv, xi–xix, xi.
53. The Hon. Sybil Hardyman 291. This was the cliff-hanger line of the episode. Aileen's prostrate corpse graces the front of the number; the next illustration ("A glutinous drop of greenish liquid appeared upon the point of the bodkin") shows a young woman with a horrified expression in fashionable dress surrounded by potted plants (291). Mrs. George Augustus Sala's column ran weekly in the early years of the decade.
54. James Davis was a sports journalist, dilettante, and general man-about-town, who allegedly chose the pseudonym "Owen Hall" because he "owed all" to London's bailiffs and duns.
55. I draw here on Endelman's thorough survey, esp. 127–34.
56. G. Frankau 224. It seems, from the subtitle, and from Gilbert's own account in his autobiography, that he did not realize the pieces had been published twenty-seven years earlier, in the *Gentlewoman.*
57. "Medicoes under the Microscope" 786.
58. *Gentlewoman* (4 July 1891): 22.
59. See [Shaw,] "Literary and Art Notes, Etc." 5; for discussion, see Tyson 253–54. Shaw references the fact that Dr. Phillips was thought to be based on a real-life doctor, who threatened to sue. Few original copies of the first edition are in existence (the British Library holds one); this may be because, according to popular myth at least, the doctor destroyed every copy he could get his hands on.
60. See "At the Play," *Hearth and Home* 119. The *Gentlewoman* published a collaborative novel, *The Fate of Fenella,* in 1891, the chapters of which were published by authors in alternating gender order: Frank Danby took a place between Florence Marryat and Mary Eliza ("Mrs. Edward") Kennard, suggesting that the paper was maintaining the artifice at least up to this point.
61. Frankau excoriated Moore for a dangerous "lack of reticence" in his fiction, a "grossness" that "is nauseating and un-English"; "unless he can contrive to disguise its quality he must fail again and again with a failure that no industry can avert and no logrolling obscure." Danby, "Mr. George Moore's New Novel" 106. Danby's remarks were not atypical; the *Whitehall Review* observed that any reader who opens a book by George Moore must be "prepared for requiring a strong dose of disinfectant after some of the passages, and a shower-bath after others." "Mr. George Moore's Latest Surprise" 19. Julia did plenty of "logrolling" for her son, paying Chatto and Windus

fifty pounds to publish his first novel—as Gilbert later admitted, with some chagrin. See G. Frankau 162–64.

62. Moore, "Correspondence: Mr. George Moore's New Novel" 143. Moore liked the comparison so much he repeated it twice in the letter, first in the first paragraph, again in the last.

63. In the landscape of Jewish London life, new migrants tended to head to the East End. Older Jewish families lived in areas like Bayswater and Maida Vale. The first synagogue was opened in 1863, as a branch synagogue of the Great Synagogue and the New Synagogue. The population soon began spreading west, so that by "the 1880s at least 1,000 and possibly 2,000 out of Maida Vale's estimated 10,000 residents were Jewish." Baker, Bolton, and Croot, "Paddington: Judaism."

64. I have not been able to confirm the reference in *Punch.* It is the only review Julia's son quotes, more than fifty years later, in his impressionistic autobiography; it may have been either untrue, misattributed, or misremembered. See G. Frankau 23. Other reviews were more positive: see, for instance, in the *Pall Mall Gazette,* "A Couple of Novels" 5: "It is well-written, plainly and straightforwardly."

65. Galchinsky, "Permanently Blacked" 174–75, 171.

66. In a typical comment, Frankau remarks that hypochondriacs and hysterics are "at once the bane of the honest physician, and the blessing and chief source of income of the unscrupulous ones." Ariel [Julia Frankau], "Physicians: No. X—Dr. Hughlings Jackson" 358. In the previous column, a week earlier, Frankau recalled admiringly the perspicacity of a doctor who recommended that a nineteen-year-old girl who suffered fits of incessant shaking, screaming, crying, and unconsciousness should receive dry bread and water and corporal punishment. Dr. Hughlings Jackson's dining room, meanwhile, is distinguished by "a high dado" with "a low frieze enclosing the paneled walls" which "are strict eighteenth century; the large fireplace with a dog stove is of the same period" (358).

67. Medicos [Julia Frankau], "Medicoes under the Microscope: Sir Andrew Clark" 44.

68. Medicos [Julia Frankau], "Medicoes under the Microscope: Sir Andrew Clark" 44. In a profile of "Derrick," Frankau pours scorn on a mother who, desperate for excitement, restless at home, fails to act as a tender mother to her son. The mother takes to her bed regularly, with "violent neuralgia," and in the end her son despises her. It may be worth noting that Gilbert said of his mother that she put her writing career to one side to focus on mothering. See Ariel [Julia Frankau], "Derrick" 530. Her unwillingness to seek medical help caused Frankau to allow her own diabetes to progress; she also refused all advice to stop eating sweets.

69. G. Frankau, *Mothers and Children,* v–xiii.

70. Arnold ed. Collini 65.

71. Arnold ed. Collini 65.

72. Danby, *Dr. Phillips* 5, 40.

73. G. Frankau 77.

74. The sexual advances Moore made toward Frankau must have played a part in the fraying of their friendship—Gilbert Frankau later claimed Moore told him, "If your mother had only become my mistress when I asked her to, she would write better

English." (Moore also told Gilbert that he and Eliza, Julia's sister, were briefly lovers; Julia referred to Moore at home, for reasons one can only imagine, as the "White Slug"). G. Frankau 100, 101.

75. Danby, "Correspondence" 174.
76. Moore, "Correspondence" 143.
77. Danby, "Correspondence" 174.
78. Frankau, *John Raphael Smith* v, vi, vii. I owe this reference to Endelman 134. The Julia Frankau, "Mumsy," of Gilbert Frankau's autobiography is a superb hostess—for an account of her society friends and hospitality skills see, for example, 152–53; for an account of her energy as a writer, mother, wife, and woman-about-town, 17.
79. G. Frankau 76–77. Gilbert recalls that improved financial circumstances, partly enabled by a family bequest, further allowed Julia to purchase a seaside residence in Eastbourne. His father, however, had "no zest for the Mayfair game" (G. Frankau 77). Gilbert himself displays a lively awareness of the gradations of suburban life: after financial problems forced him, years later, to move his own family to a semidetached house in St. John's Road, Harrow, he remarked laconically: "Dolly and I moved down several rungs of the suburban ladder. Few women appreciate that" (G. Frankau 161).
80. Danby, "Gospel" 226. Frankau policed her demeanor rigorously to the end. Her son's account of her final months (she died slowly, of diabetes and consumption) stresses her absolute determination to avoid any appearance of sentiment or fuss. See G. Frankau 188–89.
81. Danby, "Correspondence" 174.
82. Aria, *My Sentimental Self* 158–59.
83. In *The Year's Mind: Hamworth Happenings* (1913), Panton tells the story (thinly disguised as that of someone she "knows") of meeting Mary as a child, in 1854; of her mother's forgiveness; then of the shock and horror of Frith's second marriage in vivid detail:

> I was a bare six years of age when the deed occurred, yet how well I recollected the bright, crinolined ringletted and merry girl who became the lost creature she was to the end of her days. How well I remembered, one bitter cold day, when it rained as it is raining now, and she caught me up to her warm young breast and carried me into the firelit shelter of her own home. I can see her merry, laughing face, looking out of her window which was almost covered with some luxuriant creeper, a wisteria, I think, but am not sure, and how she pelted me with parcels of hardbake and other simple sweets because we called to her to come out and she wanted to be lazy and read.
>
> Then her name was forbidden to us, we were never to ask for her any more, and the next time I met her, her laughter and curls and merriment were gone. I was her judge, not her child-lover, and I hated her as I hate her now and ever shall as long as I remember the dreadful deed she did. Tempted? Not she, she was the temptress, sinner, cruel, unscrupulous: she never saw another's happiness but she snatched at it; well, conscience must have troubled her, too, for drink ended her days, and left her a victim old and lonely, and the children she had robbed to curse her very name. (*The Year's Mind* 45–46)

Vivien Knight reports that the first time Jane met Mary was, indeed, in 1854, when Jane was six, during a stay at Hampton, when the family was taken to recuperate after a bout of whooping cough (see Knight 16). There is no evidence that Mary Alford ended her life plunged into alcoholism; Panton's determination to take charge of the story is at play once more.

84. Danby, "Gospel" 226.
85. Aria, *My Sentimental Self* 159. Davis Aria actually died, quite literally, at the Adelphi Theatre, shortly before the curtain went up on *Grand Hotel.* See G. Frankau 25.
86. G. Frankau 33; A. Bernstein 83–84, 83, 84.

CONCLUSIONS

1. Besant qtd. by Strong 235; Crosland 188–89.
2. Crosland 35, 15–16.
3. Pope 5.
4. Pope 13, 56.
5. Crosland 50, 54.
6. Whelan, "Clash" 155.
7. Wolseley, *Gardens* 145.
8. Lethbridge 3, 4, 5, 23–25.
9. For more on Birmingham's Victorian growth see Lethbridge passim; for a study of the many cultural societies in Manchester see Rose 103–17, and for discussion of Manchester magazines see Beetham 167–92. *Leeds and Suburbs: An Illustrated Monthly Magazine* was first published in 1894.
10. "The newly built villas of England's Victorian cities, seen beyond high-walled lanes, certainly formed one of Grimshaw's most memorable creative images." Robertson 86. For more on Grimshaw's "suburban lane theme" see Robertson 94–95, 102, 118.
11. "Our Views," *Amateur Photographer* (1884) 3.
12. Nine of her medals were auctioned in 2010: see https://www.cowanauctions.com/lot/90654/. She was also a talented cyclist.
13. For more discussion see Whelan, "Clash" esp. 154–60. "The right kind of person had Culture; the 'jumped-up' middle and lower middle classes had the suburbs and material goods." Whelan argues that the suburbs were firmly on the wrong side of the culture debate—"the work of the new suburban" is "seen as meaningless, empty, mindless and more of a burden to the surrounding culture than a necessity." Whelan, "Clash" 159, 160.
14. Wolseley, *Gardens* 271, 274.
15. Pionke's definition of professional rituals is generated by a close study of male professional experience, and as such is not immediately applicable to women (Pionke defines professional ritual as "any scripted, repeatable, highly formalized and self-conscious collective activity that strives for a level of meaningfulness not found in quotidian life," 6). My point, then, is not that women were doing the *same* thing as men but rather that the rituals of suburban life could be approached by women as possessing a similar degree of public importance and meaningfulness.

16. *Loan Exhibition* 8.
17. *Loan Exhibition* 3.
18. *Loan Exhibition* 3.
19. *Loan Exhibition: Minutes,* 3 November 1884.
20. A Woman, But Not an Exhibitor 4; "Exhibition of Women's Industries, Bristol" 247.
21. Woolf 102.

Bibliography

Adams, Annmarie. *Architecture in the Family Way: Doctors, Houses, and Women, 1870–1900.* London: McGill–Queen's University Press, 1996.

Alderman, Geoffrey. *Controversy and Crisis: Studies in the History of the Jews in Modern Britain.* Boston: Academic Studies Press, 2008.

Allport, Douglas. *The Collections, Illustrative of the Geology, History, Antiquities and Associations of Camberwell, and the Neighbourhood.* Camberwell: H. Trate, 1841.

Aria, Eliza Davis. *My Sentimental Self.* London: Chapman and Hall, 1922.

Ariel [Julia Frankau]. "Derrick." *Gentlewoman* II, no. 42 (25 April 1891): 530. See also Danby, Frank; Medicos; and Frankau, Julia.

Armstrong, W. A. "The Flight From the Land." In *The Victorian Countryside,* edited by G. E. Mingay. Vol. 1. 1981; repr. London: Routledge, 2000. 118–30.

Arnim, Elizabeth von. *Elizabeth and Her German Garden.* London: Macmillan, 1898.

Arscott, Caroline. "William Powell Frith's *The Railway Station:* Classification and the Crowd." In *William Powell Frith: Painting the Victorian Age,* edited by Mark Bills and Vivien Knight. New Haven: Yale University Press, 2006. 79–93.

"The Art of Puffing." *Dublin Review* 27 (1849): 146–62.

"At the Play." *Hearth and Home* 56 (9 June 1892): 119.

Baker, T. F. T., D. K. Bolton, and P. E. C. Croot. "Paddington: Bayswater." In *A History of the County of Middlesex: Volume 9, Hampstead, Paddington,* edited by C. R. Elrington. London, 1989. 204–12. *British History Online* http://www.british-history.ac.uk/vch/middx/vol9/pp204–212

———. "Paddington: Judaism." In *A History of the County of Middlesex: Volume 9, Hampstead, Paddington,* edited by C. R. Elrington. London, 1989. 264–65. *British History Online* http://www.british-history.ac.uk/vch/middx/vol9/pp264–265

Bardswell, Mrs. F[rances] A. *The Book of Town and Window Gardening.* London: John Lane, 1903.

Barker, Lady Mary Anne. *The Bedroom and Boudoir.* London: Macmillan, 1878.

Barratt, Nick. *Greater London: The Story of the Suburbs.* London: Random House, 2005.

Barson, Susie. "Infinite Variety in Brick and Stucco: 1840–1914." In *London Suburbs,* edited by Andrew Saint. London: Merrell Holberton, 1999. 61–102.

Barthes, Roland. "The Rhetoric of the Image." In *Image, Music, Text,* translated by Stephen Heath. New York: Hill and Wang, 1964; repr. 1977. 32–51.

Batson, H. M. "The Vogue of the Garden Book." *Nineteenth Century* 98 (1900): 974–87.

Beauvoir, Simone de. *The Second Sex.* 1949. London: Picador, 1988.

Beecher, Catharine E., and Harriet Beecher Stowe. *The American Woman's Home: Or, Principles of Domestic Science; Being A Guide to the Formation and Maintenance of Economical, Healthful, Beautiful, and Christian Homes.* 1869; repr. New York: J. B. Ford, 1872.

Beetham, Margaret. "'Healthy Reading': The Periodical Press in Late Victorian Manchester." In *City, Class and Culture: Studies of Social Policy and Cultural Production in Victorian Manchester,* edited by Alan J. Kidd and K. W. Roberts. Manchester: Manchester University Press, 1985. 167–92.

Bell, Susan G., and Karen Offen, eds. *Women, the Family, and Freedom: The Debate in Documents, Volume 1: 1750–1880.* Stanford: Stanford University Press, 1983.

Bennett, Arnold. *A Man from the North.* 1898; repr. New York: George Doran, 1911.

Bernstein, Aline. *An Actor's Daughter.* London: Knopf, 1941.

Bernstein, Susan David. "Too Common Readers in the British Museum." In *Victorian Vulgarity: Taste in Verbal and Visual Culture,* edited by Susan David Bernstein and Elsie B. Michie. London: Ashgate, 2009. 101–17.

Bernstein, Susan David, and Elsie B. Michie, eds. *Victorian Vulgarity: Taste in Verbal and Visual Culture.* London: Ashgate, 2009.

Besant, Walter. *London in the Nineteenth Century.* London: Adam and Charles Black, 1909.

Bhabha, Homi. "Of Mimicry and Man: the Ambivalence of Colonial Discourse." *October* 28 (1984): 125–33.

Bilston, Sarah. *The Awkward Age in Women's Popular Fiction, 1850–1900: Girls and the Transition to Womanhood.* Oxford: Clarendon Press, 2004.

[Boulger, George Simonds.] "Jane Loudon." *Dictionary of National Biography.* Vol. 34. London: Smith and Elder, 1885–1900. http://www.oxforddnb.com/index/17/101017030/

[———.] "John Claudius Loudon." *Dictionary of National Biography.* Vol. 34. London: Smith and Elder, 1885–1900. http://www.oxforddnb.com/index/17/101017031/

Booth, Michael. "Introduction." In *The Lights O'London and Other Victorian Plays,* edited by Michael Booth. Oxford: Oxford University Press, 1995. ix–xxvi.

Boyd, Andrew. *Recreations of a Country Parson.* 1861; repr. Boston: Ticknor and Fields, 1866.

Boyle, Eleanor Vere (E.V.B.). *Days and Hours in a Garden.* London: Elliott Stock, 1884.

———. *Seven Gardens and a Palace.* London: John Lane, 1900.

Bourdieu, P. *Distinction: A Social Critique of the Judgement of Taste.* 1979; repr. London: Routledge, 2013.

Braddon, Mary Elizabeth. *Dead-Sea Fruit.* 1868; repr. 2 vols. Leipzig: Tauchnitz, 1868.

———. *The Doctor's Wife.* 1864; repr. Oxford: Oxford University Press, 1998.

———. "Good Lady Ducayne." In *Nineteenth-Century Stories by Women: An Anthology,* edited by Glennis Stephenson. Peterborough, Ontario: Broadview, 1997. 71–104.

———. *Lady Audley's Secret.* 1862; repr. Peterborough, Ontario: Broadview, 2003.

———. *A Lost Eden.* London: Hutchinson, 1904.

———. *Lost for Love.* 1874; repr. 2 vols. London: Tauchnitz, 1874.

———. *The Story of Barbara.* 2 vols. Repr. Leipzig: Tauchnitz, 1880.

———. *One Thing Needful.* London: John and Robert Maxwell, 1887.

Bradley, Katherine, and Helen Sweet, eds. *Women in the Professions: Politics and Philanthropy, 1840–1940.* Victoria, B.C.: Trafford, 2009.

Branca, Patricia. *Silent Sisterhood: Middle-Class Women in the Victorian Home.* London: Croom Helm, 1975.

Bright, Michael. *Cities Built to Music: Aesthetic Theories of the Victorian Gothic Revival.* Columbus: Ohio State University Press, 1984.

Brooks, Michael W. *John Ruskin and Victorian Architecture.* New Brunswick, N.J.: Rutgers University Press, 1987.

The Builder's Practical Director: Or, Buildings for All Classes, Containing Plans, Sections and Elevations for the Erection of Cottages, Villas, Farm Buildings, Dispensaries, Public Schools, &c., with Detailed Estimates, Quantities, Prices, &c. London: J. Hagger [1855–57].

Bulwer-Lytton, Edward. *The Disowned.* 1829; repr. Boston: Little, Brown, 1893.

———. *Night and Morning.* 1841; repr. Philadelphia: J. B. Lippincott, 1865.

Burgess, Henry. "Ladies Page." *Florist and Garden Miscellany* 2 (1849): 191–92.

Burnett, John. *A Social History of Housing, 1815–1985.* London: Methuen, 1986.

Bushnell, Rebecca. "The Gardener and the Book." In *Didactic Literature in England 1500–1800: Expertise Constructed,* edited by Natasha Glaisyer and Sara Pennell. Aldershot, Hampshire: Ashgate, 2003. 118–36.

Buxton, B. H. *Great Grenfell Gardens: A Novel.* 3 vols. London: Tinsley Brothers, 1879.

Cannadine, David. "Conclusion: Urban History in the United Kingdom: The 'Dyos Phenomenon' and After." In *Exploring the Urban Past: Essays in Urban History by H. J. Dyos,* edited by David Cannadine and David Reeder. Cambridge: Cambridge University Press, 2003. 203–22.

Cannadine, David, and David Reeder, eds. *Exploring the Urban Past: Essays in Urban History by H. J. Dyos.* 1982; repr. Cambridge: Cambridge University Press, 2003.

Carey, John. *The Intellectuals and the Masses: Pride and Prejudice Among the Literary Intelligentsia, 1880–1939.* New York: St. Martin's Press, 1993.

Carter, Tom. *The Victorian Garden.* London: Bell and Hyman, 1984.

Chalklin, Christopher. *The Rise of the English Town 1650–1850.* Cambridge: Cambridge University Press, 2001.

Chamberlain, Edith L. *Town and Home Gardening.* London: J. S. Virtue, 1893.

Chamberlain, Edith L., and Fanny Douglas. *The Gentlewoman's Book of Gardening.* London: Henry, 1892.

Chancellor, Edwin Beresford. *The History and Antiquities of Richmond.* Richmond: Hiscoke, 1894.

Chaucer, Geoffrey. *The Canterbury Tales.* In *The Riverside Chaucer*, edited by Anthony Burgess. Oxford: Oxford University Press, 1991. 3–328.

Cherry, Gordon E., and John Sheail. "Town and Country: An Overview." In *The Agrarian History of England and Wales*, Volume 2: 1850–1914, edited by E. J. T. Collins. Cambridge: Cambridge University Press, 2000. 1540–80.

Clubbe, John. "Byron's London Revisited." In *Byron in London,* edited by Peter Cochran. Newcastle: Cambridge Scholars, 2008. 2–20.

Cohen, Deborah. *Household Gods: The British and Their Possessions.* New Haven: Yale University Press, 2006.

Cohen, Monica F. *Professional Domesticity in the Victorian Novel: Women, Work and Home.* Cambridge: Cambridge University Press, 1998.

Collini, Stefan, ed. *Matthew Arnold: Culture and Anarchy and Other Writings.* Cambridge: Cambridge University Press 1993.

———. *Public Moralists: Political Thought and Intellectual Life in Britain 1850–1930.* Oxford: Clarendon Press, 1991.

Collins, W. *Basil.* 1852; repr. Leipzig: Tauchnitz, 1862.

Colón, Susan E. *The Professional Ideal in the Victorian Novel: The Works of Disraeli, Trollope, Gaskell, and Eliot.* New York: Palgrave Macmillan, 2007.

Corkran, Alice. "A Chat with the Girl of the Period." *Girls' Realm* 1 (1899): 965.

"A Couple of Novels." *Pall Mall Gazette* (13 April 1887): 5.

Cowling, Mary. "Frith and His Followers: Painters and Illustrators of London Life." In *William Powell Frith: Painting the Victorian Age,* edited by Mark Bills and Vivien Knight. New Haven: Yale University Press, 2006. 57–77.

Coyne, Joseph Stirling. "Did You Ever Send Your Wife to Camberwell?" In *The Lights O'London and Other Victorian Plays,* edited by Michael Booth. Oxford: Oxford University Press, 1995. 33–48.

Crosby, Christina. "Reading the Gothic Revival: 'History' and *Hints on Household Taste.*" In *Rewriting the Victorians: Theory, History, and the Politics of Gender,* edited by Linda M. Shires. London: Routledge, 1992.

Crosland, T. W. H. *The Suburbans.* London: John Long, 1905.

Cunningham, Gail. "Houses in Between: Navigating Suburbia in Late Victorian Writing." *Victorian Literature and Culture* 32 (2004): 421–34.

———. "The Riddle of Suburbia: Suburban Fictions at the Victorian Fin de Siècle." In *Expanding Suburbia: Reviewing Suburban Narratives,* edited by Roger Webster. New York: Berghahn, 2000. 51–70.

Cunningham, Peter. *London in 1853.* London: J. Murray, 1853.

Daly, Nicholas. "Fiction, Theatre, and Early Cinema." In *The Cambridge Companion to Popular Fiction,* edited by David Glover and Scott McCracken. Cambridge: Cambridge University Press, 2012. 33–49.

———. *Literature, Technology, and Modernity, 1860–2000.* Cambridge: Cambridge University Press, 2004.

Danby, Frank [Julia Frankau]. "The Brixton Gospel." *Saturday Review* 83 (27 February 1897): 226–27.

———. "Correspondence: *Celibates* and Mr. George Moore: To the Editor of the Saturday Review." *Saturday Review* 80 (August 10 1895): 174.

———. *Dr. Phillips: A Maida Vale Idyll.* London: Vizetelly, 1887.

———. *Mothers and Children: Hitherto Unpublished Stories by the Late "Frank Danby."* London: W. Collins, 1918.

———. "Mr. George Moore's New Novel." *Saturday Review* 80 (27 July 1895): 105–6.

See also Ariel; Medicos; and Frankau, Julia.

D'Arcy, Ella. "A Marriage." *Yellow Book* 11 (1896): 309–42. Repr. in *Modern Instances.* London: John Lane, 1898.

Davidoff, Leonore, and Catherine Hall. *Family Fortunes: Men and Women of the English Middle-Class, 1780–1850.* Chicago: University of Chicago Press, 1987.

Dew-Smith, A[lice] M. *Confidences of an Amateur Gardener.* London: Seeley, 1897.

DiBattista, Maria, and Emily O. Wittman, eds. *Modernism and Autobiography.* Cambridge: Cambridge University Press, 2014.

Dickens, Charles. *Barnaby Rudge.* London: Chapman and Hall, 1841.

———. *Dombey and Son.* 1848; repr. Oxford: Oxford University Press, 1996.

———. *Hard Times.* London: Bradbury and Evans, 1854.

———. *The Old Curiosity Shop.* London: Chapman and Hall, 1841.

Dyos, Harold J. *Victorian Suburb: A Study of the Growth of Camberwell.* Leicester: Leicester University Press, 1961.

Dyos, Harold J., and David A. Reeder. "Slums and Suburbs." In *The Victorian City: Images and Realities,* edited by H. J. Dyos and Michael Wolff. Vol. 1. London: Routledge, 1973. 359–86.

Earle, Mrs. Theresa. *Pot-Pourri from a Surrey Garden.* 1896; repr. London: Thomas Nelson, n.d.

Eden, Emily. *The Semi-Attached Couple and The Semi-Detached House.* 1859; repr. London: Virago, 1979.

Editor. "Other Folk's Houses. By Mrs. Panton." *Gentlewoman* (11 April 1891): 504.

Elliott, Brent. *Victorian Gardens.* London: Batsford, 1986.

Endelman, Todd M. "The Frankaus in London: A Study in Radical Assimilation, 1837–1967." *Jewish History* 8 (1994): 117–54.

"Exhibition of Women's Industries, Bristol," *Queen* 77 (7 March 1885): 247.

Federico, Annette R. *Idol of Suburbia: Marie Corelli and Late-Victorian Literary Culture.* Charlottesville: University of Virginia Press, 2000.

Feldman, David. "Migration." In *The Cambridge Urban History of Britain: 1840–1950,* edited by Martin J. Daunton. Cambridge: Cambridge University Press, 2000.

Field, Geoffrey C. "Anti-Semitism with the Boots Off." In *Hostages of Modernization: Studies on Modern Antisemitism, 1870–1933/39,* edited by Herbert Arthur Strauss. Berlin: de Gruyter, 1992. Vol. I. 294–325.

Finney, Gail. *The Counterfeit Idyll: The Garden Ideal and Social Reality in Nineteenth-Century Fiction.* Tübingen: Niemeyer, 1984.

Flanders, Judith. *The Victorian House: Domestic Life from Childbirth to Deathbed.* London: HarperCollins, 2003.

Flint, Kate. "Fictional Suburbia." In *Popular Fictions: Essays in Literature and History,* edited by Peter Humm, Paul Stigant, and Peter Widdowson. London: Methuen, 1986. 111–26.

———. *The Woman Reader, 1837–1914.* Oxford: Clarendon Press, 1993.

Forster, E. M. *Howards End.* 1910; repr. New York: Knopf, 1921.

———. *A Room with a View.* 1908; repr. Norfolk, Conn.: New Directions, 1922.

Frankau, Gilbert. *Self-Portrait: A Novel of His Own Life.* London: Hutchinson, 1940.

Frankau, Julia. *John Raphael Smith: His Life and Works.* London: Macmillan, 1902. See also Ariel, Medicos, and Danby, Frank.

Frith, William Powell. "Crazes in Art: 'Pre-Raphaelitism' and 'Impressionism.'" In *Magazine of Art* XI (June 1888): 190–19.

———. *My Autobiography and Reminiscences.* 2 vols. 2nd edition. London: Bentley, 1887.

Galchinsky, Michael. *The Origin of the Modern Jewish Woman Writer: Romance and Reform in Victorian England.* Detroit: Wayne State University Press, 1996.

———. "'Permanently Blacked': Julia Frankau's Jewish Race." *Victorian Literature and Culture* 27 (1999): 171–83.

Galinou, Mireille. *Cottages and Villas: The Birth of the Garden Suburb.* New Haven: Yale University Press, 2010.

Garrett, Rhoda, and Agnes Garrett. *Suggestions for House Decoration in Painting, Woodwork, and Furniture.* 2nd edition. London: Macmillan, 1877.

Garson, Marjorie. *Moral Taste: Aesthetics, Subjectivity and Social Power in the Nineteenth-Century Novel.* Toronto: University of Toronto Press, 2007.

Gaskell, Elizabeth. *North and South.* 1852; repr. Leipzig: Tauchnitz, 1855.

Gates, Barbara T. *Kindred Nature: Victorian and Edwardian Women Embrace the Living World.* London: University of Chicago Press, 1998.

Girouard, Mark. *Sweetness and Light: The Queen Anne Movement, 1860–1900.* Oxford: Clarendon Press, 1977.

Geller, Jay. *The Other Jewish Question: Identifying the Jew and Making Sense of Modernity.* Ashland, Ohio: Fordham University Press, 2011.

Gissing, George. *In the Year of Jubilee.* London: Lawrence and Bullen, 1894.

———. "The Prize Lodger." 1898; repr. in *Human Odds and Ends: Stories and Sketches.* London: A. H. Bullen, 1901. 133–54.

———. *The Whirlpool.* New York: Frederick A. Stokes, 1897.

Gray, Thomas, to Mr. Palgrave. 24 July 1759. In *The Works of Thomas Gray, Collated from the Various Editions.* London: J. F. Dove, 1827.

Grosmith, George. *The Diary of a Nobody.* 1892; repr. Bristol: Arrowsmith, 1905.

Hadjiafxendi, Kyriaki, and Patricia Zakreski. "Artistry and Industry: The Process of Female Professionalization." In *Crafting the Woman Professional in the Long Nineteenth Century: Artistry and Industry in Britain,* edited by Kyriaki Hadjiafxendi and Patricia Zakreski. London: Ashgate, 2013. 1–24.

———, eds. *Crafting the Woman Professional in the Long Nineteenth Century: Artistry and Industry in Britain.* London: Ashgate, 2013.

Hammerton, A. James. "The English Weakness? Gender, Satire and 'Moral Manliness' in the Lower Middle Class, 1870–1920." In *Gender, Civic Culture and Consumerism: Middle-Class Identity in Britain 1800–1940,* edited by Alan J. Kidd and David Nicholls. Manchester: Manchester University Press, 1999. 164–83.

Hapgood, Lynne. *Margins of Desire: The Suburbs in Fiction and Culture 1880–1925.* Manchester: Manchester University Press, 2005.

Hardyman, The Hon. Sybil. "The Hertfordshire Horror—II." *Gentlewoman* IX, no. 218 (8 September 1894): 290–91.

Haweis, Mary Eliza Joy. *Beautiful Houses: Being a Description of Certain Well-Known Artistic Houses.* New York: Scribner and Welford, 1882; repr. London: Forgotten Books, 2012.

Haynie, Aeron. "An Idle Handle That Was Never Turned: The Decay of the Country Estate in *Lady Audley's Secret.*" In *Beyond Sensation: Mary Elizabeth Braddon in Context,* edited by Marlene Tromp, Pamela K. Gilbert, and Aeron Haynie. Albany: SUNY Press, 2000. 63–74.

Helmreich, Anne. *The English Garden and National Identity: The Competing Styles of Garden Design, 1870–1914.* Cambridge: Cambridge University Press, 2002.

Hibberd, Shirley. *Rustic Adornments for Homes of Taste.* 2nd edition. London: Groombridge, 1857.

Homans, Margaret, and Adrienne Munich, eds. *Remaking Queen Victoria.* Cambridge: Cambridge University Press, 1997.

Horsten, Leon, and Richard Pettigrew, eds. *The Bloomsbury Companion to Philosophical Logic.* London: Bloomsbury, 2014.

Horwood, Catherine. *Gardening Women: Their Stories from 1600 to the Present.* London: Virago, 2010.

"Houses to Let." *Times* (Thursday, 20 July 1826): 1. *Times Digital Archive.*

Howard, Ebenezer. *Garden Cities of To-morrow.* London: Swan Sonnenschein, 1902.

———. *Tomorrow: A Peaceful Path to Real Reform.* 1898; repr. London: Routledge, 1998.

Howard, Keble [John Keble Bell]. *The Smiths of Surbiton: A Comedy Without a Plot.* London: Chapman and Hall, 1906.

"How Our Leaders Work: No. 6: Mrs. Jeanie A. Welford." *Practical Photographer* II, no. 21 (1 September 1891): 232–34.

Huddart, David. *Homi K. Bhabha.* London: Routledge, 2006.

Hunting, Penelope. "Dr. John Coakley Lettsom, Plant-Collector of Camberwell." *Garden History* 34 (Winter 2006): 221–35.

Hurtado, Shannon Hunter. *Genteel Mavericks: Professional Women Sculptors in Victorian Britain.* New York: Peter Lang, 2012.

Irigaray, Luce. *Speculum of the Other Woman.* Ithaca, N.Y.: Cornell University Press, 1985.

Jameson, Fredric. *The Political Unconscious: Narrative as a Socially Symbolic Act.* 1981; repr. London: Routledge, 2002.

Jahn, Michael. "Suburban Development in Outer West London, 1850–1900." In *The Rise of Suburbia,* edited by F. M. L. Thompson. Leicester: Leicester University Press, 1982. 93–156.

Jann, Rosemary. "Breeding, Education, and Vulgarity: George Gissing and the Lower-Middle Class." In *Victorian Vulgarity: Taste in Verbal and Visual Culture,* edited by Susan David Bernstein and Elsie B. Michie. London: Ashgate, 2009. 85–100.

Jekyll, Gertrude. *Children and Gardens.* 1908; repr. Woodbridge, Suffolk: Antique Collectors' Club, 1982.

———. *Home and Garden: Notes and Thoughts, Practical and Critical, of a Worker in Both.* London: Longmans, Green, 1901.

———. "The Idea of a Garden." *Edinburgh Review* (July 1896). Repr. in *A Gardener's Testament: A Selection of Articles and Notes.* London: Country Life, 1937. 10–38.

———. "Some Decorative Aspects of Gardening." *Empire Review* (May 1924). Repr. In *A Gardener's Testament: A Selection of Articles and Notes.* London: Country Life, 1937. 39–50.

———. *Wall and Water Gardens.* London: George Newnes, 1901.

———. *Wood and Garden: Notes and Thoughts, Practical and Critical, of a Working Amateur.* London: Longmans, Green, 1899.

Jenkins, Simon. *Landlords to London: The Story of a Capital and Its Growth.* London: Faber, 1975.

Johnson, John. *Typographia or the Printer's Instructor: Including an Account of the Origin of Printing.* London: Longman, 1824. 2:658–59.

Johnson, Louisa. *Every Lady Her Own Flower Gardener.* London: W. S. Orr, 1839.

Jovchelovitch, Sandra. *Knowledge in Context: Representations, Community and Culture.* London: Routledge, 2007.

Kellett, J. R. *The Impact of Railways on Victorian Cities.* London: Routledge, 1969.

Kintz, Linda. "In-Different Criticism: The Deconstructive 'Parole.'" In *The Thinking Muse: Feminism and Modern French Philosophy,* edited by Jeffner Allen and Iris Marion Young. Bloomington: Indiana UP, 1989. 113–135.

Knight, C., ed. *The English Cyclopaedia: Geography.* Vol. IV. London: Bradbury and Evans, 1867.

Knight, Vivien. "The Private Life of William Powell Frith." In *William Powell Frith: Painting the Victorian Age,* edited by Mark Bills and Vivien Knight. New Haven: Yale University Press, 2006. 1–28.

Kuchta, Todd. *Semi-Detached Empire: Suburbia and the Colonization of Britain, 1880 to the Present.* Charlottesville: University of Virginia Press, 2010.

Kucich, John. "Afterword: How Victorian Was Vulgarity?" In *Victorian Vulgarity: Taste in Verbal and Visual Culture,* edited by Susan David Bernstein and Elsie B. Michie. London: Ashgate, 2009. 241–52.

Lampard, Eric E. "The Urbanizing World." In *The Victorian City: Images and Realities,* edited by H. J. Dyos and Michael Wolff. Vol. 1. London: Routledge, 1973. 3–58.

Lane, Christopher. "Bulwer's Misanthropes and the Limits of Victorian Sympathy." *Victorian Studies* 44 (2002): 597–624.

Lees, Lynn Hollen. *Exiles of Erin: Irish Migrants in Victorian London.* London: Cornell University Press, 1979.

Lethbridge, J. P. *Victorian Birmingham.* Birmingham: Newgate Press, 2002.

Levitt, Laura. *Jews and Feminism: The Ambivalent Search for Home.* London: Routledge, 1997.

Loan Exhibition of Women's Industries: Address Book. (Book.) Bristol, 1885. From the Blackburn Collection, Girton College, Cambridge.

———: *Minute Book.* (Book.) Bristol: 1885. From the Blackburn Collection, Girton College, Cambridge.

———: *Report and Balance Sheet.* (Pamphlet.) Bristol: 1885. From the Blackburn Collection, Girton College, Cambridge.

———: *Exhibition of Women's Industries, in Queen's Villa, Queen's Road, Bristol.* 2nd edition. London: J. W. Arrowsmith, 1885. From the Blackburn Collection, Girton College, Cambridge.

Loftie, W. J. *A Plea for Art in the Home.* Philadelphia: Porter and Coates, 1876.

Long, Helen C. *The Edwardian House: The Middle-Class Home in Britain, 1880–1914.* Manchester: Manchester University Press, 1993.

Loudon, Jane. *The Ladies' Companion to the Flower Garden.* 1841. 4th edition. London: William Smith, 1846.

———. "On Flower Gardens: II." *Ladies Magazine of Gardening* 1 (1842): 200–206.

———. *Practical Instructions in Gardening for Ladies.* London: Murray, 1841.

Loudon, John Claudius. *The Suburban Gardener, and Villa Companion.* Edinburgh: Orme, Brown, Green, Longman's, 1838.

———. *A Treatise on Forming, Managing, and Improving Country Residences.* London: Longman, Hurst, 1806.

———. *The Villa Gardener: Comprising the Choice of a Suburban Villa Residence,* edited by Jane Loudon. London: William S. Orr, 1850.

Mallett, Philip. "The City and the Self." In *Ruskin and Environment: The Storm-Cloud of the Nineteenth Century,* edited by Michael Wheeler. Manchester: Manchester University Press, 1995. 38–57.

Marcus, Sharon. *Apartment Stories: City and Home in Nineteenth-Century Paris and London.* Berkeley: University of California Press, 1999.

———. "The Profession of the Author: Abstraction, Advertising and *Jane Eyre.*" In *The Brontës,* edited by Patricia Ingham. New York: Pearson, 2003. 146–68.

Marshall, Gail. "Henry James's Houses: Domesticity and Performativity." In *The Oxford Handbook of Victorian Literary Culture,* edited by Juliet John. Oxford: Oxford University Press, 2016. 702–16.

Maryon, Maud. *How the Garden Grew.* London: Longmans, 1900.

Maxwell, John. "The Thames at Richmond." *Times* (5 September 1873): 6. *Times Digital Archive.*

McClintock, Anne. *Imperial Leather: Race, Gender, and Sexuality in the Colonial Contest.* London: Routledge, 1995.

McGinn, Colin. *The Meaning of Disgust.* Oxford: Oxford University Press, 2011.

Medicos [Julia Frankau]. "Medicoes under the Microscope." *Gentlewoman* I, no. 22 (6 December 1890): 786.

———. [Julia Frankau]. "Medicoes under the Microscope: Sir Andrew Clark." *Gentlewoman* II, no. 27 (10 January 1891): 44.

———. [Julia Frankau]. "Physicians: No. X – Dr. Hughlings Jackson." *Gentlewoman* II, no. 36 (14 March 1891): 358.

See also Ariel; Danby, Frank; and Frankau, Julia.

"Memorabilia of Two Literary Men of the Last Century." *Chambers's Edinburgh Journal* (15 January 1842): 413–14.

Miller, William Ian. *The Anatomy of Disgust.* Cambridge, Mass.: Harvard University Press, 1997.

———. *Humiliation: And Other Essays on Honor, Social Discomfort, and Violence.* Ithaca, N.Y.: Cornell University Press, 1993.

Mitchell, Sally. *Daily Life in Victorian England.* London: Greenwood, 1996.

Montwieler, Katherine. "Marketing Sensation: *Lady Audley's Secret* and Consumer Culture." In *Beyond Sensation: Mary Elizabeth Braddon in Context,* edited by Marlene Tromp, Pamela K. Gilbert, and Aeron Haynie. Albany: SUNY Press, 2000. 43–61.

Moore, George. "Correspondence: Mr. George Moore's New Novel. To the Editor of the *Saturday Review.*" *Saturday Review* 80 (3 August 1895): 143.

Morris, John. "Introduction: On Stereotypes and Stereotyping." In *Exploring Stereotyped Images in Victorian and Twentieth-Century Literature and Society,* edited by John Morris. New York: Edwin Mellon, 1993. 1–26.

"Mr. George Moore's Latest Surprise." *Whitehall Review* no. 582 (7 July 1887): 19.

"Mr. W. P. Frith Speaks." *Whitehall Review* no. 597 (20 October 1887): 17–18.

Muthesius, Stefan. *The English Terraced House.* New Haven: Yale University Press, 1982.

———. *The High Victorian Movement in Architecture 1850–1870.* London: Routledge, 1972.

"M. Vitet's Essays on the Fine Arts." *Reader* IV (29 October 1864): 538–40.

Neiswander, Judith. *The Cosmopolitan Interior: Liberalism and the British Home, 1870–1914.* New Haven: Yale University Press, 2008.

Newman, B. "The Vulgarity of Elegance: Social Mobility, Middle-Class Diction, and the Victorian Novel." In *Victorian Vulgarity: Taste in Verbal and Visual Culture,* edited by Susan David Bernstein and Elsie B. Michie. London: Ashgate, 2009. 17–34.

Nord, Deborah Epstein. *Walking the Victorian Streets: Women, Representation, and the City.* New York: Ithaca UP, 1995.

"Novels of the Week." *Athenaeum* no. 3099 (19 March 1887): 375–77.

"Obituary: Mrs. J. E. Panton." *Times* (21 May 1923): 11. *Times Digital Archive.*

Olsen, Donald. *The Growth of Victorian London.* London: B. T. Batsford, 1976.

———. "House Upon House." In *The Victorian City: Images and Realities,* edited by H. J. Dyos and Michael Wolff. Vol I. London: Routledge, 1973. 333–57.

"On the Mischievous Effects of Fairs in the Neighborhood of the Metropolis." *Times* (20 August 1819): 3. *Times Digital Archive.*

Ottewill, David. *The Edwardian Garden.* London: Yale University Press, 1989.

"Our Views." *Amateur Photographer* I, no. 1 (10 October 1884): 3–5.

"Our Views." *Amateur Photographer* XXII, no. 579 (8 November 1895): 297–300.

[Panton, J. E.] *The Building of Whispers (Being the History of the Making and Ending of a Home).* London: Heath, Cranton and Ouseley. [1915].

———. *The Cannibal Crusader: An Allegory for the Times.* 1889; repr. Bristol: Arrowsmith, 1909.

———. *Fresh Leaves and Green Pastures.* London: Eveleigh Nash, 1909.

———. *From Kitchen to Garret: Hints for Young Householders.* 1887; repr. London: Ward and Downey, 1898.

———. *In Garret and Kitchen: Hints for the Lean Years.* London: Heath, Cranton, 1919.

———. *A Gentlewoman's Home: The Whole Art of Building, Furnishing, and Beautifying the Home.* London: "Gentlewoman" Offices, 1896.

———. *Homes of Taste: Economical Hints.* London: Samson, Low, 1890.

———. *Leaves from the Countryside: An Episode.* London: Heath, Cranton and Ouseley, 1914.

———. *Leaves from a Garden.* London: Eveleigh Nash, 1910.

———. *Leaves from a Housekeeper's Book.* London: Eveleigh Nash, 1914.

———. *Leaves from a Life.* London: Eveleigh Nash, 1908.

———. *Less Than Kin: A Novel.* London: Ward and Downey, 1885.

———. *More Leaves from a Life.* London: Eveleigh Nash, 1911.

———. *Most of the Game.* London: Eveleigh Nash, 1911.

———. *Nooks and Corners.* London: Ward and Downey, 1889.

———. *The River of Years.* London: Heath, Cranton [1916].

———. *Suburban Residences and How to Circumvent Them.* London: Ward and Downey, 1896.

———. *The Way They Should Go: Hints to Young Parents.* London: Downey, 1896.

———. *The Year's Mind: Hamworth Happenings.* London: Eveleigh Nash, 1913.

Perkin, Harold. *The Rise of Professional Society: England Since 1880.* London: Routledge, 1989.

Peterson, Linda. *Becoming a Woman of Letters: Myths of Authorship and Facts of the Victorian Market.* Princeton: Princeton University Press, 2009.

———. *Victorian Autobiography: The Tradition of Self-Interpretation.* New Haven: Yale University Press, 1986.

"Philosophers and Negroes." *Saturday Review* 22 (15 September 1866): 325–26.

Pionke, Albert D. *The Ritual Culture of Victorian Professionals: Competing for Ceremonial Status, 1838–1877.* London: Routledge, 2016.

Pope, Ged. *Reading London's Suburbs: From Charles Dickens to Zadie Smith.* London: Palgrave Macmillan, 2015.

Pugin, Augustus. *Contrasts; or, A Parallel Between the Noble Edifices of the Fourteenth and Fifteenth Centuries, and Similar Buildings of the Present Day; Shewing the Present Decay of Taste: Accompanied by Appropriate Text.* London: St. Marie's Grange, 1836.

Ragussis, Michael. *Figures of Conversion: "The Jewish Question" and English National Identity.* Durham, N.C.: Duke University Press, 1995.

Raitt, Suzanne. *Vita and Virginia: The Work and Friendship of V. Sackville-West and Virginia Woolf.* Oxford: Clarendon, 1993.

Rappaport, Erika Diane. *Shopping for Pleasure: Women in the Making of London's West End.* Princeton: Princeton University Press, 2000.

Ravetz, Alison, and Richard Turkington. *The Place of Home: English Domestic Environments, 1914–2000.* Oxford: Taylor and Francis, 1995.

Rawcliffe, J. M. "Bromley: Kentish Market Town to London Suburb, 1841–8." In *The Rise of Suburbia,* edited by F. M. L. Thompson. Leicester: Leicester University Press, 1982. 28–91.

Reader, W. J. *Professional Men: the Rise of the Professional Classes in Nineteenth-Century England.* London: Weidenfeld and Nicolson, 1966.

Review of *The Suburban Horticulturalist. Gentleman's Magazine* 175 (1843): 171–72.

Review of *Suggestions for the Formation of a New Style of Architecture. Athenaeum* no. 1829 (15 November 1862): 633.

Riddell, Charlotte Eliza [F. G. Trafford]. *City and Suburb.* 3 vols. London: Charles J. Skeet, 1861.

"R.G." "On The Natural Love of Flowers." *The Ladies Magazine of Gardening* 1 (1842): 69–70.

Robertson, Alexander. *Atkinson Grimshaw.* Oxford: Phaidon, 1988.

Rodger, Richard. "Slums and Suburbs." In *The English Urban Landscape.* Edited by Phillip Waller. Oxford: Oxford University Press, 2000. 233–68.

Rose, Michael E. "Culture, Philanthropy and the Manchester Middle Classes." In *City, Class and Culture: Studies of Social Policy and Cultural Production in Victorian Manchester,* edited by Alan J. Kidd and K. W. Roberts. Manchester: Manchester University Press, 1985. 103–19.

Rosenberg, Edgar. *From Shylock to Svengali: Jewish Stereotypes in English Fiction.* Stanford: Stanford University Press, 1960.

Ruskin, John. *Modern Painters.* Part II: "On Ideas of Beauty." 1843; repr. Sunnyside: George Allen, 1883.

———. "Of Queens' Gardens." In *The Complete Works of John Ruskin,* edited by E. T. Cook and Alexander Wedderburn. 39 vols; vol. 18. London: George Allen, 1903–12 [1905]. 109–44.

———. *The Seven Lamps of Architecture.* Vol. I. London: Smith, Elder, 1849.

Saint, Andrew, ed. *London Suburbs.* London: Merrell Holberton, 1999.

Sala, George Augustus. *Gaslight and Daylight: With Some London Scenes They Shine Upon.* London: Chapman and Hall, 1859.

Savinson, Richard. *Royal Richmond: An Introduction to the History of Richmond.* Richmond: Richmond Local History Society, 2005. 12–13.

Schaffer, Talia. *The Forgotten Female Aesthetes: Literary Culture in Late-Victorian England.* Charlottesville: University of Virginia Press, 2000.

———. *Novel Craft: Victorian Domestic Handicraft & Nineteenth-Century Fiction.* Oxford: Oxford University Press, 2011.

———. "The Sensational Story of West Lynne: The Problem with Professionalism." *Women's Writing* 23, no. 2 (2016): 227–44. DOI: 10.1080/09699082.2015.1130287.

Schnare, Susan E., and Rudy J. Favretti. "Gertrude Jeykll's American Gardens." *Garden History* 10 (1982): 149–67.

Schwarzbach, F. S. "Newgate Novel to Detective Fiction." In *A Companion to the Victorian Novel,* edited by Patrick Brantlinger and William B. Thesing. London: Blackwell, 2005. 227–43.

Scocpol, Theda. *Diminished Democracy: From Membership to Management in American Civic Life.* Norman: University of Oklahoma Press, 2004.

Scott, Peter. *The Making of the Modern British Home: The Suburban Semi and Family Life Between the Wars.* Oxford: Clarendon Press, 2013.

Scott, Sir Walter. "Landscape Gardening." *Quarterly Review* 37 (1828): 303–44.

[Shaw, Bernard]. "Literary and Art Notes, Etc." *Pall Mall Gazette* no. 6871 (25 March 1887): 5.

Simmons, Jack. "The Power of the Railway." In *The Victorian City: Images and Realities,* edited by H. J. Dyos and Michael Wolff. Vol. I. London: Routledge, 1973. 277–310.

Simo, Melanie Louise. *Loudon and the Landscape: From Country Seat to Metropolis, 1783–1843.* New Haven: Yale University Press, 1988.

Smith, Sidonie. "Construing Truth in Lying Mouths: Truthtelling in Women's Autobiography." In *Women and Autobiography,* edited by Martine Watson Brownley and Allison B. Kimmich. Wilmington, Del.: Scholarly Resources, 1999. 33–52.

Smyth, Elizabeth, Sandra Acker, Paula Bourne, and Alison Prentice, eds. *Challenging Professions: Historical and Contemporary Perspectives on Women's Professional Work.* Toronto: University of Toronto Press, 1999.

Steinbach, Susie. *Understanding the Victorians: Politics, Culture, and Society in Nineteenth-Century Britain.* London: Routledge, 2012.

Strong, Roy. *London: A Social History.* London: Hamish Hamilton, 1994.

Swift, Jonathan. "The Lady's Dressing Room." In *The Poems of Jonathan Swift.* Edited by Harold Williams. Volume II. Oxford: Clarendon Press, 1958. 525–30.

Tabaroff, June. "'Wife, unto Thy Garden': The First Gardening Books for Women." *Garden History* 11 (1983): 1–5.

Taylor, Charles. *Sources of the Self: The Making of Modern Identity.* 1989; repr. Cambridge: Cambridge University Press, 2006.

Taylor, William H. *The Vital Landscape: Nature and the Built Environment in Nineteenth-Century Britain.* London: Ashgate, 2004.

Thomas, R. R. "Poison Books and Moving Pictures: Vulgarity in *The Picture of Dorian Gray.*" In *Victorian Vulgarity: Taste in Verbal and Visual Culture,* edited by Susan David Bernstein and Elsie B. Michie. London: Ashgate, 2009. 185–200.

Thompson, F. M. L. "Introduction: The Rise of Suburbia." In *The Rise of Suburbia,* edited by F. M. L. Thompson. Leicester: Leicester University Press, 1982. 2–25.

———, ed. *The Rise of Suburbia.* Leicester: Leicester University Press, 1982.

Tosh, John. *A Man's Place: Masculinity and the Middle-Class Home in Victorian England.* 1999; repr. New Haven: University Press, 2007.

Tyson, Brian. *Bernard Shaw's Book Reviews, Originally Published in the Pall Mall Gazette 1885–1888.* London: Pennsylvania University Press, 1991.

Wagner, Tamara S. "Sensationalizing Victorian Suburbia: Wilkie Collins's *Basil.*" In *Victorian Sensations: Essays on a Scandalous Genre,* edited by K. Harrison and R. Fantina. Columbus: Ohio State University Press, 2006. 200–211.

Waters, Michael. *The Garden in Victorian Literature.* Aldershot: Gower, 1988.

Weedon, Alexis. *Victorian Publishing: The Economics of Book Production for a Mass Market 1836–1916.* London: Ashgate, 2003.

Weltman, Sharon Aronofsky. "'Be No More Housewives, but Queens': Queen Victoria and Ruskin's Domestic Mythology." In *Remaking Queen Victoria,* edited by Margaret Homans and Adrienne Munich. Cambridge: Cambridge University Press, 1997. 105–22.

Whelan, Lara Baker. "The Clash of Space and Culture." In *Gissing and the City: Cultural Crisis and the Making of Books in Late Victorian England,* edited by John Spiers. London: Palgrave, 2006. 152–61.

———. *Class, Culture and Suburban Anxieties in the Victorian Era.* New York: Routledge, 2010.

Whitehead, Charles. "The Suburban Retreat." *Bentley's Miscellany* 22 (1847): 119–25.

Whiting, J. B. *Manual of Flower Gardening for Ladies.* London: David Bogue, 1849.

Wiener, Martin J. *English Culture and the Decline of the Industrial Spirit, 1850–1980.* 1981; repr. Cambridge: Cambridge University Press, 2004.

Witz, Anne. *Professions and Patriarchy.* London: Routledge, 1992.

Williams, Raymond. *The Country and the City.* Oxford: Oxford University Press, 1973.

Williamson, Jeffrey G. *Coping with City Growth During the British Industrial Revolution.* Cambridge: Cambridge University Press 1990.

Wittman, Emily O. "'Death Before the Fact': Posthumous Autobiography in Jean Rhys's *Good Morning, Midnight* and *Smile Please.*" In *Modernism and Autobiography,* edited by Maria DiBattista and Emily O. Wittman. Cambridge: Cambridge University Press, 2014. 185–96.

Wolff, Robert Lee. *Sensational Victorian: The Life and Fiction of Mary Elizabeth Braddon.* New York: Garland, 1979.

Wolseley, Hon. Frances. *In a College Garden.* London: John Murray, 1916.
———. *Gardening for Women.* London: Cassell, 1908.
———. *Gardens: Their Form and Design.* London: Edward Arnold, 1919.
A Woman, But Not an Exhibitor. "A Novelty in Exhibitions." *Pall Mall Gazette* (26 February 1885): 4.
Woodcock, Sally. "'Very Efficient as a Painter': The Painting Practice of William Powell Frith." In *William Powell Frith: Painting the Victorian Age,* edited by Mark Bills and Vivien Knight. New Haven: Yale University Press, 2006. 145–55.
Woods, R. I. *The Demography of Victorian England and Wales.* Cambridge: Cambridge University Press, 2000.
———. "The Population of Britain in the Nineteenth Century." In *British Population History from the Black Death to the Present Day,* edited by Michael Anderson. Cambridge: Cambridge University Press, 1996. 281–358.
Woolf, Virginia. *Three Guineas.* 1938; repr. *A Room of One's Own and Three Guineas.* Oxford: Oxford University Press, 2015.
A Working Man. "The Working Man's Way in the World." *Tait's Edinburgh Magazine* 18 (1851): 224–29.

Index

Illustrations are indicated by italicized page numbers.